TO RUSSIA WITH FRIES

TO RUSSIA WITH FRIES

GEORGE COHON

with David Macfarlane

FIRST PUBLISHED IN THE U.S.A. 1999

Canadian Cataloguing in Publication Data

Cohon, George, 1937 –
To Russia with fries
ISBN 0-7710-2198-4

1. Cohon, George, 1937 – . 2. McDonald's Corporation. 3. Fast food restaurants – Russia (Federation). 4. Fast food restaurants – Canada. I. Macfarlane, David, 1952 – . II. Title.

TX945.5.M33C63 1997 338.7'6164795'092 C97-931600-6

Printed and bound in Canada

McClelland & Stewart Inc.
The Canadian Publishers
481 University Avenue
Toronto, Ontario
M5G 2E9

To what has always been most important
in my life –
family:
especially
Susan, Mark, Craig and Jeanette

CONTENTS

A WORD ABOUT THE AUTHOR

Unlike many of the readers of this book, I know the remarkable man who wrote it. When George Cohon told me that he was planning to write a book about his life, I welcomed the idea with enthusiasm.

For the people who have met him, George Cohon is literally synonymous with McDonald's in Russia. His strong personal identification with McDonald's is one indication of how much people need and appreciate this successful business.

George is an interesting man – vigorous, imaginative, charming, courageous, and kind. Starting out with small personal savings, he went all the way to create a huge business with $2 billion in annual sales and hundreds of outlets in Canada and Russia. The secret of his success lies in his unique personal qualities and his ability to do business in all kinds of conditions and, perhaps most importantly, to find good partners and employ the right kind of people.

The secret of George's success is that he is a thoroughly modern man who thinks big and is able to detect the trends in people's way of life and their interests and to foresee how their needs will change.

George Cohon's activities in our country deserve special mention. It is quite a story, and a fascinating one at that. He first came to Moscow ten years before *perestroika*. Here, he demonstrated his exceptional business abilities and human qualities.

At the height of the period of stagnation, when the free spirit of the market was totally non-existent, George enthusiastically pursued the idea of starting a business here, and he succeeded, despite having to fight his way through the bureaucratic jungle. Incidentally, this is a truly instructive example for those in the West who are still hesitant whether to come and bring their capital to Russia.

After the adoption of joint-venture legislation, made possible by *perestroika*, the business really got off the ground. The first McDonald's restaurant opened on Pushkin Square in Moscow on January 31, 1990. It was an extraordinary event, which was covered by reporters from around the world.

This was not just a personal triumph for George. It was a breakthrough which demonstrated that new economic relations between our country and the rest of the world were possible. It was a symbol of the good will of international business which would be important in helping us build a democratic society.

At that time, consumer services were a badly neglected sector of our economy, and thus we also benefited by learning how a consumer-oriented enterprise is run in a market environment. The important thing for us was that it was not an exhibition but a real business, operating on the highest international standards.

A large number of people are involved in the McDonald's system, deriving both enjoyment and practical benefit from it. This group includes not only those working in the restaurants, but also the suppliers, whose co-operation with the company means the inflow of new technologies and new ways of providing service and also challenges them to improve quality, which in turn contributes to the development of civilized modern markets.

The example and experience of George Cohon go well beyond business and commerce. They promote democratic and humanitarian values. In George, the company has a leader who has done much to help Russian children, including orphans, the very needy, and physically and mentally handicapped children.

And the merry clowns, the Big Mac signs, the colourful, unique decorations and ideal cleanliness in and around the restaurants, the welcoming smiles and helpful service – all of this complements the hamburgers whose great popularity is well deserved. That is why McDonald's has no problems with the customers.

George Cohon is a man of action. He has been able to make his own work and the work of his countless employees and associates a truly fascinating experience and a source of food and fun for millions of people. He is also a real humanitarian.

It is very good that he has written a book about himself. I am sure that many of his admirers will find it both interesting and instructive.

Mikhail Sergeyevich Gorbachev
Moscow, 1997

Introduction

The way I introduce myself is always the same. Whether I'm in a McDonald's in Moscow, or St. Petersburg, or Toronto, people come up to me all the time. I guess I'm approachable that way. I like to talk to customers. I like to know what they think. No, it's more than that. I *need* to know what customers think. I'm a front counter kind of guy. I always have been. We have people in the company who are better with numbers and spreadsheets than I am. And there are people who are better with the technical side of things. I prefer to operate a little less formally. But Ray Kroc, the founder of McDonald's, used to say, "Don't worry about making money. Love what you're doing, and always put the customer first." So when people come up to me in restaurants and say, "Mr. Cohon . . ." I always say, "George. My name is George. Mr. Cohon was my father."

Actually, my father's real name was Kaganov. My grandparents escaped from the Ukraine during the pogroms of 1906, when my father was six months old. An immigration officer at

Ellis Island wrote Cohon down on a form, and Cohon it stayed. But that's another story.

A good story, though. I have to tell you. When my grandparents were waiting in Bremen to get tickets for passage to America, the line they were in seemed to stretch forever. It was moving slowly. You can just picture it, can't you? Everything dim and gloomy, and all those people – huddled masses, like it says on the Statue of Liberty. My grandparents were anxious. Very anxious. They weren't sure how many berths were left, and it didn't look to them as if it was possible for all these people in this endless lineup to be crammed onto one boat. There didn't seem to be any way in the world they were going to get on. So, underneath the blankets in her arms, my grandmother kept pinching my father. The baby howled, of course. Just howled. The noise was driving the people all around them crazy, or perhaps they were afraid something was wrong with the little boy, so they let the Kaganovs move forward. The Russians in the line said, "*Da prokhodite zhe Vy vperyod, prokhodite!* – Go on, go on. Get up there."

Now, let me jump forward about ninety years. You'll notice I jump around a lot. That's just the way I am. It's the way I think. It's the way I do things. Fred Turner, when he was CEO of the entire McDonald's Corporation, once called me a butterfly. I was constantly excited about this project and that project, this idea and that idea, this proposal and that proposal. Fred said, "George, slow down. You're floating around like a butterfly in a garden." And Susan, my wife, and our two sons, Craig and Mark, won't let me forget what Fred said. They're always telling me I'm doing six things at once. Which is true. It drives the people in my office crazy. I can't seem to think of one thing without something else popping into my head. I'll be visiting a potato farm outside of Moscow and suddenly get an idea for a fundraiser for Ronald McDonald Children's Charities of Russia and at the same time I'll be thinking about a speech I'm going to give for a *Business Week* seminar for chief executive officers in London, England, and making plans for a restaurant opening in St. Petersburg and worrying about some new tray-liners I saw at a McDonald's in Toronto. Somebody once said I have a multi-track mind. It's true. You'll see. One minute I'm telling you the story about my grandparents' escape from the Ukraine. Next thing, it's ninety years later, and Susan and our two sons and I have decided we want to take a holiday on a cruise ship.

We made up our minds at the very last minute, and we were eager to go. But our travel agent said, "Impossible. These things are booked years in advance. There's no way in the world you can get on."

I thought to myself, we'll see.

Maybe I was thinking of my grandmother and the ticket line-up in Bremen. Maybe it's just the way I am. Or maybe my grandmother is one of the reasons I am the way I am. Who can say? At any rate, the next morning I called the cruise line's head office in San Francisco.

The booking agent said, "Mr. Cohon . . ."

"George. Call me George."

"George, look. The cruise is five weeks from now. People book these cruises at least a year in advance. I'm sorry. I'd love to help you. But there's just no way."

"Okay," I said. "Okay. I understand. But if anything opens up, keep me in mind, will you?"

"Of course."

"And, by the way, do you ever eat at McDonald's?"

"Sure," he said. "There's one in our building. It's very popular. Actually, we'd eat there more often, but at lunch time there's always a long line-up."

"How many people are in your office?"

"About twenty-five."

"So what do you think the odds are of me getting lunch for everyone in your office delivered at precisely twelve o'clock?"

"Impossible," he said.

"Well," I said, "it's like this. It's tough getting on that boat. And it will be tough for me to get your office lunch. But let's both do the best we can, okay?"

So I made another phone call to San Francisco. This time, to the McDonald's in the building. I explained what I wanted. And at twelve o'clock sharp, lunch for the cruise line's head office was delivered to their door. About an hour later, the booking agent called me back.

"Mr. Cohon," he said.

"George."

"George. The most amazing thing has just happened. There's been a cancellation. A suite. I just got a call from St. Louis."

I thanked him and asked him to place our booking through our travel agent. And I thought: That's the power of Big Macs. And of grandmothers.

I like to tell stories about the things that have happened to me because I like hearing stories. I think people's lives are stories. People's days are stories. People's dreams are stories. Some of my friends say I think in stories. They could be right.

There are some stories I've told often over the years. Like the one about Mikhail Gorbachev and my T-shirt. Or the one about the time my wife took the wife of the former Israeli Defence Minister Moshe Dayan shopping in Toronto. Or about the time I got a little carried away in an overly competitive tennis match with the head of the KGB. Or the story about my visit, in 1991, as an honoured guest, to the town of Dnipropetrovs'k in the Ukraine – the same town, then called Yekaterinoslav, from which my grandparents and their young family fled in 1906.

The stories of my life bump up against one another. They connect: like my grandparents escaping by boat from the Ukraine and, ninety years later, a cruise ship in San Francisco. They have their own order, but it's not necessarily the obvious order. Things with me don't ever begin at A and work their way slowly to Z. I don't start at the beginning and plod patiently to the end. I'm not that kind of guy. Maybe that's why I enjoy the bustle of a McDonald's restaurant so much: Whether I'm at the front counter at a busy lunch hour, or back at the grill, or over at the drive-thru, there are always twenty things going on at once. I love it. There's no beginning and no end to it. It's my kind of place.

I've found that in business and in life, it isn't always clear where beginnings are – especially when you're doing something new. That's when things are really fun.

We didn't know where the beginning was in 1967 when I got the McDonald's franchise for most of Eastern Canada and gave up my law practice, and Susan and our two young sons, Craig and Mark, and I left Chicago for Toronto. We didn't know a soul, we didn't have much money, and McDonald's then was far from being the household word it is today. How do you start a new business and a new life in a strange new country? No-one knew – or, if they did, they weren't telling us. We had to find our own way. Certainly, no-one knew where the beginning was when, in 1976, at the height of the Cold War, I decided that we should open McDonald's in what was then the Soviet Union. Where do you start when you decide to introduce one of the most potent symbols of Western capitalism into a system dedicated to the very opposite? No-one knew. There was no order to doing something like that. There were no rules. But just the fact that no-one knew how didn't seem to me a good reason not to do it. So we invented our own rules. We took off in all directions at once, and as we went we learned which directions led somewhere and which ones didn't. Which, to tell you the truth, suited me fine. I don't have a very linear mind.

So, be warned. The book you have in your hands is not going to be very linear, for the simple reason that its subject – me – is anything but. It's not going to begin with George A. Cohon being born in 1937 on the South Side of Chicago, and end sixty years later, with me as the Senior Chairman and Chairman of the Executive Committee of McDonald's Restaurants of Canada Limited and Senior Chairman of McDonald's-Russia. It's not going to begin in the early 1950s, when a milkshake-machine salesman named Ray Kroc got to know two brothers – Mac and Dick McDonald – who were operating a small chain of drive-in restaurants in California, and end forty years later, with more than 21,000 McDonald's restaurants in more than 100 countries, serving more than 35 million customers a day. It's not going to begin in the 1930s with people like my parents involving themselves in all kinds of community charities because they believed it was the right thing to do, and then end in the 1990s, with my personal involvement in charitable work, or, well beyond that, with an institution like Ronald McDonald Children's Charities that has given more than $100 million to organizations around the world benefiting children.

Of course, this book will tell you these stories, but in my way, my order. If you and I were sitting together. . . . Well, actually, I don't sit anywhere very much. So, let's say you and I were in my car right now – that would be more like it. And suppose we're on our way to Variety Village, a wonderful place for handicapped kids in which McDonald's is very involved. Or to a Ronald McDonald House. Or to a Royal Bank of Canada directors' meeting. Or to my country house north of Toronto, where Susan and I enjoy the peace and quiet and where I like to go mountain biking. Or maybe you and I are just on our way to a McDonald's for lunch. Let's say you were the ghost writer, and we were talking about this book. A ghost might want to talk about how this book should begin. He might say, "Mr. Cohon . . ."

"George, please."

"George. You should start in the Ukraine. Or on the South Side of Chicago. Or maybe in Toronto, the day you arrived to start your new career with McDonald's."

I'd be listening. I don't want to give the impression I don't listen. I'd be listening to what you were saying, but I might have a sudden thought. They come out of the blue sometimes.

"Excuse me," I'd say. "I just have to make a quick call."

It's a habit. I use the car phone a lot. Something comes to me, and I pick up the phone and call Nancy Serblan, my assistant.

"Nance. Get through to our people in Moscow and get me some information on the Hotel Metropol, will you? Background, you know. Historical stuff. Architectural details. That kind of thing. Yeah. Soon as possible. Thanks."

The ghost might ask, "Where were we?"

And I'd say, "Where else? We're at the beginning."

• 1 •

A Foot in the Door

The Metropol is the most beautiful hotel in Moscow. Designed in 1898 by the British architect William Walcott, it stands in the very centre of the city, a short walk from Red Square and the Kremlin, and across Teatral'naya Square from the Bolshoi Theatre. From the day it opened its doors, the Metropol was a magnet for Moscow society. Its art exhibitions and concerts were legendary, and, in the early years of this century, if you spent a day sitting in its flower-laden, chandelier-hung Art Nouveau lobby, you might well have seen Nijinsky or Rachmaninoff come through the front doors.

In 1917, everything changed. After the Revolution that year, the Metropol was used by the new Bolshevik government as the second House of Soviets. Lenin often delivered speeches from the balcony overlooking the Metropol Restaurant – the same restaurant, by the way, where, half a century later, Julie Christie and Rod Steiger had dinner in one of my favourite movies, David Lean's *Dr. Zhivago*.

In the 1930s, the Metropol was converted back to a hotel. During the Second World War it became a temporary press centre, housing foreign correspondents from Western newspapers and magazines. After the war, it continued to be a hub for foreign visitors – the few foreign visitors that there were in those days.

I made my first trip to Moscow in 1976. In view of the upheavals in Russia in the 1990s, 1976 seems like a long, long time ago. Light years have passed since. Today, Russia is still exotic, still exciting, still unique. To the foreign visitor it remains a little strange and unfamiliar, and I never fail to feel a shiver of excitement when I walk into Red Square at night. It is an awesome sight.

But in 1976, Russia was another world. The year before, Andrei Sakharov, the famous dissident, had been denied permission to leave the USSR to accept the Nobel Peace Prize, and two years earlier, the writer Alexander Solzhenitsyn had been expelled for his criticisms of the Soviet Union. Brezhnev was in power and, although this was officially the period of détente, the tensions between the United States and Russia were still considerable. Between 1976 and 1979 I was travelling to Moscow an average of six times a year, which was a little unusual for a Western businessman. I had this crazy idea: I thought we could open a McDonald's there.

Going to the USSR, pre-*perestroika*, was always fascinating, but it was hard to feel welcome there. It sometimes seemed as if the basics of service, hospitality, and plain old-fashioned friendliness – the kinds of things that are so important to McDonald's – had been dumped in the Moscow River in 1917. Whenever I arrived at the Moscow airport, I had to wait in a queue for hours to clear customs. Everything was grey and grim. Young soldiers with steely-eyed stares would go through all my luggage, piece by piece. They'd go through everybody's luggage piece by piece. I got the feeling they'd go through their mothers' luggage piece by piece.

They would inspect every page of my passport slowly and methodically. I always wondered what they were looking for: Invisible ink? Secret codes?

When they were finally done with me, I would get a cab into the city – a few packages of Marlboros was the usual fare – to the Intourist Hotel, where I would have to line up again.

I'd wait. And I'd wait. Finally, when I'd get to the check-in desk, all too often the woman there would say, "No more rooms." Just like that. No apology. No nothing – even though I had a prepaid voucher for a room, for that specific date, in my hand. *Ne znayu, nichego ne mogu podelat'*. It was just too bad.

I would be exhausted from the trip. All I'd want was to get some sleep. And I'd be sent to another big dump of a government-run hotel – the Belgrad, or the Rossiya, where my room was not much bigger than my suitcase, where the toilet paper (if there was any) could have sanded down what little paint there was on the window-sills, and where, of course, the telephones didn't work.

It didn't take me long to learn that the McDonald's pins and the twelve-dollar Ronald McDonald watches that I always carried were more useful than the official vouchers when it came to getting a room at the Intourist. I'd produce pins or a watch and suddenly, as if by magic, an empty room would be found. McDonald's pins and watches were my American Express card in Moscow. I never went anywhere without them.

On top of all this, like all Western visitors to the Soviet Union in those days, I constantly felt that I was being watched. We treated this as a bit of a game sometimes – looking under rugs and lampshades for bugs, stepping outside for particularly important discussions with my Moscow team. It was like something out of James Bond. But, in fact, it wasn't a joke. It wasn't uncommon to be tailed by a classic black Volga. The American Embassy actually issued documents to visitors advising them that they should act on the assumption they were under surveillance. We were warned that if we left papers in our rooms they would be looked at, that our telephone calls would be monitored, and that we would always be followed. It was disconcerting, to put it mildly.

After a few visits, I started to find my way around. Gradually, I got to know the ropes. And by 1978 I had shifted from the Intourist Hotel and its long line-ups to the more accommodating, and much more interesting, Metropol. It became my Moscow home. It was, by far, the best hotel in Moscow – even if it did have the fiercest-looking floor-lady I had yet encountered in all my visits. Typically, in Russian hotels, these women sit sternly beside the elevator door on each floor. They boss around the maids. They keep the keys to the rooms. They make certain that order prevails, and they keep a watchful eye on everyone. They are grandmother types, classic Russian *babushkas,* and nothing happens on their floors – no extra towel is handed out, no message is left, no arrangements for a trans-Atlantic phone call are made, no guests arrive – without their knowledge. They know everything that's going on.

Dounia sat in the Metropol's second-floor corridor like a rock. She was a force to be reckoned with. She wore her steel-grey hair in a bun that looked as if bullets would bounce off it. She had a bulky, shapeless build, as if she were wearing several coats under her dark-blue hotel smock. She looked as if all the hardships of Russia's twentieth century were etched on her wrinkled old face. She glowered at me whenever I got off the elevator. I'd manage a smile, and then hurry into my room.

It was a corner room – Room 2264 – on the second floor, overlooking Teatral'naya Square. It was a suite that, in the fall of 1979, I got to know all too well. It had vast, high ceilings, a massively heavy desk, and a grand piano which, while very elegant, was not a lot of use to me. Perhaps it had been used by Rachmaninoff. Perhaps Bernard Shaw had doodled around on it when he came to the Metropol and met with Stalin. Maybe Van Cliburn had practised on it before winning the Tchaikovsky Piano Competition in 1958. Whatever the piano's heritage, I would have happily traded it for a shower that worked, or for enough hot water to shave, or for an extra towel.

The room also had a telephone. It never, ever worked. But, in the worst of all possible worlds, it rang constantly. Day and night. No-one was ever on the line.

And, of course, the room had grim, unyielding Dounia guarding it. I was never sure if she was keeping outsiders out, or guests in. She was always there, sitting in the corridor like Mother Russia.

I spent a lot of time in Room 2264. In fact, in 1979, I stayed there for seventeen days straight. There isn't a hotel room in the world that I know quite as well.

My stay at the Metropol all began with a story I like to tell. A story about a bus.

It was at the time of the 1976 Olympics in Montreal. Some time before the Games, I got a call from the Canadian Department of External Affairs. An official explained that the Government of Canada would be entertaining a group of Soviets who were in charge of the 1980 Olympic Games. The 1980 Olympics were going to be held in Moscow, and a delegation from the USSR would be visiting Montreal. Could I help?

Somehow the Department knew that McDonald's had a custom coach. It was a very nice, very comfortable bus that we used for charity events. We didn't usually let anyone else use it, but I felt that since it was the Government of Canada that was asking, we should do what we could to help.

So the Department of External Affairs got the bus. And, as it happened, my wife, our two sons, Craig and Mark, and I got a chance to go to Montreal that summer to see the Games. (I'm a big Olympics fan; I went to Los Angeles in 1984, Barcelona in

1992, and Atlanta in 1996.) The Montreal Olympics were the Games at which the Canadian high-jumper Greg Joy won the silver medal, and we were there, cheering our heads off, when he did. They were great Olympics, and a great event for Canada to be hosting. It had been less than two years since I had become a Canadian citizen, and that summer, in Montreal, with the eyes of the world on Canada, I felt real pride in the achievements of my adopted country.

Late one afternoon, after a track and field event, Susan and the boys and I were leaving the Olympic Stadium. It was a hot, sunny day. We were dressed in jeans and T-shirts, making our way through the crowd, when I looked across the street, and there was the McDonald's bus. The Soviet delegation was just getting off. On the spur of the moment, I said to Susan, "Let's go meet the Russians."

So we walked over. As we approached, we were stopped by two plain-clothes officers. One was RCMP; the other, KGB. We were stopped a few yards from the bus. Perhaps for fear they might defect, the Soviet delegation was being guarded very closely. The officers stepped in front of us, and I did what I have done many times since in similar situations: I produced my business card.

It is not an ordinary-looking business card. It's shaped like a Big Mac, and it's good for one free Big Mac. This caught the attention of the RCMP officer. Then, once the card's meaning became clear to him, it really sparked the interest of the man from the KGB.

The card did what it almost always does. It broke the ice. Soon we were talking. It might be a hold-over from one of the many part-time jobs I took on when I was a student – I worked for a while as a Fuller Brush salesman – but I know that once you engage people in conversation, the barriers come down soon enough. You establish contact. You make a few jokes. You humanize the situation. And you do what all salesmen are always trying to do: You get your foot in the door. My foot was almost in. We were well on our way, at that point, to talking our way past the two officers, when, hurrying through the crowd toward us, like a grey-suited bundle of worry, came a third obstacle. He was a very officious-looking bureaucrat from Ottawa – all clipboards and protocol and official itineraries. He could see what was going on, and he didn't like it. By this time, a few of the Russians had gathered around, and the Canadian official took it upon himself to intervene.

He told us that he was from External Affairs. He told us that these were very important people, very busy, and couldn't be bothered. He told us that we wouldn't be allowed to get anywhere near them. He cited all kinds of international this and intergovernmental that. And he told me that I would have to go through the Protocol Department of External Affairs to request permission to speak with the visiting delegation from the Soviet Union.

This kind of thing always rubs me the wrong way.

I looked at him straight through his spectacles. "My friend," I said. "The protocol is, I own the bus."

One of the Russians there had worked at the United Nations. He was fluent in English. He heard what I said to the Canadian official, and because Russians had to deal with such extraordinary levels of bureaucracy, because they were always being told they couldn't do this and couldn't do that, he thought that what I had said to the officious man from External Affairs was hilarious. He broke out laughing and immediately told the other Russians, who also found what I had said very funny.

Needless to say, the Canadian bureaucrat wasn't very amused by this. But by then it was too late; the Russians were swarming around us. Soon we were all talking, and they were joking with our young boys. In no time we were all the best of friends, and the

Russians, being Russians, decided that they would invite us out to dinner. When a Russian offers you a dinner invitation, proposes a toast, or suggests opening a bottle, it is always difficult and usually impossible to decline.

We agreed to go. But I had an idea. It was a little odd, but it turned out to be a pretty good one. I said, "Let's have a snack first."

Susan looked at me as if I'd lost my mind. "George. We're going out to dinner. They don't want to have a snack before going out to dinner."

But the Soviets were game. When it comes to questions of appetite, Russians usually are.

We drove to the McDonald's at St. Catherine and Atwater, across the street from the old Montreal Forum. Just a few months earlier, Ray Kroc, Fred Turner, and I had cut the ribbon, opening this restaurant – the four thousandth McDonald's in the world.

There was an Olympic final on at the Forum, and there were huge line-ups along the sidewalks and across the streets. One of the Russians asked, "What are the queues for?"

I said, "To make you feel at home."

We went into the McDonald's. Now, when most people go into a McDonald's they don't really think very much about it. It's a McDonald's. It's clean. It's bright. It's lively. They know what to expect. Those of us who work for McDonald's look closely at things, of course. How many customers are there? How fast are the lines moving? How's the communication between the front counter and the grill? Are the crew members neatly turned out? But most customers don't bother with these kinds of details. They just want to get their food quickly and then enjoy it.

It was different with the Soviets we met in Montreal. You have to remember that going into a McDonald's was something absolutely new to these people. To them, a restaurant was either a dark little hole in the wall where, maybe, you could get a sausage sandwich, a boiled potato, and a cup of tea, or else it was a vast, coldly formal dining room that was always out of everything and where the waitresses or waiters seemed physically incapable of smiling. To our new friends from the Soviet Union, the quality, service, and cleanliness of McDonald's was a revelation. They couldn't believe it, and they couldn't believe that so many ordinary Canadians could afford to be there that night, enjoying themselves with friends and family. Such an outing – something we take for granted – was, at that time, unheard-of in their country.

And so, over Big Macs, and french fries, and Cokes and milkshakes, we began to talk about McDonald's and about the Soviet Union. It was a friendly chat, and I asked the delegation a question that would change my life. I asked whether Russians would enjoy going to a McDonald's if there was one, say, in Moscow.

"*Konechno, poydyom*," they said. "Of course we would."

Looking back, I suppose we all must have thought that at first we were talking hypothetically. After all: McDonald's in the USSR! On the face of it, it seemed a pretty improbable notion.

You'll recall that I described myself as a front counter kind of guy. Spreadsheets and technicalities are not my strong suit. But I'm always at the front counter, in my mind at any rate. It's important to know what people think, and at the front counter you learn quickly enough about what customers like and what they don't like. Executive offices can be very nice, but the front counter is where the rubber meets the road: the point where every aspect of McDonald's – all the company's philosophy, all of its quality control, its service training, its emphasis on standards and friendliness, all of its innovations and its employees' efforts – boil down to a single question: Does it make the customer happy? If you had been at the front counter of the McDonald's at St. Catherine and Atwater on the night of July 23, 1976, you would have met some very, very happy Russian customers.

In the days after our encounter with the Soviet delegates, I found that I couldn't get their enthusiasm for McDonald's out of my mind. I couldn't stop thinking about how much they enjoyed the restaurant and how much they enjoyed their food. I kept hearing them – "*khorosho*," "*otmenno*," "*vkusno*." Good. Delicious. Tasty – and I found myself thinking ahead to the 1980 Olympics, scheduled for Moscow. Who was going to provide food services for the Games? From what I'd heard, the Soviet Union didn't seem very adept at providing food services for its own citizens, much less thousands of hungry visitors. So why couldn't it be McDonald's?

That simple question raised the prospect of many complications – complications that, for a lot of people, might have kept the whole notion of McDonald's in the USSR stuck in the starting gate. Some might have worried more about the demographics of the Soviet population, or the economy, or the political situation. Others might have stalled on the problem of suppliers – with Soviet agriculture in a perpetual state of crisis, where would we find product that would consistently meet our standards? How could we guarantee the volume of supply that we would require? Certainly we weren't going to run the kind of restaurants that Soviets were used to – restaurants that never had half the items on their menu. Telling customers that we were out of Big Macs was just not on.

Some people might have decided that finding cheerful, energetic, and efficient personnel was simply not possible in the Soviet Union. Still others might have worried about how unlikely it was that the USSR would welcome so high-profile a symbol of Western capitalism into Russia.

I was not unaware of these potential problems. But my thinking was much more straightforward.

I thought: There is a huge population in the USSR. People get hungry and they like to eat. Their diet is largely made up of meat, bread, potatoes, and milk, and McDonald's provides meat, bread, potatoes, and milk of the highest quality. At an affordable price. I couldn't forget how taken my Soviet friends in Montreal were with what we at McDonald's call "QSC & V" – Quality, Service, Cleanliness, and Value. It's our mantra at McDonald's – it's something that everyone, from the newest employee to the most senior executive, has to take to heart. The Soviets took one look at QSC & V and they loved it.

Perhaps I was being naive. Certainly, some people thought I was. I remember Victor Bychkov, the deputy minister of internal trade of the USSR, telling me in the early 1980s that the entire notion of McDonald's in the Soviet Union was preposterous. Still, the issue seemed pretty straightforward to me. They want the food. We have the food. So, I thought. Why not?

I like to do things directly. And quickly. I like to strike while the iron's hot. And that may be a key difference between myself and many other people. There are lots of people who might have had the bright idea of, say, McDonald's in the USSR, but for them, an idea like that flits briefly through their minds and then disappears, along with a lot of other unacted-upon ideas. It's not a matter of talent. Ray Kroc used to say, "Nothing is more common than unsuccessful men with talent." It's a matter of action, of doing, of taking advantage of the moments history offers to us. Catch the wave. Take the plunge. Just do it. These are modern versions of something William Shakespeare wrote four hundred years ago: "There is a tide in the affairs of men, which, taken at the flood, leads on to fortune."

So I took the tide at the flood. When I got back to Toronto, I picked up the telephone. I called Fred Turner.

Fred Turner was then chairman and CEO of the McDonald's Corporation. Tenacious, intense, detail-oriented, Turner was someone whose advice I often sought.

I told Fred about our chance encounter with the Soviet delegation in Montreal. I told him about their response to McDonald's. I said, "Fred, this may sound crazy, but I'd love to go for it. I'd like to try to get us into the Soviet Union."

People often ask why McDonald's-Canada went into the Soviet Union. They often imagine that it was some kind of dark plot – that the Americans thought that it would be advantageous to use the Canadian company as a smokescreen. People think that somewhere, in some vast McDonald's headquarters, some clever Machiavellian schemer decided that the Soviets would probably feel less threatened by a Canadian operation than an American one. It would make a nice thriller, I suppose. Unfortunately, it isn't true. There was no secret American plan. There was no ultra-sophisticated strategy. There was no Machiavellian scheming. There was just a phone call between Fred Turner and me. And Fred Turner is someone who likes to make decisions as quickly and as firmly as I do. He knows how things work; he started at McDonald's in 1956 as a grillman. He knows McDonald's from the bottom up. He trusts his instincts.

He thought for a minute. Then he said, "Okay. Why don't you go for it, George."

And that changed everything.

It was never my intention only to go after the 1980 Olympics. My goal was to establish McDonald's in the USSR for the long run. In military terms, providing food services for the 1980 Olympic Games was going to be our beach-head. Or, to use a Fuller Brush metaphor, showing the Soviets that we could serve fifteen thousand meals a day near the Luzhniki Stadium was our way of getting our foot in the door.

This approach is absolutely consistent with McDonald's philosophy. Whether a new McDonald's is being opened in Ontario, or Connecticut, or Pushkin Square, managers (if the restaurant is owned by McDonald's) or owner-operators (if it is franchised) are strongly encouraged to become involved in their community. We don't believe that a short-term commitment ever makes sense – which is why there are community bulletin boards on the walls at McDonald's and why you will see a local McDonald's sponsoring a softball team or a kids' soccer league. It's why McDonald's will help out with local fundraisers, and charities, and schools, and community events. Our success has always been based on long-term commitment to the community. And so, the notion of a quick in-and-out in the USSR – set up, do the Olympics, and then blow town – was quite contrary to our way of doing things.

It was understood from the beginning that our bid for the food services at the Olympics would not earn us any profit. In fact, we had to think of it as an elaborate and possibly costly R & D project. It was a chance for us to impress upon the Soviets what McDonald's was and what kind of a contribution we could make. In his foreword to this book, Gorbachev points out that, for the Soviets, it was important that we were "not an exhibition but a real business, operating on the highest international standards." And we wanted to make this clear.

The specific nature of our negotiations was that we would build temporary facilities at each of the sports venues for the Games. "Temporary" was a word that made our approach to the USSR seem pretty innocuous. It was like coming in on tiptoes. But "temporary" was pretty much the last thing we had in mind – particularly when it became apparent that the negotiating process was going to be long, and difficult, and expensive. We began talking in 1976. By 1979, we were still talking, and McDonald's-Canada had already invested millions in our pitch to the USSR. For that reason, we wanted to leave the door open to more than a temporary presence in the USSR.

From our point of view, the potential market in Russia was just too big to pass up. The population of the USSR was 258 million. On its own, Moscow's population was nearly 35 per cent of the entire population of Canada – and by 1979, in Canada, there were more than three hundred McDonald's in operation, all doing extremely well. That year, McDonald's opened in Brazil and Singapore, bringing the company's international presence to a total of twenty-seven countries – a 900 per cent increase over what it had been a decade earlier. Shares in McDonald's were trading, after several splits, for $43.50 U.S., and, also in 1979, McDonald's served its 30 billionth hamburger. "Nobody Can Do It Like McDonald's Can" was our advertising refrain that year, and that catchy little jingle seemed to sum up the way we were approaching the world. We had every confidence in our product and in its market appeal.

Our instincts told us that in time the Soviet Union might prove to be one of the most profitable parts of McDonald's world. It was, at first, little more than a hunch – but a hunch we were willing to pursue. At first, we weren't certain to whom, exactly, we should be talking. And so we decided to talk to anybody who would listen. Here, for instance, is a telegram I sent in 1977 to several officials at the Ministry of Food for the USSR – one of dozens of similar telegrams I sent: "I am heading a top level delegation to Moscow on behalf of McDonald's Restaurants. McDonald's operates 4,500 restaurants around the world serving over 1.9 billion meals annually. We will be in Moscow Sept 26–30 to make a written and a 16mm movie presentation explaining the McDonald's Restaurant system. We would be pleased to have you and your representatives attend our presentation. . . . Looking forward to meeting you. George A. Cohon, President and Chief Exec. Officer, McDonald's Restaurants of Canada Limited."

Sometimes they came. Sometimes they didn't. And usually, at each of these presentations, we would have to explain to someone what a hamburger was.

The Soviets we'd met in Montreal were members of the organizing committee for the 1980 Olympic Games, and it was that committee with which we did most of our negotiating. The person with whom I dealt most frequently in those days was a fellow named Vladimir Koval. He was friendly and jovial. His emotions were never too far below the surface. He had been a basketball player in his day, and he was now the coach for the Soviet Olympic team.

Although we didn't ever address our long-term goals directly across the negotiating table, Koval and his team understood that a permanent position in the Soviet market was our objective. They knew how high the stakes were for us. I was convinced that the USSR represented one of the largest potential markets for McDonald's in the world. They would have been blind had they not seen what we had in mind.

The negotiations from 1976 to 1979 were extremely difficult. We were working in a vacuum. The two economic systems were so radically different that there was little or no common ground for our discussions. Our basic team consisted of Ron Cohen, executive vice president; John Huhs, our first lawyer; Peter Misikowetz, assistant vice president; and myself. Across the table, we were facing a constantly changing line-up of negotiators and advisors. Koval and the Olympic Organizing Committee were the most consistent players, but the situation was complicated. There were three parties involved in the discussions – the Olympic Organizing Committee, the Main Administration for Public Catering of the Moscow City Executive Committee, and McDonald's Restaurants of Canada. To further complicate matters, the Executive Committee, through its chairman, who was effectively the mayor of Moscow, got its orders from the Kremlin and the Politburo. As a result, there were a lot of people involved in the negotiations on their side. We'd often go off in the morning to Koval's office in Gorky Street and confront a whole new team.

"Where's Ivan?" I'd ask. "And Tanya?"

"They are not here." Which did not exactly come as news.

This sort of manoeuvre often seemed to occur the day after a long, difficult negotiating session in which I had finally given way on a couple of sticky points in order to keep things moving. I remember that once, when it was getting late in the day, I backed off on a boycott protection clause that our lawyer, John Huhs, insisted we include in the agreement. "These are the Olympics," I said. "Who's going to boycott the Olympics?"

Famous last words. This was a major concession (as things turned out, it was almost a disastrous concession), but my hope was that when the next morning's talks began, the Soviets would respond with a concession or two of their own.

Nyet.

That morning, in the boardroom of Koval's office, I found myself facing a table of strangers. "But yesterday . . ." I began.

"Yesterday was yesterday. Today is today."

And off, once again, slowly, painstakingly, we would go.

The Soviets were very good at making it seem as if we were making progress. Just enough to keep you from giving up, but never enough actually to get anywhere. We would have meetings that we would think were important, but probably, in the scheme of things, weren't important at all. For instance, we'd have meetings to sign protocols – a protocol being an agreement to meet again to try to reach an agreement. Bureaucrats are very big on protocols. Protocols inspire lots of meetings, produce lots of paper, promote endless discussion – and almost never get down to anything as definite as a result. Which is why bureaucrats like them so much. So here we were, a handful of pretty unbureaucratic guys from Toronto finding their way through the tangles of what Mikhail Gorbachev calls the USSR's "bureaucratic jungle."

So we met. And met again. And we agreed to continue to discuss mutually advantageous ideas. In the initial protocol between McDonald's-Canada and the organizing committee of the 1980 Olympics, we agreed to work toward "establishing a fast food service restaurant on the territory of Luzhniki stadium." That was the easy part. Under discussion – and sometimes under heated discussion – were such items as a $100,000 fee we would have to pay to the organizing committee, the cost of the transportation and housing of our personnel, and the requisite licences and clearances to import the product we needed.

Still, there were lots of things on which we agreed – not that our various agreements ever meant very much. We agreed on co-operation, on exchanges of information, on establishing a dialogue. We agreed to strive for this and work toward that. There was one meeting at the offices of the Olympic Organizing Committee at which we couldn't quite understand what the interpreter was saying. We kept looking at one another in bewilderment. It seemed extremely complicated and we kept asking for clarification. Eventually we realized that we were being asked to agree to keep trying to agree.

And so, after we stopped laughing – we agreed.

And all of these agreements were signed with typically Russian ceremony.

Part of the process of signing protocols is responding to toasts, proposing toasts, drinking toasts – vodka, of course. Clear, cold, liquid dynamite. We drank toasts to East–West co-operation, to world peace, to international co-operation. And I proposed a few – a few thousand. I'm not a big drinker – certainly not a big vodka drinker – but I realized very quickly that this was the way the Soviets do things. So, when in Rome. . . .

You name it, we toasted it. Before long I got the nickname Pop-up. At the slightest provocation, I'd jump to my feet. "*Tovarishchi* – Comrades," I'd say. "To General Secretary Brezhnev." "To international co-operation." "To a good harvest."

There was sometimes something almost dream-like about those first four years of negotiations. Something unreal. For instance, I used to like to begin meetings with something that would catch the Soviets' attention. I would say, "I'm a capitalist. I believe in free enterprise. Competition and profit are not dirty words."

This was a kind of cocky thing to say back then. It was a little provocative. I didn't want to get into a big ideological debate with the people with whom we were negotiating, but I didn't want them to get the impression that I was in some way in sympathy with their system, either. My own personal politics generally hover somewhere between Liberal and Conservative on the Canadian spectrum, and the way I vote depends on the qualifications of individual candidates.

Thinking now of the way events unfolded in the Soviet Union over the succeeding fifteen years, I suppose that when I stood up and said, "I believe in free enterprise and in pay based on performance," I must have been hitting a responsive chord in many of the people with whom we were talking – much more responsive than I could have imagined, or that they could have let on, at the time. The communist system was about to enter the decade of its collapse, and the seeds of its eventual failure had long been sown. The fact that the system was breaking down was apparent everywhere: in the broken-down buses and trucks at the sides of the highways, in the empty, gloomy stores, in the line-ups that would immediately collect at a street corner whenever word got out that somebody was bringing a truckload of food in from the country. The break-down was apparent, yes; openly discussed, no. And in the late 1970s, stating my belief in capitalism so bluntly was more bravado than anything else. Or so I thought. It was a way of catching people's attention, of pulling their chain a little, of waking up a sleepy table of Soviet bureaucrats who didn't know a Big Mac from a peanut butter sandwich. That I could speak frankly during our business negotiations sometimes lulled me into a false sense of security about how tolerant the system was. But then something would happen to remind me of the true nature of the state.

I remember once attending the Bolshoi Ballet. The famous theatre is across Teatral'naya Square from the Metropol, and I attended performances there whenever I could. The Bolshoi was built in 1824, and the greatest dancers in the world have appeared there over the years. One night, a father and daughter shared a box with me. They were from Riga in Latvia. The daughter was a medical student, twenty-three or twenty-four years old. They both spoke English very well, and during the intermission we struck up a conversation. He was a distinguished-looking gentleman; she was a classic Eastern European beauty. After the ballet, I invited them back to the hotel for a drink.

As we walked into the hotel, the daughter was stopped by security police. They asked for her papers. She'd left them at her hotel, but the police were not going to let her off the hook. The father started to get angry. The police identified themselves – KGB – and threatened to take him to the station. By this time, the daughter was terrified. So I tried to intervene.

I said, "Look. She's a medical student. I'm a Canadian businessman and they are my guests. We met at the ballet. I invited them here for a drink . . ."

"*Spokoino, ne nado shum podnimat,*" they said. Which, in rough translation, means "Shut your trap, buddy!" They said that if I didn't, I'd end up in trouble, too. The way they said "trouble" had a particularly ominous ring. I got the distinct impression that, in this situation, a Ronald McDonald watch was not going to help. The one who spoke to me had eyes with all the friendliness and charm of a pair of ball bearings. And that's when I started to get frightened. I realized that these bastards weren't fooling around.

They took the girl away. I remember the sheer terror on her face. They wouldn't let her father go with her. It seemed completely unreasonable – especially to a foreigner. Unreasonable and unnecessary. The helplessness and the fear that I felt knocked me out of the secure world of the tourist and visiting businessman. I caught a sudden and very disturbing glimpse of a reality of Soviet life.

They threw her in the back of their Volga, and about two hours later, they brought her back. She was petrified. The father and I had sat in the lobby, waiting. He was beside himself. And when, at last, the police returned her to the hotel, they made no apology. They just dumped her off. I couldn't believe their attitude. They seemed interested in nothing other than throwing their weight around, exerting their influence, making sure that we knew who was the boss.

Unreal. That's the word that kept passing through my mind. Something else that struck me as unreal during our early negotiations was how differently we were received, depending on who was receiving us. McDonald's, by then, was a household word throughout much of the world. There were two hundred McDonald's in Japan by 1979, one hundred in Germany, and we had just opened in Portugal. Everyone had heard of McDonald's – everyone, it seemed, except the officials of the Soviet Union with whom we were negotiating.

We might as well have been from another planet. We often met with officials who had absolutely no notion – not the vaguest idea – what we were talking about. So, as a result, we had to explain over and over and over again what it was we were trying to do. We had to spell out everything: This is a hamburger; this is an order of french fries; this is ketchup; this is somebody who smiles and says, "Thanks. Please come again." All Greek to them.

And meanwhile, of course, the cost of our efforts in the USSR kept climbing – a cost that I was called upon frequently to defend before a sometimes impatient board of McDonald's directors. Fortunately for me, my boss, Fred Turner, had visited the USSR in the late 1970s. He had seen the potential, and he supported me during many a board meeting.

In Moscow, we were often kept waiting. We were often told at the last minute that our appointment was cancelled. Initially, we were often obliged to meet with such low-level officials, I half-expected them to start polishing the floors while we were talking. We were not taken to be the representatives of a celebrated, world-wide corporation. Rather, we were all too often dealt with like irritatingly persistent gnats.

Occasionally, everything changed. We found that whenever the right person pressed the right button for us, we would be treated like veritable heroes of the Revolution. I remember once, after a particularly long stretch of negotiations, Ron Cohen and I decided that we needed to get out of Moscow. We needed a break. As executive vice president, Ron was a key player in the negotiations. People often think we're related, but of course we're not. I'm Cohon, thanks to a clerk on Ellis Island who wasn't a very good speller. He's Cohen – a name that can be traced back through 3,300 years of Jewish history to Aaron, the first high priest – which would be pretty impressive lineage, except for one thing: Ron's an Irish Catholic. That day, we decided that we would head off to

Sochi, a city about 1,000 miles from Moscow on the Black Sea for the weekend, just for a little R & R.

We had, by then, worked our way well up the ladder, and we had been engaged in some pretty intensive negotiations with Vsevolod Pavlovich Shimansky, the minister of trade for the Russian Federation. Unbeknownst to us, Shimansky wired ahead to the Sochi City Council, saying that two nice businessmen from Canada were coming in, and would every courtesy be extended.

Now, it probably didn't matter to the officials in Sochi that Ron was executive vice president of McDonald's-Canada, and that I was the CEO. But it mattered – and mattered a lot! – that the minister of trade for the Russian Federation sent a wire to the Sochi City Council from Moscow, requesting that something be done. Jump? How high?

When Ron and I arrived at the Hotel Kameliya in Sochi we were both exhausted. It had been a rough week. The meetings had been endless and unproductive. We were ready for a rest. We had dinner. We went to our rooms. We fell into our beds. For the first time in quite a long while we were going to be able to sleep in.

But very early the next morning my phone rang. I was still only half awake when what the desk clerk was saying began to sink in.

"Come again?"

"*Gospodin Kohon, Vas tut vnizu zhdyot delegatsiya.*" My Russian wasn't very good. But it sounded to me as if she was saying that a government delegation was there to meet us.

I called Ron's room. He is only marginally better in the early morning than I am. He pulled on a pair of cut-off jeans and a T-shirt and sandals and stumbled to the elevator. When he walked into the lobby, still rubbing the sleep out of his eyes, he was greeted by the Mayor and the City Council and about twenty local dignitaries. Young girls with flowers to present. Gifts from the city of Sochi. Official welcomes. Speeches. The whole bit.

Ron called up to my room. "Remember that sleep-in we planned?"

"Uh-huh."

"Well, George, the plans have changed."

We were the honoured and official guests of the Mayor and the City Council of Sochi. They wined us and dined us, and that night they took us to a circus that was on in the town. We sat in the VIP box, and at intermission – while all the regular folk had to line up for their chunks of bread and sausage – we were taken to a private room where we feasted on caviar, and cold cuts, and smoked salmon, and champagne. It was the Mayor's wife's birthday, and so we started making toasts. As usual, Pop-up was popping up like a toaster. To Pushkin. To the next five-year agricultural plan. To the Red Army hockey team. By then, I'd had a lot of practice.

After a while, it occurred to me that the intermission had been going on for rather long. But none of our hosts seemed in any hurry. So we carried on – more toasts, more smoked salmon. Eventually Ron and I thought maybe we should head back toward our seats. There were only a few kilos of Beluga caviar left, and although the champagne supply looked healthy enough, no-one could think of any more toasts to make. Followed by the Mayor and all the councillors, we left the VIP lounge, came down a long, empty corridor, stepped back into the stadium – and there found thousands of people sitting quietly and patiently, waiting for our return. You could have heard a pin drop as we made our way down the aisle. They had held the circus for about fifteen minutes – for us! When we sat down, the second half of the program was allowed to begin.

"Unreal," Ron said.

"Unreal," I replied.

Soon we were back in Moscow. Negotiations continued. They were complex, minutely detailed – but at long last, it seemed that the Olympic Organizing Committee was on side; it appeared to be favourably disposed to our servicing sites during the Olympic Games. The City of Moscow's Main Administration for Public Catering, Glavobshchepit, an important partner in any arrangement, still had some concerns. Nevertheless, negotiations looked promising. We pressed on. And although there were times when I thought this negotiating process would go on forever, finally, by late fall of 1979, it seemed we had a deal to provide the food services for the 1980 Games. It had been a long, hard haul, and, logistically speaking, 1980 was not very far away – but we had reached an agreement at last! It was an extremely intricate deal. It spelled out everything: the number of McDonald's that would open in different venues; the design of these McDonald's; the hours they would be open; the role the Soviets would play in their operation and management.

It hadn't been easy. But on a cold early winter day we rose from the table in Koval's office. The two teams shook hands. The Soviets said that now it was just a question of typing up the agreement and of having it translated. This process would take several days.

"Fine," I said. "I'll sign whenever it's ready. Just let me know."

"We'll call you on Wednesday. At ten o'clock in the morning. Where will you be?"

"Room 2264. The Hotel Metropol."

The two days passed pleasantly enough. In the hotel corridor, I scurried past Dounia's stony expression. On the streets, I enjoyed just walking. I enjoy walking through cities. I especially enjoy walking through Moscow – Red Square, the Arbat, Gorky Park, the Pushkin and Tretyakov galleries. There is something about the place that never fails to excite me, and I often wonder whether my attraction to the culture and to the people has to do with my own heritage. I was born in Chicago only three decades after my family left this part of the world. They had been in the Ukraine for generations. The Ukraine isn't Russia, but it's a lot closer than the corner of 71st Street and South Shore Drive, and I don't believe these kinds of deep-rooted, centuries-old connections disappear very quickly. Perhaps I enjoy my travels throughout Russia, the Ukraine, Belarus, Georgia, and the Baltics because at some subconscious level I feel as if I'm coming home.

On Wednesday morning, I was in my hotel room. At ten o'clock the phone rang. The message was a little disappointing. They weren't quite done yet. They would call me back at two in the afternoon.

At two they called, as promised. Apparently, there was some technical problem with the translation. They said: We'll call you tomorrow, at ten in the morning.

They called the next day at ten in the morning. Same thing.

I was starting to get anxious. "What's the problem?"

"*Tekhnicheskaya neuvyazka*," they said. A technical problem. "Don't worry. We'll call you this afternoon."

Which they did – but only to say: We'll call you tomorrow morning.

I had no idea what was happening, and all the attempts I made to get an answer were stonewalled. The Russians are masters at stonewalling. So, I waited. Every day they called. At ten a.m. Then at two. And I waited.

Ten in the morning: We'll call you at two.

Two in the afternoon: We'll call you tomorrow at ten.

And I waited. In Room 2264 of the Hotel Metropol. With a grand piano I couldn't play, with a view of the vast, monolithic KGB headquarters, with a shower that didn't work, and with the indomitable Dounia posted outside my door. I was beginning to get an insight into the concept of house arrest.

I waited for *seventeen* days.

I kept making plane reservations, and then cancelling them. After the first week, I devoted a lot of time to trying to figure out how to get some laundry done – no easy task in those days. I walked the streets. I wandered through GUM – the big Soviet department store – and bought a pair of blue jeans. They measured my waist with string, then they measured the jeans. I've never yet been able to get them on.

I stood in Red Square at midnight and watched the guard change at Lenin's tomb. There was something eerie and frightening about the blank-faced, goose-stepping automatons who made up the guard.

I got to know Moscow pretty well during that period. The Borodinskii Bridge. Gorky Street. The Pushkin Museum. The Tretyakov Gallery. But I spent much of the time in Room 2264. The room was always too hot. I couldn't open a window. I sat, reading, listening to the pipes bang and the vacuum cleaners droning in the hall. Every night, when I came back from my walk, the last person I saw was Dounia. Once, I thought I saw her smile back at me when I said goodnight. Every morning I woke up and looked out my window, and every day I wondered: "What the hell is going on?"

After about a week of this, I began to feel not-quite-myself. Then a little woozy. Then downright sick. I'm not sure what kind of a bug I had picked up. Perhaps food poisoning. Perhaps the flu. Whatever it was, it laid me low.

Getting sick in Moscow in those days was no laughing matter. I knew that if Russian hospitals were as well run and as organized as their restaurants I was in big trouble. I took to my bed, thinking I would just weather the storm.

On the second day of my illness, I heard a knock at my door. I thought it was the chambermaid. I called out to tell her not to bother making up the room. But, to my surprise, I heard the jingle of keys in the corridor and the click of my lock being turned.

The door opened. It was Dounia.

I had never seen her standing before, and she was shorter than I had imagined. Still, she was a powerful-looking figure, about the size, shape, and general cuddliness of the boulders you sometimes see in national parks with historical plaques on them.

I raised my head from my pillow. I thought: Oh-oh, she's here to do a towel count, or to reprimand me for not folding my clothes properly, or to order me out of the room because some *apparatchik* needs it.

She came to the side of my bed. She reached out and put a hand on my forehead. It was cool and gentle, like a grandmother's. "*Da Vy i vpryam sovsem zaboleli*," she said. "You're really sick."

Dounia looked after me. She was like a wonderful nurse – friendly, efficient, helpful – and every day she arrived at my room with some sort of hot Russian brew that she had concocted for me. It wasn't exactly my grandmother's chicken soup, but it was some kind of curative broth that was very settling. For three or four days, she brought this in to the hotel from her home. She heated it up in the hotel's kitchen and brought it to my room. She nursed me back to health.

This was an important lesson. As a visitor, I heard constantly from other foreigners about how unfriendly and unhelpful the Russians were. When I told them what I was trying to do in Moscow, invariably their response was: You'll never teach the Russians to put the customer first; they have no understanding of the service industry. And so Dounia, at the Metropol, was kind of an inspiration to me. Judging by what she had done for me, I couldn't see that we would have any difficulty teaching Russians how to work in a McDonald's, and how to teach them to go the extra mile, cheerfully, for our customers. There is nothing inherently unfriendly about Russians. On the contrary. I sipped Dounia's broth and wondered: If I had fallen ill in the most luxurious and expensive Western hotel, how many members of the staff would have voluntarily gone to such lengths to help me?

Finally – finally! – the phone message was different. Instead of asking me to wait for another call, they told me to come to Koval's office for a meeting. Seventeen days late, but I was healthy, thanks to Dounia, and feeling quite buoyant. I took a cab to Gorky Street. But when I walked into the Moscow Olympics committee offices at 22-A, my heart sank. I could tell by the tone of conversation, and by the look in Koval's eyes, that something was terribly wrong.

"George," he said. "There is a problem. The deal's off."

I was stunned. "How can it be off? You and I agreed to terms. We shook hands."

I'm not sure that there is any expression that is much sadder than the one that crosses a Russian's face when something is so mysteriously Russian, it cannot be explained to a Westerner. "A riddle wrapped in a mystery inside an enigma," was how Churchill once described Russia. And Koval's sad eyes and despondent, apologetic shrug seemed to imply that the explanation of why the deal had fallen through would be just as impenetrable, just as murky.

"I can't tell you why," Koval said. "But the deal is off. It's dead."

Four years of negotiations. Millions of dollars. Every "t" had been crossed. Every "i" had been dotted. Ron Cohen, Peter Misikowetz, and I had put everything into this. Every detail had been ironed out. But now, none of that mattered. For reasons that I couldn't guess, the deal was down the drain.

We went back to the Metropol. I called the airport. I packed my bag. I said goodbye to Dounia.

"*Schastlivogo puti*," she said. "Goodbye."

On the way to the airport I thought of how often I had told the McDonald's boards not to worry, the deal would happen. Of how often Fred Turner had supported me. Of how often I had said that, in the end, it would be worth all the money, all the time, all the effort.

I paid the cab driver. In rubles. I was, by then, out of McDonald's pins and watches. I had no American cigarettes. He was disappointed. That made two of us.

I would have a lot of explaining to do when I got home.

• 2 •

Born in the U.S.A.

It must be something that everyone daydreams about now and then. Going back. It's impossible, of course. Thomas Wolfe said it: You can't go home again. But the impossibility of returning doesn't stop people from wondering what it would be like. Certainly, it doesn't stop me. I often think about the old neighbourhood, the aunts and uncles and cousins, the friends, the schoolyard, the movie theatres, the drugstore where they used to make strawberry sodas and Coke with a thick, wonderful syrup. Once, a few years ago, I actually did go back – to the apartment where I grew up, to the streets where we used to play and ride our bikes, to the sidewalk where my dad used to walk home from work.

Of course, it wasn't the same any more. Everything had changed. Thomas Wolfe was right.

But it hasn't stopped me from thinking about the old days. Just for a moment – a passing thought in the middle of a pretty busy life. I find myself, just for an instant, whisked back fifty years.

To 6744 south Chappel Avenue. Chicago. The South Side. Where I was born in 1937. Home.

I can see my Dad coming along Chappel on his way back from the bakery. He went into law as a young man, but when my grandfather died he took over a small bakery on the northwest side of Chicago, called Northwestern Bakery, renamed it Cohon's Rye Bread, and turned it into a thriving enterprise. The best rye bread in Chicago. He always wore a suit and tie. He worked long hours. He started early and it was usually seven or eight o'clock before he got home.

Jack Cohon. Serious-looking, hard-working, conservative. A little formal. A little stiff. In some ways, very different from me. I don't think you could have paid him to put on a pair of the blue jeans that I wear so often. Certainly not a T-shirt, certainly not in public. He'd probably still give me a good talking-to if he were around today and found out that often I go in to the office without a tie or without a jacket. "George, you're the head of the company," he'd say. "Dress right."

In other ways, he's not so different. In truth, the older I get, the more I see certain similarities. For instance, when people tell me they can't find work, I hear my father's voice in my own response. I know it's a different world today. I know there are people who want to work but who are caught in the trap of welfare, and who have children to look after, and who, often, are trying to better their education at the same time that they are trying to provide for a family. I often think that corporations could be doing more than they do to help people get on their feet and off welfare. But I also meet people who will only consider certain kinds of jobs, and who complain about how hard those jobs are to find – and when I talk to them, I hear my father's voice ringing in my head: Go drive a cab, work part time in a hospital, work for free if you have to, go volunteer, go help somewhere, go do something until the right job comes along. Make things happen. Just don't sit around whining about how hard work is to find.

My father always worked. When he saw an opening he took it. When the law firm where he wanted to set up his practice told him that although they could use him, they were sorry, they simply didn't have enough space in the office for him, he told them not to worry. He'd move in his own desk and sit in the hall.

When my grandfather's bakery suddenly needed someone to run it, my father decided he'd learn how to run a bakery. He'd learn how to make the best rye bread in the city. This attitude sank in with me.

I've always worked. When I was eleven, my grandfather – my mother's father – had a plumbing store, Sol Ellis and Sons at 21st and State Street. He would hire me on a Sunday to sit and count inventory. I'd get a ladder and climb up to the big bins, and sit there all afternoon counting bolts and washers. It was boring, just counting. It was especially boring on beautiful sunny days, but it was a job. It was something I did to earn my own money – and that made me quite proud. My job. It had a nice ring to it.

I took other part-time jobs when I grew older. I sold shoes, I worked construction, I worked night shifts in a bakery, I was a Fuller Brush salesman. People who know me are never surprised that I was an excellent Fuller Brush salesman. Once a salesman, always a salesman. It's something you have in your blood. I remember that in 1989, at a big fundraising dinner for cystic fibrosis that Mila Mulroney had organized, the salesman in me really came out. In the Museum of Civilization, in Hull, there were several hundred people in attendance who had already made generous donations to the campaign. But my friend Doug Bassett, of Baton Broadcasting, and I decided we were going to up the ante a little, and during the dinner we worked the room, table by table. It wasn't so very different from going door to door when I was a kid. It was just a matter of being persuasive – which, in the case of a cause like cystic fibrosis, wasn't difficult. We must have been pretty convincing, because we managed to double the amount of money that had been raised for the campaign, from $500,000 to $1,000,000, in about fifteen minutes. When the emcee, the world-renowned Canadian musician David Foster, stood up and announced what we had just done, Mila, seated at the head table next to Barbara Bush, burst into tears.

Anything is possible.

So, work? You're having trouble finding work? Here's what my father would say, in a voice that comes right out of the Great Depression: Don't tell me there's no work. Set up your desk in the hall. Learn how to make the best rye bread. There's always work. Go find it.

It sounds a little harsh to modern ears, but Dad wasn't harsh. He wasn't unfriendly. It's not as if he'd bite your head off or anything. He was quiet. He was firm in his convictions. He was solid. Old-fashioned, you might say – but some of those old-fashioned ideas had a lot of merit. They still do. My parents taught my sister and me to be fair. If we were arguing over some dessert – a piece of pie or cake, or the last schnecke – my father would always say that one of us could divide it in two, and the other would choose which half to take. "That's fair," he'd say. They also taught us to be polite, to be respectful of our elders, to be considerate of other people. My father's manners were always impeccable. He always said hello to people. South Shore was a real neighbourhood in those days. There were neighbourhoods like it throughout Chicago – blocks of decent, hard-working people, where everyone knew everyone else. In the summer, it was an especially closely knit community. There was no air-conditioning then, and windows were open. People strolled along the street. My father would be coming home from work, and he'd always say, "Hello, Mrs. Mannister." "Good evening, Mr. Eisenburg."

"Hello, Jack," they'd say. "How's Carolyn?"

Everyone loved my mother. She had a real spark of personality – a little more flair for life than my father had. She had a giving nature, which is something I can only hope I've inherited. She also had something which I have no doubt she passed on. She had the same gap between her two front teeth as I have – an heirloom from the Ellis side of the family.

My father was a real gentleman. A solid citizen. A good man. He taught me and Sandy, my older sister, that it was our responsibility to help those less fortunate than ourselves; I suppose my interest in charitable organizations comes from my parents' attitude toward those who really needed assistance. It wasn't anything special to them. No big deal. It was just part of life, part of being a citizen, part of being a member of a community. But Dad also had a kind of toughness to him – it was the way many people were in those days. It was a kind of toughness for which a lot of people today don't have much sympathy.

He didn't have any patience for people who thought they deserved a free ride. This was the era of Roosevelt and the New Deal. Times were hard. Everyone knew that. But welfare? The dole? He had no time for it. He'd put himself through law school. He'd studied at night. He took over a small bakery when my grandfather died and steadily increased its business. He got up at five and, after dinner, after helping us with homework, he fell into bed, exhausted, by ten. He worked hard. He knew, from his father's example, that it was possible to start with nothing and to end up with something. What could possibly be more difficult than what my grandparents managed to do: escape from the violence and hatred of the pogroms, arrive in a strange new land with a young family, with no money, with only a very few English words, and still, against all those odds, establish themselves? I never knew my grandfather, although I was named after him. I think that being his namesake and listening to my father's tales of admiration for his father's rugged self-determination have instilled in me a work ethic which, in turn, I have passed on to my sons.

My mom, Carolyn, was always waiting for him in the evenings – with dinner ready. She usually stood at the open window, in the evening light. Tall, attractive, she had light brown hair and clear blue eyes.

I remember the time – I must have been six or seven years old – we drove to a movie downtown in the bakery truck. Delivering bread was considered an essential service during the war, so we could always get gas for the truck. My sister and I felt a little self-conscious, embarrassed even, pulling up in front of the crowd at the theatre in a bread delivery truck. My mother noticed, and she said, "Be proud. It doesn't matter whether we arrive in a bread truck or a sedan. Just be proud."

I remember my mother in our tiny kitchen, preparing a weekly favourite, lamb chops. I ate so much cabbage as a child that I decided I would never eat it again. We weren't poor. But we weren't well-to-do, either. We lived in a three-storey, six-apartment building. A second-floor walk-up – five rooms, one bath, one telephone. Middle-class, I guess you would have said then.

One bath. Now that's a vivid memory. The other day I counted how many bathrooms we have in the houses we own now. I'd never actually counted them up before. The total surprised me a little. I mentioned this to Susie. She said, "Just don't count the telephones."

I can imagine what my father would say about our bathrooms. "What are you running here, a hotel?" So I asked myself a question: How does owning so many bathrooms affect who I am? How does being wealthy affect who I am? And I decided: I'm still the same guy who lived in an apartment with one bath. I just don't have to wait in line any more.

But money was tight back then. There were no cruise ship holidays, no trips to Hawaii, no season tickets to Wrigley Field. Even so, there was never any suggestion that Mom should go out to work. That just wasn't done in those days. She stayed at home and kept house. She had her charities, and volunteer work, and her literary club that met regularly to discuss books. She was a great fan of Eleanor Roosevelt's books. And she looked after my older sister, Sandy. And she looked after me.

Even the fact that she could drive – she got her licence when she was sixteen – raised a few of the more old-fashioned eyebrows in the neighbourhood. After the war, we had a Dodge, and I can still see my mother and my grandmother in the front seat rolling sedately past the sidewalk where I was playing. My grandmother would want to go a friend's place, or maybe shopping at Marshall Field's, and Mom would drive her. This was considered unusual. A driver's licence was thought to be a little too much independence for a woman back then.

And what of the neighbourhood? Well, in some ways it was nothing special. There were neighbourhoods like it in most big American cities in those days. There was a real mix of people, although people on our street were mostly Jewish – families who were, like ours, from traditional Jewish backgrounds, where ritual and observance were instilled in children, and who regularly attended the South Side Hebrew Congregation on the Sabbath and on High Holidays. The older people still had rich Russian or German accents when they struggled with English. Many spoke Yiddish. You could picture yourself back in the old world when the iceman delivered his sawdust-covered blocks on his horse-drawn cart. On Sunday evenings, in the warm weather, we gathered in Jackson Park for picnics.

As in a lot of urban neighbourhoods in those days, if you went a few streets over from ours, there were blocks that were more Irish. Others more Italian. Others were more African-American. At schools – and on the football teams I played on – everyone was thrown together. But people had their turf.

I don't remember much anti-Semitism or out-and-out racism in those days, but the neighbourhood was divided into its cliques. It wasn't anti-Jewish so much as anti whatever you were not. If you were Jewish, you didn't quite trust the Irish – that kind of thing. This was a far cry from the kind of multi-culturalism you see in almost any McDonald's in North America today – a white counterperson, a Hispanic manager, serving African-American customers, Asian customers, you name it – but in those days everyone thought that social fragmentation was perfectly natural. You just stuck with your own. Family, friends, business associates, clubs. People held together, which was good. But on the other hand, they sometimes held together by holding other people away, which wasn't so good. Still, these kinds of divisions weren't regarded as particularly serious, and, at the adult level, the tensions between different groups were usually held in check. A balance was maintained. Civility usually prevailed. At the level of school kids, though, these rivalries were often a little more out in the open. I had some interesting walks home – interesting as in hair-raising. I had to learn some pretty basic survival skills. Until my third year in high school, when – almost overnight, it seemed – I turned into a big, strong, tall kid, I did more running and fast talking than fighting.

Today, in business, people always talk about street smarts: how to size up people or a situation quickly, how to think on your feet, how to make the right move at the right time. This is an invaluable asset in business – because business, when you get right down to it, is mostly about understanding people: knowing how to assess business relationships, how to separate real intentions from fabricated ones, how to read a situation accurately, how to guess motives and ambitions, how to know who you can count on and who you can't, knowing who to trust on a handshake deal. Knowing who will honour the handshake when the chips are really down.

Street smarts. I think the term is pretty accurate, although I'm not so sure that many of the people who use it these days ever learned any smarts on any actual streets. There aren't many corners and sidewalks and alleys at most MBA programs.

I've had a look at what business schools do, the times I've been invited to speak at Harvard, Northwestern's Kellogg School, the University of Western Ontario, and at INSEAD in Fontainebleau, France. I'm always happy to talk to students, and I think that business schools have many strengths. But one thing they can't teach is the kind of instinctual response and reliance on gut feelings that some people are lucky enough to learn at a young age.

I remember once, in 1989, driving to work in Toronto, and hearing a young woman, a Canadian rower, talking on CBC Radio's *Metro Morning* about how difficult it was to get the support she needed to compete on the world scene. She was saying that after a disastrous Olympics in 1988, rowing had experienced cutbacks so devastating that it looked as if top Canadian rowers would have to cover a considerable portion of their own training, equipment, and travel costs for the 1989 World Championships. I'd never heard of this young woman before. I knew nothing about her. I wasn't even particularly interested in rowing, to tell you the truth. But somehow, in my gut, I knew she was going to go places. I could tell by something in her voice, something in her conviction, that she was a winner. So when I got to the office, I called the CBC. She was still there. I asked how much money she thought she needed. She was a little surprised, but eventually she told me: about $2,000. I told her the cheque was in the mail. I think the thud I heard was her keeling over.

It was just a hunch. But, all things considered, it wasn't a bad call. Silken Laumann went on to become one of Canada's best-known and most courageous athletes, one of the best rowers in the world, and the winner of three Olympic medals.

So why was I so sure about Silken Laumann? I'm not sure I can explain it. A feeling. An instinct. Street smarts.

Business schools can teach the most sophisticated management techniques. They can teach the most advanced forms of corporate structuring and financial projections. They can teach you everything you need to know about Nasdaq and the Dow Jones and the Federal Reserve. But they can't teach you the kind of quick, creative thinking the average ten-year-old Jewish kid on the South Side of Chicago had to learn when he came around a corner and found four big Italian kids coming his way.

Hang tough. Cut and run. Stare down the competition. Take a beating. These are terms you see bandied about in business magazines and on financial pages. These are things you hear business-people say at conferences. They are metaphors. But when I was a kid, their meanings were quite literal. If you took a beating, you took a beating. There was nothing metaphorical about a black eye and a bloody nose. If you encountered a bully – and I particularly remember one kid who picked on me and who beat me up constantly when I was going to elementary school – "taking one on the chin" was not an abstraction. You knew who your friends were; you knew who your enemies were. And the line between them was pretty clear.

There are two stories that come to mind. The first is about the bully. He picked on me, and on a lot of the little kids at the school, relentlessly. He was a big kid – big for his age – so there wasn't much we could do about it. Year after year, he was just a sort of fixture in our lives – mean, cruel, and really, when you got down to it, cowardly, because he always picked on kids who were smaller than he was. He'd wait for us. He'd jump us. He'd beat the hell out of us.

This went on well into high school – and I'd become so used to thinking of him as being bigger and stronger than I was that, for a while, during the year that I had a real growth spurt, I didn't realize that I was actually just as big, just as strong. Until one day, I was going to get a drink at the school drinking fountain, and he barged in front of me. I stood there for a moment, thinking of all the times he had pushed me and my buddies around, all the times he had beaten us up, all the nasty things he had done – and I suddenly realized: Hey, I can take this guy. It was a kind of revelation. I stepped up and cracked his teeth into the fountain. When he turned around, there I was. Standing my ground. Staring down the competition. And that was that. He told his father. And his father came over one night and talked to my father. I denied everything, but that kid's bully days were over. From that day on, whenever he saw me, he was the one who did the running. He never bothered me again.

Let bygones be bygones? That's not the way things were when I was growing up. That's not the way I am, even today. For instance, here's the second story I can tell you – the story about Don Smith.

Don was one of the top officers of McDonald's in the U.S.A. throughout the 1970s. We were quite friendly. I always used to see him when I was in the States, and when he was in Canada we would get together. He was a frequent visitor at our house over the years.

If someone I know leaves McDonald's and goes into another business, I always wish them well. I stay in touch, and if there's anything I can do to help, I'm always happy to do so.

But McDonald's is not a place for hired guns; people who work there don't just move around the industry from one company to the next. It's a question of friendship, of loyalty. It's almost family. So if someone leaves McDonald's and stays in the same business – if they go to work for a competitor – I just write them off. In my books, they're gone.

Don Smith left McDonald's in 1977 to become the head of one of our direct competitors. As far as I was concerned, that was that. Finito. Somebody works through the company – the company that I've helped to build, the company on which my livelihood is based – and then tries to take business away from us – I have no time for him. Period.

After Don went to the competition, one day he was in Toronto, on business. He came by our house, as he had so many times when he had been working at McDonald's. As it happened, I was out of the country. The doorbell rang, and Susie went to the intercom.

Susie knew Don quite well. She also knew how I felt, and, as a matter of fact, she felt the same way. She said, "George isn't home."

"Well, I just wanted to say hi."

Susie said, "I'll tell George you stopped by." Click. She wouldn't even open the door for him.

You sometimes hear businessmen talk about payback time. About being a team player. When I was a kid I learned about both – literally. It sometimes helps, I find, to be able to remember what metaphors really mean.

Not that our neighbourhood was all fights and bullies. Far from it. Mostly, I felt safe there. I felt at home.

The beach was only six blocks away. Lake Michigan. That was our swimming pool. I've seen some of the best beaches in the world – Nevis, South Africa, Hawaii, the South of France – but I'm not sure I've ever had more fun than we did on those summer afternoons playing touch football at the 67th Street Beach.

You could play baseball or basketball in the yard of O'Keeffe Elementary School. I loved playing basketball. Just loved it. When I got to high school, I had my heart set on making the team. I made the first cut, and the second, and the third, and the fourth. But on the very last cut, with only five players left to go, I got the axe. I was devastated. I think it was the first real failure I had to face in my life.

There was always something to do in the neighbourhood. You could play in the schoolyards, or you could walk down the street looking in shop windows. People strolled down 71st on warm summer evenings: young couples holding hands, older couples arm in arm, kids trotting along behind, licking ice-cream cones or whizzing secret spitballs at one another. Cars went by, but not many. Not like today. Everything was slower. In the evenings it was like a kind of promenade. Music coming from radios at open windows. Voices chattering, or joking, or – this being a Jewish neighbourhood – arguing loudly and passionately about politics, about sports, about whether Victor's Deli had the best knishes. No televisions, of course.

In some ways our neighbourhood was like a small town. We never ventured very far away. I don't think we knew a soul in the suburbs – the suburbs where, in many cases, no Jews were allowed to live anyway. Once I had a girlfriend who lived in a suburb west of Chicago, and on one occasion I went out to visit. While I was there, I was asked if I would help her father put up the Christmas lights, of all things. And there we were, hanging up the lights, and he said to me, "You know, you're the only Jew I've met that I like." My girlfriend was a really pretty girl, and we got along well – but I got the hell out of there as fast as I could.

Comments like that cut to the bone. To this day. To show you, here's a story about something that happened to me. Not in Chicago. Years later, in Toronto.

Once, in 1971, I came home from a business trip. Things were going well for the company – we had just introduced the famous "You Deserve a Break Today" jingle; McDonald's stock had just split for the fourth time. I was president and CEO of McDonald's in Eastern Canada. We were opening new restaurants, looking for real estate, hiring. Ron Cohen, Ed Garber, and I were steadily building the company. I was extremely busy – in the middle of the negotiations over whether I would go public with the McDonald's rights I owned for Ontario or sell the licence back to the McDonald's Corporation. I was travelling a lot in those days, criss-crossing the country, and on this particular occasion I'd been away for four or five days.

Wherever I was, and however much I was travelling, I always made a point of trying to get home for the weekends. And on this occasion, I'd come in from the airport. I got out of the cab in front of the house, and I was starting up toward the front door. As I walked across the drive, I heard a voice. It was the woman who lived one door south of us. We'd moved from our first house in Toronto on Lowther Avenue to this house on Forest Hill Road in 1970. She had lived next door for years.

She was calling to her husband, and it so happened a window was open. I heard her say, "The dirty Jew is home."

Those were her words. "The dirty Jew." Clear as a bell. This wasn't the first time I had heard disparaging comments from next door, but this was certainly the worst. I walked into our house. I said hi to the kids. I sat down with Susie. We had a drink. I must have seemed a little quiet.

She said, "Is something wrong?"

I said, "We're going to buy the house next door."

"We're going to *what?*"

"Buy the house. The one next door." And I told her what I had heard our neighbour say.

Susie said, "Oh, no. That's awful. Really awful. But George, you can't just buy it. For one thing, we probably can't afford it. For another, it isn't for sale."

"We'll see," I said.

The next day I went to work. I called a lawyer friend who works for one of the biggest WASP law firms in the city. I told him the story.

He said, "That's terrible. But what do you want me to do?"

I told him. I wanted him to form a shell corporation. I wanted him to act for it. I wanted him to approach our neighbours and say that he was representing an undisclosed client. An undisclosed client who wanted to buy their house. I said, "Make them an offer."

So he did.

No dice. The house wasn't for sale.

I said, "Jack it up."

So he did.

We raised it by about 25 per cent. Enough to catch their attention. And when they saw the offer jump like that, they began to think, well, maybe the house was for sale after all. They signed back this time – asking pretty much twice my original offer. So we negotiated a little, and finally sawed it off at $115,000, $120,000 – something like that.

I called Susie. "We have the house."

"Great. We have the house. Now what?"

Good question.

It wasn't actually my intention to tear it down. I didn't want to get carried away – at least, no more carried away than I had already been. Buying the house seemed revenge enough; getting rid of it altogether seemed a little excessive. Still, I wasn't quite sure what I was going to do with the place. We thought we might lease it, but Susie and I were both busy with other things. It sat empty for a while, which, in and of itself, I took to be an improvement.

And then, later that year, during a very cold night in the middle of the winter, the heating went off in the next-door house. We didn't know about it until it was too late. The pipes froze and burst. I was away in Montreal and Susie called to say everything was covered in water and ice. It was a mess.

"Now what?" Susie asked.

Good question.

I'd had to borrow money to buy the house in the first place; the cost of extensive repairs was beyond my budget. So I called a friend of mine – a guy who owns the biggest wrecking firm in Toronto.

And that was that. Gone. The lot is now a lovely side garden to our home. There is a reflecting pool where our neighbours' house once stood. I sit by it sometimes and enjoy the quiet. To the north, our neighbour has been a friend for over twenty-five years. But to the south, not a single voice from a single open window ever disturbs my peace. The lot – 50 by 175 feet in a very prestigious part of Toronto – also happens to be worth about ten times what I paid for the house and the lot in 1971 – which makes me smile when I stop to think about it.

There are some people, when I tell them this story, who think I over-reacted. I can see them cringe a little. I can see them thinking: One unkind word, one slip of anti-Semitism – and bang! he pulls out all the stops. But I don't think I over-reacted. I didn't cheat our next-door neighbours. On the contrary, I paid more than market value for their house. But I felt strongly about the matter. I still do. There is nothing that upsets me more than bigotry – bigotry of all sorts. The slips of anti-Semitism that I have encountered in my life serve to remind me of the prejudice that so many people suffer. The division of insult that so often comes between Catholics and Protestants, whites and blacks, Jews and Arabs is a profoundly destructive force. The cruel jokes aimed at a Sikh cab driver because he wears a turban, or the thoughtless and unfunny remarks that were made about Tiger Woods after his phenomenal victory at the 1997 Masters golf tournament, come from the same narrow-mindedness. It angers me when I hear a Jew make a derogatory comment about a black, or a WASP make a crack about a Pakistani – as much as the unkind words of my neighbour angered me as I was walking from a cab to my front door. It was particularly hurtful because it was so close – within earshot – of my own home, my wife, my children. It was on my own front step, which is about the last place I am willing to tolerate that kind of hatred. So when I sat down with Susie and told her we were going to buy the house, it was not just our next-door neighbour I had in mind. I guess I was thinking about all the little things here and there that had happened over the years. Things you just pick up now and then – that hurt, that rankle, and that perhaps, at the time they occur, you don't have the power to do anything about. Things like the kind of insults school kids throw around, not knowing how much they sting. Or the time in a Chicago suburb when my girlfriend's father thought he was paying me a compliment when he told me that I was the only Jew he had ever liked.

A compliment! I couldn't think of a worse insult. I remember standing there, a string of Christmas lights in my hand, and thinking: This is not where I belong. I was polite, though. Respectful of elders, as I had been taught. I said goodbye. And I was never happier to get back to our street and our home.

It was like a little village, our neighbourhood. A small town washed in the glow of big-city street lights.

There was Mitchell's ice-cream. It was the best, absolutely the best. And at Rosenblum's Drug Store, you could get a hot fudge sundae at the counter. I loved watching them make their famous sodas with the thick sweet syrup. My sister used to take me to the Hamilton or the Jeffrey movie theatres for Saturday matinées. Admission was ten cents; Sandy used to get an extra nickel from my parents for taking me along with her. There were times she wasn't sure it was worth it.

I always looked up to Sandy, but she was a hard act to follow. She was always a good student – much better than I ever was. She involved herself in various kinds of community work, and to this day her memories of the neighbourhood are vivid. Susie and I see Sandy and my brother-in-law and former law partner, Maury Raizes, frequently in Florida now. We have more time to be together these days; in some ways we're closer than we've ever been, and I always enjoy her company and reminiscences. When Sandy talks, memories of the old neighbourhood come flooding back.

From where we lived, you could hear the streetcar on 67th Street. We used to ride it – a gang of us, I suppose, although "gang" was a more innocent word then than it is now. Not entirely innocent, though, and looking back at the part of town where I grew up I suppose I can see early signs of the tensions that later erupted in so many American cities. I remember once playing football for our high school team. My mother came to one of the games, and a fight broke out in the stands between some white kids and some black kids. (The school I went to was mostly black.) The fight grew, and my mother, along with the other spectators, actually had to run from the field to escape. We finished the game with the field cordoned off by police. We wouldn't have known it then – in 1954 – but this wasn't just an isolated event. This was South Side Chicago – but it could have been the south Bronx, it could have been Watts. It was a sign of things to come.

We couldn't see the trouble ahead. We couldn't foresee the difficulties that so many American inner cities found themselves in during the sixties and seventies. We were a little innocent about things then. Perhaps a little naive. Perhaps just lucky – because, in those days, it was still a great place to grow up.

Sometimes we would take the Illinois Central train downtown, to the loop. I remember going in for VJ day, to the corner of State and Madison, which, in those days, was known as the busiest corner in the world. You might think that living on a quiet, ordinary street in South Side Chicago was an inauspicious beginning, but I'll tell you: I stood in front of Lenin's tomb in Red Square while the world was being transformed by Gorbachev's reforms. I was in the office of the Acting Prime Minister of Georgia, in Tbilisi on August 19, 1991, the second day of the attempted coup by the Soviet old guard, when a fax, signed by Boris Yeltsin, came through, announcing that the coup was illegal. I've been close to what seem to be important moments in history. But I'm not sure that I've ever felt closer to history than I did when I was eight years old and I stood in the crowd at the busiest corner in the world, waving a flag and cheering until I was hoarse because, at last, the war was over.

That was a long time ago. But memory is a funny thing, and sometimes the long-ago seems close enough to reach out and touch again.

A few years ago I was in Chicago on business. I sit on the board of trustees of Northwestern University, Susan's and my alma mater; my son, Mark, also attended Northwestern. Mark, interestingly enough, preceded me as a trustee – he was the youngest in the university's history. When I spoke at my first meeting I was able to say, "This is a classic case of a father following in his son's footsteps."

My sister still lives in the city. We have friends there to this day. So, I feel I have kept a connection with the place where I grew up, where I first began to practise law, and where Susie and I started our married life. Still, on that business trip to Chicago a few years ago I realized, sitting in my hotel room one evening, that it had been thirty-one years since I had actually been in the old neighbourhood. I was curious. I wondered about it. I found myself daydreaming about the sidewalks, the corners, the aunts and uncles and cousins, the friends, the schoolyard, the movie theatres, the drugstore where they used to make sodas with that thick, wonderful syrup. I found myself remembering people such as Eliot Hasan, my high school football coach. (He told us that if he ever caught us with a cigarette we'd be off the team. To this day, I have never smoked.) I decided to rent a car and go have a look at the old place. I would try to go back home again.

It's actually quite a pretty drive back to south Chappel. You take the Outer Drive by Lake Michigan, past Soldier Field, on past the Museum of Science and Industry. It brought back a lot of memories. But the closer I got to our neighbourhood, the more clearly I could see the devastation caused by poverty and urban decay. There were places that actually reminded me of the kind of systemic break-down I had witnessed in the Soviet Union. I turned the corner at 71st and South Shore Drive, and many of the stores that I remembered had long been boarded up. The area, now, was almost entirely African-American. A few of the old places were still there – Rosenblum's Drug Store had managed to survive – but mostly it was the kind of inner-city wasteland that you see on television or in the movies.

I locked my doors. I rolled up my windows. I kept driving. Past what had once been the homes of friends and relatives. Past the old schoolyard where I had so enjoyed playing basketball. Past the sidewalks where we had played. On, slowly, through the streets, until I came to 6744 south Chappel Avenue.

I parked the car. I took a deep breath. And then I got out.

Almost immediately, a big semi tractor truck pulled up right behind my car. The cab door flew open, and a big, tough-looking guy jumped down to the curb. He walked right up to me. There was nothing friendly in his voice.

"What you doing here, man?"

I assessed the distance between me and my parked car. I said, "I used to live here."

"Uh-huh. When was that?"

"Oh, a long time ago."

"You got that right. Where'd you live then?"

"Right there." I pointed. "The apartment on the second floor."

"You're shitting me, man. That's where I live now."

Jerry Metcalf turned out to be an all-right guy. We stood on the sidewalk for a while, talking about the neighbourhood, about the difficulties he was having bringing up his young son there. He talked about the efforts that people were making to get the area back on its feet. About the drugs and the crime, but also about the attempts by a local bank, South Shore, to help people get businesses started there again.

Jerry looked big and tough. He *was* big and tough. But he was also quite friendly. As is almost always the case, once the defensive barriers had come down, we were just two human beings talking to one another.

I've always enjoyed these kinds of conversations and chance encounters. I find myself with someone – a customer, a stranger at a store, a cab driver – and I start talking. This is how you learn things, this is how you find out what other people think – and whenever I run into someone who says they like a certain place in Florida or in Arizona because there are no African Americans, or Latinos, or Mexicans there, I always think: How small, how narrow, how sad to be limited by these stupid prejudices.

Jerry and I hit it off. We had something in common: an interest in the neighbourhood. I was curious about what it was like to live there now. He was curious about what it was like then. After a few minutes he invited me in to see the apartment and to have a beer.

"Sorry," he said. "It's a real mess."

"Couldn't be any worse than how I left it," I said – which put him at his ease, but which was a complete lie. The apartment had always been immaculate when my parents lived there.

It did look the worse for wear. Still, the Metcalfs were doing their best to handle difficult economic and social conditions. Their life wasn't an easy one – crime, drugs, broken families all around them. They were the kind of people who were trying to do better, but who seemed always to have so much stacked against them. The neighbourhood was a much more hostile and dangerous place for them than it had ever been for me – and yet, I thought, they're good people. They live here, go to school here, have a stake here. There must be other good people around. While I certainly don't advocate a welfare state, I do think financial assistance for people who need it should come from a combination of government aid and corporate and private initiatives. And then, maybe, with some help, neighbourhoods like this one could start capitalizing on their human resources, on their good people, and on the hope that good people always have.

Societies have their ups and downs. Economies have their ups and downs. So do neighbourhoods. I was lucky enough to live in

South Shore during an up. But the wheels of the sixties, seventies, and eighties had turned with devastating effect here. This same period of time had been the years when McDonald's had established itself, had expanded aggressively, and had steadily built on its ongoing success. In Canada alone, the number of McDonald's restaurants had gone from 2 in 1967 to 626 in 1990. Many other companies had enjoyed the same kind of growth. Fortunes had been made – mine among them – during the years that my old neighbourhood, and many neighbourhoods like it, had been caught in a sad, downward spiral.

Sitting in the apartment my parents had lived in so long ago, looking at the cracks in the ceiling, the peeling wallpaper, the faded curtains at the dirty windows, listening to Jerry talk about his life and family, I thought: This is a tough one. Maybe *the* tough one when it comes to the private enterprise system: How do you explain the existence of spectacular success somewhere, and hardship and difficulty somewhere else? My explanation would be that in a capitalist system, whatever the ups and downs of the economy over the years, the wheels don't stop. I know from first-hand experience that in a communist system they do: They go slower and slower and finally they stop, dead. For everyone. Trucks are discarded beside the road, shops are empty, nothing functions, ambition is stifled, hope is abandoned. The old joke in the former USSR was always, "We pretend to work and they pretend to pay us." In a capitalist system, there are always people who prosper and there are always people who don't, but the wheels of productivity don't stop. The energy of capitalism's successes keep them turning. It's possible to ride them upward – if you're willing to work. I don't want to be glib about this – sure, it's hard; sure, the odds seem insurmountable sometimes; my grandparents knew that well enough – but there is hope. And that's no small thing.

Ray Kroc, the founder of McDonald's, had a saying. He had read it somewhere, and he liked it a lot. He used it frequently. Ray began as a restaurant equipment salesman and ended up one of the richest men in North America. He used to say, "Press on." And these words hang on the walls of many McDonald's offices throughout the world:

> *Press On. Nothing in the world can take the place of persistence. Talent will not; nothing is more common than unsuccessful men with talent. Genius will not; unrewarded genius is almost a proverb. Education alone will not; the world is full of educated derelicts. Persistence and determination alone are omnipotent.*

I thought of Ray as I sat with Jerry. Jerry *was* pressing on. It wasn't easy, but at least in our system, Jerry's persistence could pay off. He could look after his truck, he could take on extra runs, he could make himself indispensable – and, who knows, he could end up being manager of the company. Maybe he'll end up being the owner. A big maybe – but maybe is a lot better than *nyet*, believe me. It was a maybe that Jerry seemed to have in mind.

I liked Jerry. I thought perhaps the wheels were turning again for South Shore. Maybe another up was on its way.

We sat in the kitchen and talked. It felt odd. I kept looking around. The rooms were the rooms I knew – the dimensions, the windows, the moulding were all familiar to me – and yet everything felt unfamiliar at the same time. A bit like a dream, I guess.

It had grown dark. It was time for me to go. I had to catch a flight to Toronto. Jerry said he would walk me to the car.

"Don't bother," I said. "I can find my way."

"No. It's night. You never know. I'll just walk you down."

We said goodbye on the sidewalk. I told him I'd send his kid some presents from McDonald's. He said that would be nice. We shook hands. I got in the car. He gave me a little wave and returned to his home. His home now. I locked the car doors, took a last look at the street where I had grown up, and started on the long journey back to mine.

• 3 •

Moscow Nights

The deal for the Moscow Olympics that we had worked so hard toward between 1976 and 1979 had fallen through. I thought we had it in the bag, and then, at the last second, at the end of my seventeen days at the Hotel Metropol, the answer had come: *nyet*. I was stunned. I felt completely deflated – the feeling reminded me of the time I was dropped from the high school basketball team in the very last round of cuts when I was seventeen. That may seem a trivial comparison. And it's true, the stakes aren't the same; of course, things grow bigger and more important as you grow older. But the sinking feeling that you get very deep in your stomach when you lose something on which you have your heart set doesn't change, whatever your age. Defeat is never easy.

In November 1979, I wrote to Aleksandr Yakovlev, the Soviet Ambassador to Canada. "Needless to say, we were extremely disappointed, since two and a half years of work had gone into our proposal and it had appeared that we had reached agreement on all relevant terms. Mr. Koval, on behalf of the Olympic Organizing Committee, was likewise extremely disappointed . . . and he told me that he would continue to work on our behalf to try and obtain all necessary approvals. . . ."

One week later, I received a telegram from R. A. D. Ford, the Canadian Ambassador to the USSR. "I was as disappointed as you at negative reaction of Soviets. . . . I think veto came from high up and Promyslov [the chairman of the Executive Committee of the Moscow Council of People's Deputies] was probably vehicle for it. At a recent reception he deliberately avoided me. . . . I will keep probing whenever this is feasible."

But, as it turned out, our failure to provide the food services for the Moscow Games may have been the best deal I never made. Sometimes Lady Luck is with you, even when you're absolutely sure she's working the cards at another table. Contrary to my confident prediction, the 1980 Olympics *were* boycotted. On December 25, 1979, the Soviet Union began its invasion of Afghanistan; the explicit boycott of the Games by thirty-six countries was the most prominent symbol of the West's displeasure. Had McDonald's signed the deal for the 1980 Games we would have been left in an extremely awkward spot. Without the boycott clause my lawyer had so wisely recommended – and which I had so unwisely negotiated away – and with what, certainly, would have been intense pressure from Western countries for as high-profile a company as McDonald's to join the boycott, our signature on a contract might have proven to be a pretty costly scribble of ink.

Still, there was no silver lining that I could see in November 1979 when I stood in Vladimir Koval's office on Gorky Street and heard that our deal for the 1980 Olympics was off. It was all cloud – thick, low-lying, and dark, disheartening grey. I flew home from Moscow on a grim day in November 1979. I felt beaten. And tired.

But not so beaten and tired that I decided to quit. Soon enough, I had picked myself up, put myself back together, and headed back into the fray.

There is a difference between pessimism and optimism that is obvious. Pessimism is a negative force; it can sometimes be a cautious, realistic way of looking at specific things, but if it becomes a way of life, it can only hold you back. Optimism – the attitude that Ray Kroc had in mind when he said "Press on" – is positive. It can sometimes be imprudent and risky, but as a general attitude it will move you forward. In the years I spent visiting the Soviet Union between 1980 and the rise of *perestroika* in 1986, I could see the difference. They were like day and night. Optimism is what fuels democracy. Pessimism is the gas dictators burn.

But there is another distinction between these two forces that is not quite so apparent. Again, this was something that became clear to me during my visits in the last years of the Soviet Union.

Pessimism is almost always predictable; you hear it repeat itself over and over. Pessimistic thinking gets stuck in a rut, and the rut just gets deeper. The system can't be changed; there is nothing to be done; there is no point in trying; there is no hope. I heard this refrain over and over in the USSR about everything from politics to plumbing, from the economy to telephone service. When this kind of negativity was voiced in reference to our efforts to open a McDonald's in Moscow, the naysayers repeated themselves so constantly and so consistently, I began to think of their objections as the five levels of pessimism. These were the hurdles of negativity that we had to get over.

Number One. "George, you'll never cut the deal."

I heard this everywhere. At the board meetings of McDonald's Corporation in the United States. At meetings of the McDonald's board in Canada. I heard it in North America. I heard it in Europe. Inside McDonald's, outside McDonald's. But most of all, I heard it in the USSR. Remember, this was years before *perestroika* and *glasnost*. This was the era of Ronald Reagan. Of the Evil Empire. On the streets of Moscow, propaganda posters were everywhere. They proclaimed: "The Party and the People are One." "Long Live the Soviet People, Builders of Communism." Or simply, "Glory to Work." Streets were called Karl Marx Prospekt, or Lenin Prospekt, or Fiftieth Anniversary of the Revolution Square. Loudspeakers in public parks broadcast martial music or speeches and carefully edited news reports.

A few Western companies had made tentative inroads into the USSR, but there was no real corporate presence there. It appeared that free enterprise and communism were oil and water. There were a lot of people – several of whom sat on McDonald's board of directors – who just didn't think that communists were going to make a deal with capitalists. Period.

Number Two. "You will never be able to build restaurants that meet your standards."

These naysayers would simply point to the restaurants that did exist and rest their case. This was a pretty compelling argument, I have to admit. A dining experience in Moscow in the early 1980s was almost never a happy one. Typically, a restaurant would be vast and half empty but you would have to wait fifteen minutes for a table. The menu would be as thick as a book, but almost nothing on it would be available. The vast white napkins would always leave a blizzard of fluff on your lap; the waiter or waitress would always take so long to bring you the bill that by the time you paid you were hungry again; and nobody ever, under any circumstances, smiled.

Number Three. "You will never get Soviet citizens to work the way you want McDonald's employees to work."

Many people – including, if I may say, many Soviets – believed that Russians were somehow incapable of being friendly, hospitable, efficient, and helpful. The word that came up most frequently was "surly."

Number Four. "You won't get suppliers."

Skeptics pointed out that a national agricultural system that seemed incapable of keeping grocery stores supplied with even the bare essentials was not going to be the kind of reliable partner McDonald's requires. Again, this was a compelling argument to anyone who had spent any time in the USSR. By the early 1980s the great paradoxes of the Soviet system were beginning to be very clear. Militarily, the USSR seemed to gleam with strength and efficiency; it had gained the upper hand in Europe with its mid-range SS-20 missiles. Agriculturally and economically, however, it was in the Dark Ages. Anyone visiting Moscow could see the constant line-ups outside the doors of grocery stores and markets that had almost nothing in them. It was not a system in which we could place any confidence.

Number Five. "And George, the kicker is, you won't make money."

Some of my fellow directors pointed out that the ruble was non-convertible, that it was a weak, artificially supported currency. In those days, in Moscow, there were shops called *Beriozka*. These places dealt only in hard currency – foreign cash – and there were big bronze plaques on their fronts that announced this policy in no uncertain terms. Which meant that these places dealt only with foreign visitors. It was illegal for Soviet citizens to use currency other than their own. People pointed out to me that if we went the *Beriozka* route – that is, if we opened restaurants that accepted only American dollars or German marks, or whatever – we would be limiting our sales mostly to foreigners, and cutting out the vast market that had attracted me to the USSR in the first place. From a currency point of view, critics saw a lose–lose situation.

If I heard these five objections once, I heard them a hundred times between 1980 and 1986. This was the period after we lost our bid to provide food services for the 1980 Olympics – the period during which we were continuing our negotiations for a foothold for McDonald's in the USSR. This was an extremely difficult time. And this was when I learned how predictable pessimism is.

However, it was also the period when I learned how surprising optimism can be. Optimism – the force that inspires determination, the attitude that has helped people such as Ray Kroc to press on – can sometimes come right out of the blue. When you're least expecting it – often, it seems, when you're at a low point, when you're on the verge of giving up – you can be hit with a sudden bolt of stick-to-itiveness. Suddenly, for reasons that are sometimes quite mysterious, you can be inspired to keep going.

Once, in Moscow, when I really felt I was on the ropes, I was surprised by optimism. It began with a chance encounter with Pierre Trudeau.

I was quite friendly with Trudeau. I had chaired a big dinner for him in Toronto in October of 1982. This was at a particularly low ebb in his domestic popularity, not long after the notorious finger incident. Trudeau had gestured to a group of demonstrators while on a family vacation in British Columbia earlier that year in a pretty unmistakeable way. Naturally, the press had jumped all over this. And it had not gone down well with the Canadian public – a public not exactly accustomed to seeing a Prime Minister give people the finger. For obvious reasons, Trudeau's people had been very anxious about the Toronto dinner. I think they were afraid that no-one would show up.

I have strengths and I have weaknesses – as many of one as of the other, I sometimes think. But one thing I am good at, if you'll pardon me the immodesty, is getting people to show up. For events. For fundraisers. For charity functions.

So I called people. I cajoled people. I pestered people. And when I managed to convince people, it may have been because I was coming at them with a bit of an American perspective. I became a Canadian citizen in 1975. I gave up my American citizenship; Susan and our sons have dual citizenship. But still, my American-ness is not very far below the surface – you can hear it easily enough in my accent. I still feel an intense nostalgia when I hear "The Star-Spangled Banner." But when I moved to Canada, I felt that it was important that I be able to vote in the country where I was living. This, it seemed to me, was the very bedrock of democracy, and so, ironically, I acted on a very American instinct – the love of democracy – and became a Canadian citizen.

Still, I was brought up in the U.S.A., and my American-ness came out, I think, in my sincerity about the dinner with Trudeau. It has to do with duty, and I'd felt this way before in Canada. In 1981, Trudeau asked me to sit on the board of directors of Canada Post, and at the time I couldn't think of many things I less wanted to do. Canada Post was having serious labour problems, and was dealing with the tumultuous impact of all kinds of new technologies. Frankly, I would rather have been playing tennis than worrying about Canada Post. Still, the Prime Minister had asked – and so I felt it my duty to say yes. I served on the board for four years. I like to say jokingly that it was actually a three-year term – it's just that at the end of the third year they mailed me a notice saying my term was up, and the letter took twelve months to get to me.

My point is, in Canada, if you're a Liberal, you don't rally around a Conservative Prime Minister. If you're a Conservative, you steer clear of Liberal PMs. In the United States, there is a stronger tradition of supporting the office of the President, whatever your political affiliation. It is the office that people hold in high regard – not necessarily the man who holds it – and as a result, if the President wants you to join him for dinner, you join him for dinner. You may have fought tooth and nail against him in the last election, you may have donated thousands of dollars to the other party, but if you get an invitation to a Presidential dinner, you'll be there. And you'll feel that it was an honour to have been asked – which is what I told people when I called them up and asked them to dinner with Pierre Trudeau.

"But George," people said to me. "You know I'm a Conservative."

"You're a Canadian," I replied. That usually got to them.

When Trudeau came to Toronto I not only made sure that the dinner was a success, but I managed to have a little fun with him, too. I've always enjoyed jokes and pranks and gags, particularly when they cut through some of the BS that so often surrounds formal events and high-profile personalities. I like to throw a little humanity into the mix, a little bit of humour. It almost always helps break down the barriers, even if it is, sometimes, a little irreverent.

It was in this spirit that I presented Trudeau with a pair of gloves that had the middle finger sewn down. Trudeau thought this was quite funny, and the two of us hit it off. Since then, we've met and chatted together several times. He is an extremely erudite man, but I've always found him more friendly and less cold than most people imagine him to be.

Our friendship has led a lot of people to describe me as a big Liberal supporter. Actually, I'm neither a Liberal nor a Conservative. I am somewhere between the two. I try not to spend a lot of time splitting ideological hairs.

When I ran into Trudeau in the lobby of the Sovincentr in Moscow in the early 1980s, he was relaxed and, as always, charming. He wanted to know how our negotiations with the Soviets were going, and although I am almost always upbeat, almost always cheerful, I had to admit that our negotiations were not going well.

In those days the obstacles to a deal seemed enormous – much more so after the Olympics than they had been before, actually. The political situation between East and West remained tense. The ideological gulf was extreme. But the vast potential of the Soviet market was simply too much for me to resist. The failure to get the Olympic contract had seemed a setback, but I felt we had come too far down the road to turn back. There had to be a way.

My game plan was simple. I'd talk to everybody: officials from the Ministry of Foreign Trade of the USSR; the Ministry of (Internal) Trade of the USSR; the Ministry of (Internal) Trade of the Russian Federation; the State Committee for Science and Technology; the Chairman and Deputy Chairman of the Executive Committee of the Moscow City Council; Glavobshchepit, the main Administration for Public Catering of the Moscow City Council. My address book was becoming very full, and my day-timer was crammed with appointments with names such as Sushkov, Bychkov, Shimansky, Gvishiani, Rodichev, and Zavyalov. If somebody knew somebody who knew somebody who might be able to help us, I'd be in their office.

Here's an example of our scatter-gun approach. This invitation was sent out to officials from a dozen different government agencies: "I am heading a delegation of McDonald's Restaurants of Canada Officers to Moscow. We would very much like to have you as our guest for dinner at the National Hotel on the evening of October 16th. It would be wonderful to renew our friendship."

All sweetness and light. But in the background of all our negotiations with the Soviets, there was – in the United States and in Canada – a dull rumble of doubt. We had strong supporters in both countries, but there were others who, not unrealistically, were very nervous about what we were doing.

Ray Kroc had never been very enthusiastic about our efforts to sign a deal with the USSR. He had a tough, Cold War attitude toward the Soviets – they were Communists, they couldn't be trusted. Ray was a no-nonsense, intensely patriotic American capitalist. He was about as Republican as it is possible to be. Everything he believed in and everything he lived by could be summed up in two words: private enterprise. The Soviets stood for the very opposite – which, in his view, made them the enemy. After all, it *was* the Cold War.

I have to say that I never saw the Soviets as the enemy – their treatment of Jews notwithstanding. I always thought that establishing business relations with the USSR might open things up. It might even open the door to a more liberal emigration policy.

Still, Ray and I had a very strong personal relationship. He may have worried that I was wasting my time. He may have feared that I was wasting McDonald's money. He may have thought my politics were too far to the left – which will tell you something about how far to the right Ray was! But he was willing to give me the benefit of the doubt. He knew I had a good track record in Canada, and he knew that more often than not my instincts were good. He had his doubts, but he never raised his concerns loudly enough to obstruct what we were trying to do.

Fred Turner, the chairman and CEO of McDonald's Corporation, was more supportive. His point of view on all international development, including the Soviet Union, was as direct as mine. He had seen the potential with his own eyes during a visit in the late 1970s. "The rationale for going international was as simple as determining that the market was there," he said. My thinking exactly. But even with Ray Kroc a grudging ally, and Fred Turner an active one, there was still some pretty heavy weather to sail through. And the longer the negotiations went on without resolution, the heavier the weather became. There were directors on the

Canadian and American boards who supported us, but there were others who raised objections – negotiations had already been too expensive; profitability was by no means certain – and raised them loud and clear.

By the early 1980s, we had sunk millions of dollars into our efforts to break into the Soviet market. I simply did not know how much more time and money I would be able to spend.

This was a period of aggressive expansion within Canada for McDonald's. The high profile that the company now enjoys – both as a highly successful business and as a good corporate citizen – was established during the early 1980s. Throughout the first half of the 1980s, we were opening an average of twenty-five new stores a year in Canada. In 1981, the first year that *Forbes* magazine ranked McDonald's among the top 100 U.S. companies in profit, McDonald's became the largest food-service organization in Canada. Our charitable work was becoming increasingly important to us, and increasingly prominent. We supported Terry Fox's Marathon of Hope in 1980; McHappy Days – when celebrities, politicians, media personalities, local firefighters, police, and school principals work behind our counters and we donate one dollar from the sale of every Big Mac or Pizza to local children's charities – were introduced in 1981.

But this was a two-edged sword for us. On one hand, we used our achievements in Canada as evidence that we knew what we were doing in the USSR. This seemed an obvious argument to make. On the other hand, it begged an obvious question: Why, while enjoying success in Canada, were we so intent on risking failure in the USSR?

At board meetings in Oak Brook, Illinois, and in Toronto, I was obliged to answer some tough questions. How long would all this take? How big would the payoff be? And the bottom line: Could we trust these people?

On top of this, there was some consternation within the organization, because it was McDonald's Restaurants of Canada that was spearheading the drive into the USSR, and not the international division of McDonald's Corporation. As early as the late 1960s, Ray Kroc and Fred Turner had come to the conclusion that the service industry was *the* exportable sector of the American economy. We take this for granted now, but it was a revolutionary idea then. It was also a brilliant idea that turned out to be absolutely correct. Steve Barnes had been designated by Fred Turner as chairman of the international division, and throughout the 1970s, McDonald's International oversaw very careful and well thought-out expansions into Germany, Australia, the Netherlands, Japan, England, France, Brazil, and Singapore – among other markets. McDonald's Corporation made it their business to make sure that the company's expansions were successful and that they accorded with the standards that had originally been set for the domestic market by Ray Kroc. Quality, Service, Cleanliness, and Value – QSC & V – were McDonald's passport to the world market, and McDonald's International was the arm of the company that traditionally made certain the passport was in order. Nothing less than the company's world-wide reputation was at stake every time we went into a new country. It was – and still is – McDonald's International that deserves much of the credit for the company's remarkable global success.

Typically, McDonald's International would look very carefully at a prospective market. And when I say carefully, I mean carefully. Great attention is paid to local customs and to making connections with the right local partners. The people at International understand that McDonald's success depends on the connections it makes in the market it is entering: from management, to suppliers, to crew, and, most important, to customers. McDonald's International excelled at this kind of local sensitivity and focus. The fact that the USSR had been handed to McDonald's-Canada in what seemed a pretty casual way – I had called Fred Turner with the idea of Moscow, and he had simply said to go for it – made a few people in International a little uncomfortable. I can't say I blame them for their reaction. The International people are very good at what they do. They like to approach things more cautiously and a little more scientifically than I do. But Fred Turner trusted my instincts; he knew who I was and what I was about. Others within the company didn't know me so well. Had I been in their shoes, I might have been equally nervous and equally pessimistic.

To be fair, there were all kinds of reasons not to pursue an agreement with the Soviets after the first deal fell through, and my critics – both inside and outside the corporation – made certain I knew what they were. My instincts told me that I was right and they were wrong on this one, but instincts are often difficult to articulate, to quantify, and to communicate.

When millions of dollars are at stake, a strong hunch seems a pretty shaky premise to everyone except the guy who has the hunch. Which was me. Me and the people with whom I was working. We found ourselves, in those days, constantly answering questions. Which was fair enough. That's what directors and company executives are for – to ask tough questions, to raise objections, to look on the down side, to raise gloomy possibilities, to make sure people are proceeding responsibly. My optimism was tested. It was tested, often, by good people with good intentions, but it was tested by what I came to think of as the five levels of pessimism.

Number One. "George, you won't cut the deal."

In some ways this was the hardest objection to argue against, because my conviction was based on instinct. Even though the entire bureaucracy and political philosophy of the USSR in the early 1980s were stacked against us, I couldn't help but believe that at the most basic level of supply and demand, the successful entry of McDonald's into the Soviet Union was a no-brainer. Our feasibility studies verified this. The people needed something; we had what the people needed. The world turns on that equation. And for that reason – the most elementary reason of commerce – I believed that we were more of an irresistible force than the Soviet state was an unmoveable object.

Of course, this hunch proved to be correct. It proved to be even more correct than I initially could have imagined – even in my wildest dreams. I was pushing hamburgers, but what I didn't know at first was that within the Soviet Union many other people who were pushing far more important things were thinking the same way I was. People who were pushing freedom of expression, freedom of religion, and political and economic freedom had come to the same conclusion I had. They were the force that would not be turned back. They also had what the people wanted.

Initially, my notion that there was an opening for McDonald's in the Soviet Union was based, as most of my business decisions are, on my assessment of the people with whom I was dealing. It began with the Soviets I met on that bus in Montreal in 1976. I felt instinctively about them the way Margaret Thatcher later felt so famously about Mikhail Gorbachev: I believed that they were people with whom I could do business.

Someone comes from Chicago and was brought up to believe in free enterprise. Someone comes from Moscow and was brought up to believe in Marxism. So what? Unlike some of my colleagues in Canada and the United States, I had never thought of the Russians as enemies. Once you start sharing hopes, plans, confidences, family stories, jokes – in other words, once you establish a relationship – it almost always becomes apparent that you share some common ground. Somewhere. Somehow. Common ground on which you can trust one another.

During our negotiations for the food services for the Olympics, I had come to trust and to like Vladimir Koval. I could tell from the way he told me the deal was off in 1979 that there had been some other intervention, something over which he had no control. He said he couldn't tell me what had happened, but I remember that he was almost crying when he gave me the news. At the time, this was a very bitter pill for me to swallow. But my trust in him was still there. Koval's announcement to me that day – as hard as it was to see years of negotiations go down the drain – did not dissuade me from my belief that there was common ground on which a deal could be struck.

By the early 1980s, we were talking with everyone. We made the rounds, but in those days, no-one in the Soviet Union knew what we were talking about. "We're from McDonald's." Blank. "Big Macs, Quarter-Pounders, french fries." Blank. "You know. 'Nobody Can Do It Like McDonald's Can.' Ronald McDonald. 'You deserve a break today.'" Blank. "Egg McMuffin. Chicken McNuggets." Blank. So we decided to put together a video to explain what McDonald's was – which was a terrific plan, except for one little technical blip. We couldn't find a video player. No-one in the Soviet Union seemed to know what McDonald's was, and no-one in the Soviet Union seemed to own a VCR. We eventually flew a self-contained presentation machine, complete with its own converter, in from Canada, and we put it on a little carriage so that we could drag it around from meeting to meeting. We called it Pavlov, and I can still remember the sound of Pavlov's wheels rattling over the ancient stone cobbles at the entrance to the Kremlin.

There were more than a few Soviet officials who thought we were out of our minds, who said the deal we had in mind would be impossible. I remember Viktor Bychkov, of the Soviet Ministry of (Internal) Trade, shaking his head at a meeting in his office near the Kremlin and telling us that it was virtually impossible for us to succeed. He was a pretty gruff character to begin with, and he almost laughed us out of his office – which wasn't exactly encouraging.

But Vsevolod Shimansky, at the Ministry of Trade of the Russian Federation, was always kind and attentive and interested in what we were proposing. He was a handsome, distinguished, almost aristocratic-looking gentleman. He always made time for us. His attention gave me hope and kept me optimistic about coming to an agreement.

Shimansky and I enjoyed one another's company. When we were meeting in the early 1980s, he often wanted to continue our discussions over dinner. I noticed that he preferred restaurants that had live music – particularly balalaika music. Most Russians have a soft spot for the balalaika, and often at our dinners he would sit over his cabbage rolls transfixed, listening to "Moscow Nights."

During this same period, I happened to be in a restaurant in Australia one night. The owner was entertaining his customers by playing the guitar. I thought he was very good. He'd wander from table to table, strumming away. He seemed very professional, an extremely accomplished musician. But when he stopped strumming, the guitar kept playing; he had a tape deck inside the guitar. As soon as I saw it, I thought: Shimansky.

I got a tape deck. I got a balalaika. I carefully inserted the tape deck into the body of the balalaika. The next time I came to Russia, Shimansky met us at the airport with his aides, and his big VIP car, and all the flashing lights. The big time, I thought.

"Vsevolod," I said.

"*Zdravstvuy*, Dzhordzh!" he said. "Greetings, George."

We climbed into the car, and while we were speeding into Moscow I told him that I had been studying the balalaika.

"*Na balalayke?*"

"*Da.*"

"*Tak sygrai, davai sygrai pryamo seychas*," he said. "Play it. Play it for me now."

I told him that I couldn't – not in the car, not at his office, not later when we were out. I kept this up for about four days. It drove him crazy. He kept asking me to play, and I kept saying not yet, not yet.

Finally, on our last night in Moscow on that trip, we went out to dinner at Valdai, one of Shimansky's favourite restaurants. It was a place that featured balalaika music. There were musicians going from table to table all the time, and Shimansky couldn't contain himself any longer. He took a balalaika from one of the musicians and handed it to me.

"*Nu sygrai zhe, Dzhordzh, chevo ty*," he said. "Now, George, play."

I said, "No. I can only play my own."

He looked as if he was going to explode, but we carried on with dinner. It was a formal affair: six or seven of their people on one side of the table, six or seven of us on our side. The Russians always had a very definite pecking order to these dinners. We always sat ranked, and since I was the head of our delegation, I was sitting across from Shimansky.

We continued our discussions about the possibility of McDonald's in Russia. We told them, "We'll train your people; we'll help improve your agricultural system; we'll help to make your distribution system more sophisticated." We were, at that time, just beginning to float the notion of McDonald's building a food-processing plant outside Moscow. Fred Turner had suggested the idea. It would be a departure for McDonald's; the company had never done this kind of thing before. But I liked the concept – partly because we would need one; partly because we thought such a project, constructed at our expense, would be a compelling signing incentive for the Soviets.

Shimansky and I talked over our Chicken Kiev. We talked until the sweet, gritty coffee arrived.

"Well," I said at last. "It is now time for me to play the balalaika."

We had planted my balalaika in the corner, and so I walked over to it with a sort of dramatic flourish. While my back was still to the table, I clicked on the tape, and I turned around, strumming. It was a classic balalaika tune – "Moscow Nights" – the sort of familiar, much-loved piece that will bring tears to any true-blue Russian's eyes.

I crossed back toward our table, playing this beautiful, heartfelt song, and Shimansky stared at me in complete astonishment. I could see that my stock had just gone up about ten points as far as he was concerned. I continued strumming, and he actually got up. He stood there, in amazement, moved almost to tears.

"*Krasota kakaya!*" he exclaimed. "How beautiful!"

He told me that he had loved this music as a child. When he was a soldier, during the Great Patriotic War, he had longed for the peace and happiness he associated with such music. It was the music of Russia! It was the music of the motherland! The rushing current of the Volga River, the domes of St. Basil's, the poetry of Alexander Pushkin, the sad beauty of Anna Karenina – all these were in the notes of the balalaika! It was the music of his heritage and his blood! It was the music of the steppes, of the cherry orchards, of samovars, of summer fields, of crisp winter nights! Of dachas and troikas and birch trees! It was the music of his people! He was so proud of me. "Dzhordzh, Dzhordzh," he said. "George, George." How he wished he could play such a song!

"You can," I said, still strumming.

"*Da net, net u menya takovo slukha kak u tebya*," he said. "No, no. I have not the gift of music. Not like you."

"No, really, you can learn."

"*Net uzh*, Dzhordzh, *ya dlya etovo slishkom star*," he said. "No, George, I am too old."

And I said, "Vsevolod, you are not too old. You can learn. Here, let me show you."

I took the balalaika from around my neck and handed it to him. And, of course, when I passed it to him, it continued playing.

He almost fell over his chair. He couldn't speak. Shimansky has an uproarious sense of humour. He knew immediately that he'd been had. His laughter boomed through the whole restaurant.

"It's a gift," I said. "For you."

He was delighted. Years afterward, I learned that later that night, after our dinner and after we had said our farewells, Shimansky went back to the big, exclusive apartment block where he lived on Ryleeva Street in Moscow and woke all kinds of high-powered Soviet ministers. I like to picture them standing in hallways in their nightshirts and pyjamas. He got them – city officials, members of the Politburo, generals, high-ranking bureaucrats – out of their beds so that he could play his balalaika for them.

Shimansky turned out to be a good ally for us to have. There was a young man in his office, Vladimir Malyshkov, who would eventually play a very important role in our negotiations. However, this sort of thing – friendships, dinners, toasts, gifts – seemed a little vague to some of the people at McDonald's in Canada and in the United States who wanted some tangible evidence that we were getting anywhere. The fact that I had managed to get a good laugh out of the Minister of Trade of the Russian Federation was not the sort of progress that I could use convincingly in my reports to the directors of the company.

I knew these connections were important. I knew we were moving forward. But they wanted something a little more concrete – and something concrete was one thing the Russians were good at not giving.

There was something, though – not concrete, but still more than a little promising. It was a tip that not only kept my hopes up but that was, as I eventually realized, a piece of inside information of great historical significance. I was told that things were going to change.

In 1979, Aleksandr Yakovlev was the Soviet Ambassador to Canada. Over the years that I had been negotiating with the Soviets, I had got to know him. Yakovlev, who would later be instrumental in the reforms of *perestroika* and *glasnost*, was establishing a friendship with an up-and-coming party official named Gorbachev. I found Yakovlev to be an extremely wise and interesting man. His advice was invaluable. From time to time during our negotiations with Soviet officials, he had intervened on our behalf – smoothing the way for us, opening a few doors. For instance, in 1979, I received a cable from Vladimir Koval of the Olympic Organizing Committee. "Mr. Yakovlev, the USSR Ambassador to Canada, has advised our committee of meeting he had with Mr. Paproski, Minister of Sport and National Culture. Among other subjects they touched upon the matter of the negotiations being held in Moscow with McDonald's."

Yakovlev was the dean of the diplomatic corps. I often travelled to Ottawa to see him because I regarded his counsel very highly.

After our negotiations for the 1980 Moscow Games had fallen through, one of the first things I did when I got back to

Canada was to write Yakovlev. Then I telephoned him. I told him that I had no idea what had happened. "Aleksandr," I said. "I still can't understand it. All the points of disagreement had been ironed out. All systems were go. Everything was set. We had agreed on everything in the contract. I thought the signing was just going to be a formality. And then, poof, up in smoke. Years of negotiations down the drain. And I don't know why."

Yakovlev said he would try to find out what had happened.

Two weeks later he called me back. He said he couldn't tell me everything. He paused – then continued very seriously. "What I can say is the deal was killed at a very high level."

Years later he did tell me what had actually happened. He had tried to intervene on our behalf. While still stationed in Ottawa, he had sent a cable, supporting the idea of McDonald's in the USSR, "to the top." He received no response from the Kremlin. He followed with a second cable, and a third. Each was ignored. Yakovlev told me that at this point he was embarrassed to meet with me – embarrassed by what he called "the silly position taken by chiefs in Moscow."

He said, "There was political bickering going on around this idea. The offer met with support as well as unwillingness 'to get involved in this dangerous affair.' The Soviets never punished anybody for saying *nyet*. Only those who said *da* were held responsible."

What had happened was this: At the point when we thought we had a deal, Vladimir Promyslov, the Chairman of the Executive Committee of the Moscow City Council, ran into Mikhail Suslov, the chief of ideology of the Politburo, at some Party function. The Chairman mentioned that the City had just concluded negotiations with McDonald's and that we would shortly be signing a contract for the 1980 Games. I don't think Promyslov brought this up by way of idle cocktail party chat; I think he was running the idea past Suslov in order to keep himself covered. Lucky for him he did; the winters are very long in Siberia.

Suslov was not amused with what the Chairman told him. He made it clear that the contract would not be signed. Such an arrangement, he said, would show the outside world that the Soviet Union could not provide food services itself. This was the decision that left me cooling my heels for seventeen days in the Hotel Metropol.

At the time, Yakovlev could not tell me everything. His position as the Soviet Ambassador to Canada made it necessary for him to be very careful about what he said. But he did go on to tell me something – to offer me advice – that was, in fact, an astonishing glimpse into the changes that were in store for the Soviet Union. Remember, he was a friend of Gorbachev's; the concept of *perestroika* may well have been taking shape in his mind, even then. "Don't be discouraged," he said. "Keep on it. You must not walk away. The ideology now is not right, but don't be pessimistic. The ideology will change. Something will happen."

The ideology will change. Something will happen. It seemed about as unlikely as the Berlin Wall falling. And yet, in view of the events that have since unfolded in what is now the former Soviet Union, I often think how extraordinary my conversation with Aleksandr Yakovlev was. It isn't often someone shows you the future so clearly – especially when that future seems so improbable. But it was this advice, coming as it did from a man of Yakovlev's stature, experience, and wisdom, that helped me over the first level of pessimism.

Then there was the second hurdle. "You will never be able to build restaurants to meet your standards."

It seemed clear to me that in the USSR it was the people setting and overseeing the standards that were the problem, not the people doing the actual building. I concluded that if we paid for standards, demanded standards, and oversaw standards, we would get the standards we wanted. It might be that we would need Finnish or Yugoslavian contractors to oversee jobs at first, but I couldn't see why Russian tradesmen should be any less skilled than tradesmen anywhere else in the world.

Number Three. "You will never get Soviet citizens to work the way you want McDonald's employees to work."

This objection came up a lot during our negotiations in the early 1980s. It was a favourite of the media – particularly the Soviet media. I would be on television, or being interviewed for a newspaper article, and I'd be asked: Aren't Russians too surly? Too impolite? Too arrogant? Do you really think that they can be taught to prepare the kind of food and provide the kind of service on which McDonald's insists?

I have to admit I found this a pretty easy objection to deal with. It just never made sense to me. And my answer was always the same. I always said: Who wins the Olympics?

Usually whoever was interviewing me would be taken aback by this. It certainly wasn't what they were expecting me to say. "Pardon?"

"Who usually wins the most gold medals at the Olympics?"

"Uh. The Soviets."

"Right. The Soviets. The Soviets beat the Americans. They beat the Germans. They train hard. They work hard. They run faster, they row faster, they jump higher, they do parallel bars better. They do all these things better than anyone in the world, and you're telling me that we can't teach them to make hamburgers, clean tables, wash floors, fill out orders quickly, and smile at customers? What are you talking about?" That usually ended that.

Number Four. "You won't get suppliers."

Why not? I knew by then that the Soviets were hard-working people, and I knew they wanted to do business. Although their

My grandfather's passport: In 1906, when my father was still a baby, my grandparents and their young family fled the pogroms of the Ukraine for America.

Anxious passage: My grandfather's notepad, printed by the shipping company, is filled with names of people to contact when the Kaganovs reached the new world.

Sandy and her pesky kid brother: My sister was always trying to keep me from falling into trouble – even at this young age!

No, this isn't my first day at law school at Northwestern. This is me, a few years earlier, doing a little sidewalk advertising for our family's business – the Northwestern Baking Company.

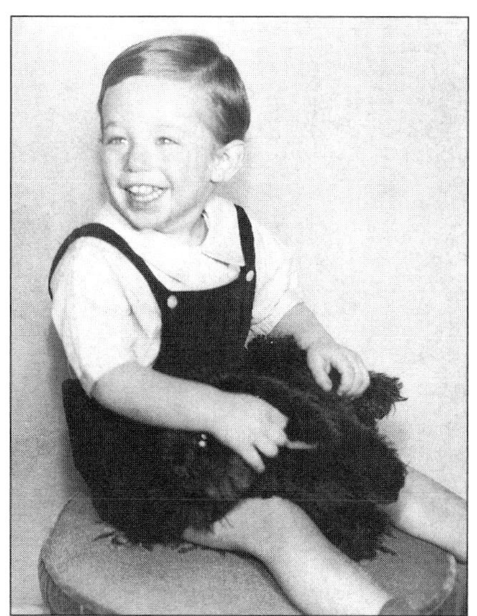

A terrible two: I still have the same mischievous twinkle and the same gap between my front teeth. The hair's another story.

Sunday in the park with George: That's me, bottom right, with my sister and our cousins. Why the frown? I probably wanted to be in the centre.

A proud day: Outside the synagogue, at age thirteen, on the day of my bar mitzvah.

The jock: I'm sporting my Hyde Park High School football letter sweater.

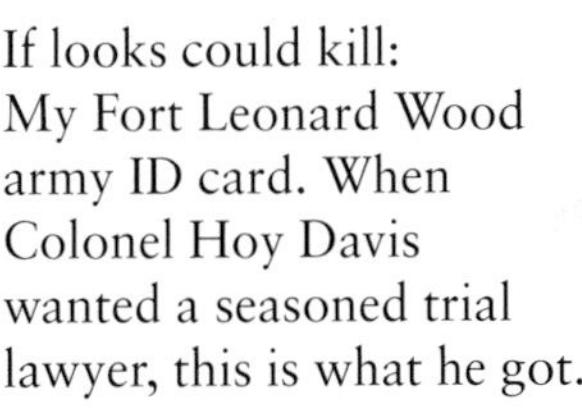
If looks could kill: My Fort Leonard Wood army ID card. When Colonel Hoy Davis wanted a seasoned trial lawyer, this is what he got.

When I was the National Campaign Chairman for the Israel Bond Drive in 1974, we invited Moshe Dayan and his elegant wife, Rachel, to a fundraising dinner in Toronto.

George Cohon (standing right), Canadian chairman of the Israel Prime Minister's Club, tickles the funny bone of Prime Minister Meir after he invited her to become a charter member of the Toronto club which bears her name. The incident took place at a dinner in Tel aviv climaxing the Israel Bonds Prime Minister's Conference. Seated at Mrs. Meir's left is Julian Venezky, a U.S. Bonds official. Next to Cohon is Sam Rothberg, Israel Bonds world-wide chairman.

Smiles are free – even for world leaders. I have often wondered whether this is the kind of clipping that found its way into the dossier that Soviet officials kept on me.

An absent friend: with Yitzhak Rabin in 1979.

September 4, 1960: The bride was radiant. (She still is.) The parents were happy. And the groom, by the look of things, appeared destined to go into the food business.

Canada by choice: My suit may have given the citizenship judge second thoughts, but in 1975 I became a Canadian. I celebrated in a typically quiet and understated way – with Bobby Gimby and his band.

A proud day: In 1988, thirteen years after I became a Canadian citizen, I received the Order of Canada from Governor General Jeanne Sauvé.

Where it all began: Susan, Craig, Mark, and I in Montreal for the 1976 Olympics. It was on this trip that we met a delegation from the Soviet Union. And the rest, as they say, is history.

A family favourite: I love this picture of Craig, Mark, Susan, and me, taken on one of the many happy days we still enjoy at our country house.

Heart and soul: Here I am in 1976 with family, the most important part of my life. Left to right: Dad, Mom, Susan and me, Mark, Craig, and Susan's parents.

The power of Big Macs: Mark, Craig, Susan, and I embark on the cruise that everyone said was impossible.

Centre left: Party on: Craig and Mark had to do all the work, but Susan, her dad (in his Harley-Davidson T-shirt), and I joined them in celebrating their graduation in 1985.

Centre right: Another ho-hum day in the country: Craig, Mark, and I throw a surprise party for Susan at our summer home.

Bottom right: Roots and Wings: Craig, Mark, and me in Jerusalem.

Going for it: Mark leading the Canadian-Soviet Arctic Quest youth expedition.

At a party for Craig and Jeanette celebrating their wedding: Mark, Susan, and me, with Jeanette's parents, Elly and Stig Sundberg, are bursting with pride and happiness.

My two "best" friends: Ken McGowen (right) and me with the former head of the KGB – my good friend and tennis partner, Vadim Bakatin.

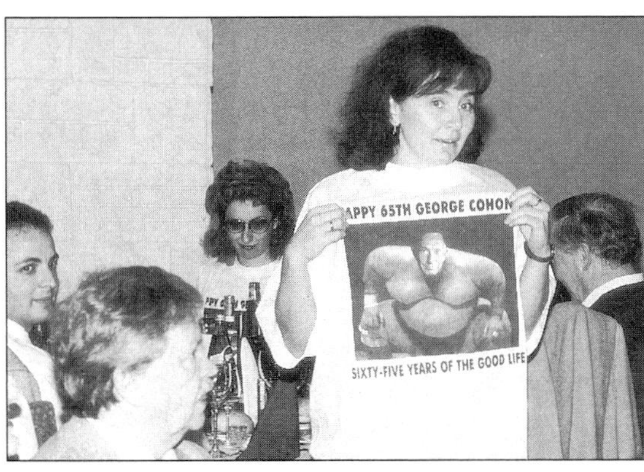

Wonders never cease: When I turned sixty, my friends and colleagues in Moscow threw a party and turned me into a sixty-five-year-old sumo wrestler!

agricultural system seemed to be in almost total disarray, we felt that its individual components were often sound. We had a team of agronomists and suppliers from Europe and North America who looked at the problems of the Soviet system thoroughly, and they believed there was a foundation on which we could build. We could help farmers on state farms and on co-ops with their crops; we could help truckers and distributors move their products efficiently; and we could establish our own processing plant. There *were* potatoes, but they were rotting in the fields. There *were* trucks, but they were stranded on the roads, out of gas. It wasn't a question of inventing the wheel so much as ensuring that gears were meshing and the wheel was turning properly. When the first rumours of McDonald's opening a restaurant in Moscow began to circulate, it didn't take long for prospective suppliers to contact us. One man, I remember, wrote to tell me that he had a cow – one cow – that he would like to sell.

Number Five. "And George, the kicker is, you won't make money."

Well, I thought we would. This, after all, was our primary reason for wanting in to the Soviet Union. The population was huge – more than ten times the population of Canada – and, from the point of view of diet, it was a population naturally receptive to our product. They eat meat, bread, potatoes, and milk; well, as it happened, we were in the business of selling meat, bread, potatoes, and milk of the highest standards. Soviet citizens desperately wanted a taste of the West; well, as it happened, that's exactly what we were.

There were some people who advised me to stick to hard currency. To them, the thought of an international operation dealing in a non-convertible currency was just too fraught with problems. But I knew from the beginning that we wanted to have rubles-only restaurants; the entire thrust of McDonald's is that it is a place for everyone – for ordinary folk, for families, for teenagers, for older people. Our success is built on inclusivity. This, in a different context, was why I argued successfully that McDonald's should never be in South Africa while apartheid was still in place. In the same way, I could see that excluding the bulk of the Soviet population by insisting on hard currency would be a catastrophic mistake. Opening a hard-currency McDonald's in Moscow would have been like opening a McDonald's in a mall in some small North American town and telling people that they had to wear tuxedos and ball gowns if they wanted to get served. It was a non-starter.

I could see that there were going to be financial complications that had to do with the instability of the ruble. You didn't have to be an economist to figure that out: The Soviet economy was limping from one unsuccessful five-year plan to the next, and on the streets in Moscow the black market for foreign currency was almost unavoidable. Our intention was to re-invest our rubles back into our Soviet expansion. But we would have to get some hard currency; the royalty fee that our Soviet restaurants would owe to the Canadian company, for instance, was not much good to us if it was paid in rubles. So I could see we were going to have to be creative. Bartering was a possibility: buying products for rubles that we could trade outside the USSR for hard currency. Perhaps one of our restaurants would accept hard currency. Perhaps we could invest in real estate, leasing property to Western companies and charging rent in hard currency. Whatever the solutions, we were going to have to be smart. We were going to have to think this problem through carefully – but with people such as George Mencke, the chief financial officer of McDonald's-Canada, advising me, having to think a problem through wasn't going to be insurmountable. That's what financial experts are for.

The bottom line was that, in the Soviet Union, we were looking at an enormous market – certainly one of the biggest in the world. We had an excellent product. We knew how to serve customers. We knew how to maintain standards. And we knew how to sell – we knew how to sell almost as well as we knew how to make burgers and fries. All this being the case, it was clear to me that in the long run we would make money. There were problems to overcome, certainly. But if you open an oasis in the desert, you're going to make money. As Ray Kroc always used to say to me, "If you concentrate on doing what you do well, the rest will follow."

These were the concerns I had on my mind throughout the early 1980s. I had answers for each of the five hurdles of pessimism. On my good days I could see my way clear of all of them, and I could remain hopeful. Still, the negotiations during this period were slow and difficult. Endless meetings. Endless protocols. I had never thought it would be easy. But after the fourth, fifth, sixth year of negotiations there were times, I have to admit, when my optimism began to fail me.

Then I met Don Kendall in Moscow. Kendall was the chairman of PepsiCo, a huge company that controls Pepsi Cola and, at that time, also controlled Pizza Hut and KFC among other companies. Years before, Kendall had made a deal with Brezhnev to bring Pepsi Cola to the Soviet Union. It was a very tough, very hard-nosed deal that completely blind-sided his competition. Which isn't all that surprising; Kendall is a tough, hard-nosed guy. Figuratively speaking, look the other way for a second with a guy like Kendall and you won't know what hit you. Coke looked the other way, and as soon as they did, Kendall signed a ten-year exclusive with the Soviets that successfully kept Coca-Cola out of the Soviet market until the 1980s. Don Kendall is a legendary figure. I had never met him, but I had certainly heard of him.

My meeting with Kendall occurred when I was standing in the lobby of Armand Hammer's hotel complex, the Sovincentr. It is a large, modern combination of hotel, conference centre, and office building. It was intended to be a centre for Western businessmen, and it is built in a kind of splashy Western style around a vast central atrium. As it happened, I was talking with Pierre Trudeau at the time. He wanted to know how our talks with the Soviets were going.

I was about to tell Pierre Trudeau how I was feeling. I don't believe I was quite at the point of throwing in the towel, but I was getting close. I was just about to answer his question when Don Kendall interrupted us.

Kendall may have looked like a gentleman. As a matter of fact, he looked exactly as if he had stepped out of the pages of *GQ*. But there was nothing gentlemanly about the way he interrupted us. He just barged into our conversation. He stepped between us and addressed himself to Trudeau. He acted as if I wasn't there.

Trudeau and I were both a little surprised. Kendall practically had his back to me. Finally, Trudeau said, "This is George Cohon, a friend of mine from Canada."

Kendall turned to me. It was as if he had just seen me for the first time. He didn't look at all pleased that I was there. He sort of glared. He looked me up and down, as if I was the one who was interrupting his conversation. "What do you do?" he asked.

There was something about his manner that was getting under my skin. But I didn't show it. I could hear my parents: Be polite to your elders. Show respect.

I replied, "I work for a company called McDonald's."

"So," he said. "You're the kid who's trying to bring McDonald's to Russia. Well, all I can say, fella, is, good luck."

I stared at him. He was rude. He was cold. He was pompous and self-important. I stood there, in the lobby of the Sovincentr, and I felt something shift inside me. It came right out of the blue, at a moment when I least expected it. You could call it determination. I knew then that I was going to keep digging and driving. It was something quite unpredictable. You could call it optimism.

I said to Mr. Kendall, "Well, thank you very much, sir. It was nice to meet you." But I was thinking: You arrogant SOB. I'm going to get you.

When Kendall eventually finished and walked away, Trudeau said to me, "So, George. The negotiations with the Soviets? You were saying . . ."

And I said, "Well, sir, they are going extremely well. I am very optimistic that we're going to close the deal."

Trudeau looked a little surprised. "Are you really?"

"Oh yes." I looked at Don Kendall's expensive suit disappearing into the crowd, and I smiled. "I have absolutely no doubt whatsoever that it will happen."

· 4 ·

Green and Growing

There are times when the answer is right in front of you – and you see it for yourself. There are other times when the answer is there, but you can't see it – until someone points it out.

When I was in the Army, after graduating from law school at Northwestern University in 1961, I did my basic training at Fort Leonard Wood, Missouri. I had decided not to go into the officer corps, so that I would do only six months of active duty followed by five and a half years of reserve.

Except for the one obvious drawback of Army life (I had married Susan the year before, and the time between furloughs was always very, very long), I actually enjoyed basic training. I was twenty-four. I was by then a pretty big, pretty strong guy, and the physical side of our training was not a huge hardship for me. I thought: Uncle Sam has no intention of letting me be anywhere else for the time being, so I might as well make the most of it. It was an opportunity to learn a few things – about me and about other people – and to get into even better shape.

I got lots of exercise. And there was no shortage of food and fresh air. But Fort Leonard Wood was no health spa. It was tough. It was demanding – and it was definitely not my friendly old neighbourhood in South Side Chicago.

"Cohon? Cohon? What kinda name is Cohon?" That was the first question our drill sergeant asked me at my first roll call. "I never heard that name before. Where's that name from?"

"It's Jewish in origin, sir," I said.

"Are you a Jew?"

"Yessir."

"I ain't never met a Jew before."

And that, more or less, established the relationship between this drill sergeant and myself. I don't want to lose any subtle shadings of character in the way I describe him. Nor do I want to present him to you as a caricature or to exaggerate. So I'll be very careful and very precise in choosing my words. Let's see. Redneck comes to mind. So does bigot. So do one or two adjectives that I'll leave to your imagination.

He rode me constantly. Jewboy this. Jewboy that. Until one day, after I'd been at Fort Leonard Wood a few weeks, after I'd had a chance to size him up a bit, and after I knew the lay of the land a little better, I actually talked back to him. It was on a break on a long-distance march. I said, "You know, I have the feeling that you hide behind your stripes."

This is not the sort of thing that a private normally says to a sergeant – even while standing easy – and I think it took him by surprise.

"Whaddya mean?"

I said, "Well, I don't mean to be impertinent. But you act like a tough guy, and you talk like a tough guy. But I think you only get away with it because you've got those stripes on your arms."

"That so?"

"With all due respect, that's my opinion. So I was thinking: If you'd like to take your stripes off for a bit, if you want to take off your shirt when we get back to the base and step out behind the barracks, we could probably get into something where we would have a little fun."

"That'd suit me just fine."

The news spread through the squad like wildfire, and so, after we got back, everyone followed us around to the back of the barracks. The drill sergeant took his shirt off. I thought: Oh-oh. He was built like a fullback. He had the demeanour of a Sherman tank. He had the friendly air of a pit-bull terrier. He was a very tough guy. Personal skills are not a big priority with drill sergeants. But toughness is a basic requirement of the job.

When we weren't doing push-ups, or marching, or climbing rope netting with full kit, we studied military theory. As a result of my new knowledge in this area, I thought a tactical manoeuvre might not be a bad idea. While I was taking my shirt off, I said, "I don't know if we should fight. Maybe we should just hand wrestle or arm wrestle or something."

"Well now."

I could tell that he thought I was having second thoughts. A relieved sort of smirk crossed his square, pink face – relieved because while I'd been sizing him up, he'd been doing the same to me. I'm six foot one, and in those days there wasn't an ounce of fat on me. I don't think he liked his view any more than I liked mine. He could see that I was not going to be a push-over.

He said, "Sure. No need for me to kill you."

A couple of my buddies went back to the barracks to get a table for arm wrestling. But while they were gone, the sergeant and

I stepped up to one another. He didn't want to wait. He held his hands up in front of him. I gave my right hand a last flex, and then took hold of his. We stood there, eye to eye, hands locked.

Back then, I had a particularly powerful grip – to this day, I have strong hands – and I had no doubt about what I was going to do.

He looked straight into my face, and he gave me a big, mean grin. I can still see his beady little eyes and his blond brush-cut. I can still smell the staleness his Lucky Strikes left on his breath.

I smiled politely back. People tell me that the gap between my two front teeth that comes from my mother's side of the family gives me a boyish, innocent look. I gave the sergeant my nicest, most youthful, most disarming smile.

Then I squeezed his right hand with everything I had. I twisted his grip as hard as I could.

And I broke three of his fingers.

Just like that. You could hear them snapping. Pop, pop, pop.

He dropped to his knees like a stone.

"I guess we're even," I said.

I went back to the barracks to finish a letter to Susan. He went to the hospital. He never bothered me again.

I've told this story a few times over the years. It usually gets a few winces at dinner parties. But I feel as if I get a little more even with that drill sergeant every time I tell it.

Not long afterward, I was in the barracks – probably counting the days, hours, minutes until my next furlough, probably writing another letter to Susan – when I got word that the camp commander wanted to see me.

Fort Leonard Wood was a large basic-training camp. There were thousands of soldiers stationed there. The commanding officer did not normally have much to do with us lowly privates, and so I knew that an order to report to the CO's office was likely to be a pretty serious matter. I was certain that the call had to do with my suddenly left-handed drill sergeant and the difficulty he would be having for the next little while tying his shoes. I didn't think it likely that the Army was going to look very kindly on privates who go around crushing sergeants' digits. I reported to the CO, fully expecting to be dressed down, or worse. I was sure I was in big trouble.

As has been the case in my life more often than I care to count (Remember my certitude that no-one was going to boycott the Moscow Olympics?), I was completely wrong. The commanding officer's interest in me had nothing to do with the drill sergeant's fingers.

The CO was a Colonel Davis – Hoy Davis. He was a big, powerful, no-nonsense guy. He was confident and decisive and he took enormous pride in the Army. He was a top-notch soldier, but he also had a friendliness and a fairness that came through, somehow, even when I was standing stiffly at attention in front of him. I liked him immediately, and sensed that if ever I were in battle, he would be exactly the kind of officer under whom I'd want to serve.

He looked up at me from the papers on his desk.

"Private Cohon, is it?"

"Yessir."

"I understand you're a lawyer."

"That's right, sir."

"Where'd you study, Private?"

"Northwestern, sir."

"When'd you graduate?"

"Just this year, sir. Class of sixty-one."

"And what kind of work have you been doing?"

"Mostly corporate, sir. In Chicago."

"Any courtroom experience?"

"No sir."

Colonel Davis sat there for a few seconds, sizing me up. I could see that he had my file in front of him.

I was all of twenty-four years old, and I thought of myself as a grown man – the very pinnacle of maturity and wisdom. I was married. I was a lawyer. As far as I was concerned, I was about as adult as it was possible to be.

But when Hoy Davis looked up from his desk he must have seen just a big, gangly kid in fatigues standing nervously in front of him. It must have been clear to him that I was still wet behind the ears. I doubt that the sight of me then could have inspired much confidence. But at that particular moment Hoy Davis didn't have a lot of options.

He said, "You're not a member of the Judge Advocate Corps?"

The Judge Advocate Corps was the officer group of lawyers. "No sir," I said.

"No, you're not," he said, as if talking to himself. He looked down at my file. "Actually, it appears that you are the only lawyer in camp who is not an officer or in officer training. Did you know that, Private?"

"No sir."

"Well, it's a fact. And it so happens that we are looking for a lawyer who is not an officer. We need a lawyer who is not in the Judge Advocate group."

He gave me a long, steady look of appraisal. His sigh was not the sigh of a man picking a first-round draft choice. "Which, I guess, leaves us with you, doesn't it, Private?"

"I guess it does, sir."

Colonel Davis explained that there was a sergeant at the camp who had been accused of being drunk on duty and of leaving his post before being properly relieved. The sergeant was going to have to face these charges in military court. "He doesn't want anyone in the Judge Advocate Corps defending him," Colonel Davis said. "He's an enlisted man, and he doesn't want an officer as his counsel. He thinks an officer's sympathies will lie with the brass on this one." Apparently, the sergeant was of the unshakeable belief that he would receive neither a vigorous defence nor a fair trial if he were represented by an officer.

Colonel Davis shrugged. I got the impression that he didn't think the sergeant was way off base in his assessment.

I said, "Let me get this straight, sir. I'm in the middle of basic training, and you want me to defend this guy?"

"That's right, soldier."

"I'm a private, and I'm going to go into court against a team of officers?"

"Uh-huh."

"And we'll get a fair trial?"

"I can't guarantee you an easy trial," Colonel Davis said. "But I can guarantee you a fair trial."

Did I think I could handle the case?

I thought I could.

"Well, then," said Colonel Davis, "why don't you just head on over to the stockade and meet your newest client."

In the Army, being drunk on duty is no joke. It is regarded as a serious breach of discipline. But not half so serious as abandoning a post while on duty. This is one of the most fundamental laws of military conduct – a soldier's responsibility for his fellows.

When a soldier is on duty, the lives of all those he is guarding are in jeopardy if he abandons his post. In a battle situation this is literally true. From a military point of view, it is treachery of the worst sort, and, in theory, the Army makes no distinction between peacetime and wartime when it comes to the duties of soldiers. Responsibilities are not altered by circumstance. A breach of military discipline is officially regarded as being just as serious at a base camp as it would be on the battlefield. Which put the accused sergeant in a very tough spot. This wasn't a game. The charges against him were serious. During wartime, the penalty for abandoning a guard post could be death.

When I met the sergeant he must have realized that it wasn't exactly Clarence Darrow who had been assigned to his case, but he was decent enough not to be unkind about my age and lack of experience. Mainly, he was relieved that his request had been granted: I may not have been God's gift to jurisprudence, but I wasn't an officer.

I soon realized that he was a good guy – a veteran of World War II and Korea – and the more I got to know him, the more upset I was that the Army was throwing the book at him. He'd made a mistake, sure. But he had served his country all his professional life. He had been a good soldier and had the decorations to prove it. And now, only a few years from retirement, he'd had a few too many beers on a dinner break and had fallen asleep. In 1961, no enemy was going to sneak into Fort Leonard Wood and murder soldiers in their sleep. But one slip, and the Army wanted the sergeant out.

Hoy Davis let me take some time off from basic training. He gave me access to the camp's library, and I hunkered down with what law books I could find. I really sweated at the case – I just didn't think it was fair that a man who had been a good soldier for so many years should be booted out so close to his retirement. I knew that no-one's life had been threatened when this poor guy had dozed off.

I became very anxious about the case. I could see that it was a legal minefield. I worked through all the law books that I could find. I learned about every possible precedent and every relevant judgment. I read case studies. I was becoming an expert in this particular area of the law, but I was aware of one very serious shortcoming in my efforts: I really didn't know how I was going to proceed. There were all kinds of arguments, leading in all kinds of directions. But no strong, single strategy was becoming clear to me.

I was like a quarterback who had the playbook memorized, and who knew every scouting report on every player on the other team, but who didn't know what to call in the huddle. I was stuck.

Stuck until, one day, sitting in the camp library and staring at the wording of the charges, almost daydreaming, the answer came to me. It was there, right in front of my face. It had been there all along.

In the camp, everyone was talking about the case. I knew that a lot of people were going to be paying attention to the proceedings – a lot of officers, to be perfectly precise. They felt there was something uppity about a young private taking on the higher ranks.

So there was a lot of anticipation when the court convened – a real buzz of excitement. People knew I had been working hard on the case, and they had cooked up the notion that I was really going to go fifteen rounds on this.

But I didn't think I was going to have to. Basically, the case I had prepared consisted of three surprises.

The first was a challenge. According to military law, both sides in a case have the right to a peremptory challenge of one member of the panel of judges. This means a counsel can have one of the judges taken off the case – without giving reasons for doing so. I had done my homework, and I knew about my client's right to a peremptory challenge; I had also learned which of the judges was the toughest and most unbending disciplinarian. He was a colonel – one tough, hard-nosed, letter-of-the-law curmudgeon of an officer. My guess was that no matter how convincing and eloquent I was, his take on the proceedings wouldn't budge an inch. The law is the law; that would be his attitude. So, the first thing I did in court was to challenge him.

He was shocked. He looked down at me. "I beg your pardon, Private?"

I said, "Colonel. I challenge you."

He sputtered. He fumed. He turned as red as my mother's beet borscht.

But he was gone. The law was the law. He had no choice.

The rumour that had spread through the camp was that my defence was going to be a marathon. People knew that I had been burning the midnight oil in the library, and they thought I was probably going to take a shotgun approach to my arguments – spray out as many legal technicalities, and precedents, and subtle, finely honed points as I could. Everyone was prepared for this to be a very long, drawn-out case. Certainly the prosecution did; they had texts and briefs piled to the ceiling.

And so, when the first charge was read out in court – being drunk on duty – and I was asked how my client pleaded, there was a gasp of amazement when I said, "Guilty."

No-one had expected this. The judges seemed a little taken aback. They consulted briefly. And the court accepted the plea.

So far, so good.

Then the second and more serious charge was read out.

Everyone in the court knew what was at stake here. Abandoning a post while on duty. There are few charges a soldier can face that are more serious. You could have cut the tension in that room with a knife.

How did my client plead?

To which I answered, "I move for dismissal."

Well, if my initial challenge to the judge had been a surprise, and if my client's guilty plea to the first charge had been a shock, my move for dismissal pretty much knocked everyone out of their chairs. The place erupted.

"Dismissal? Dismissal? What do you mean, dismissal?"

I waited for the room to calm down. I stepped before the panel of judges. I said, "A moment ago, in this court, my client pleaded guilty to the charge of being drunk on duty. And the court, in its wisdom, accepted my client's plea. It seems clear, therefore, that if my client was drunk on duty, he was on duty, and had not left his post. He might have been inebriated at his post; indeed, we have conceded that he was. But in accepting our plea, the court has already acknowledged that he was there."

They went crazy. The prosecution lawyers went absolutely nuts. They'd been snookered – worse than that, they'd been snookered on the break. They were furious. They had my guy on the first charge, but they couldn't touch him on the second, which was the heavy one. That was the one they were after – the one that would have cashiered my client, that would have finished his career, that would have left him in disgrace, that would have cut off his hard-earned pension – but they didn't get it. They didn't get it because I was lucky enough on that occasion, sitting in the library at Fort Leonard Wood, Missouri, to see what was staring me right in the face.

In his book *Grinding It Out*, Ray Kroc described the thoughts that went through his head on the fateful day in 1954 when he saw the McDonald brothers' operation in San Bernardino, California, for the first time. Ray had left his job with the Lily Tulip Company in 1939 and had gone into business on his own. It took some gumption to switch gears. Ray was thirty-seven years old when he struck out on his own, but he wasn't someone who had ever been short on gumption. He left the security of Lily Tulip and tied his prospects to the Multimixer – a five-spindle machine that made milkshakes in those days. Anyone who ever sat at a lunch counter in the 1950s or 1960s has probably seen one. With typical enthusiasm, Ray had, as he put it, "plunged gleefully into my campaign to sell a Multimixer to every drug store soda fountain and dairy bar in the nation."

Ray was the consummate travelling salesman – his eyes were always wide open and his ears were always to the ground. He liked to say, "When you're green you're growing; when you're ripe, you rot" – by which he meant you should never stop learning, never stop expanding your horizons, never get so caught up in yourself that you stop hearing what people around you are saying. And when Ray was travelling on the West Coast in 1954, what he kept hearing was talk about the little operation the two McDonald brothers were running near San Bernardino. He decided to go have a look.

"It was a restaurant stripped down to the minimum . . ." Ray wrote, "the prototype for legions of fast-food units that later would spread across the land. Hamburgers, fries, and beverages were prepared on an assembly line basis, and, to the amazement of everyone, Mac and Dick [McDonald] included, the thing worked! Of course, the simplicity of the procedure allowed the McDonalds to concentrate on quality in every step, and that was the trick. When I saw it working that day in 1954, I felt like some latter-day Newton who'd just had an Idaho potato caromed off his skull."

Computers are astonishing machines, but not half so astonishing as the human brain. I often wonder about the combination of information, calculation, and intuition that flashed through Ray Kroc's brain that day in San Bernardino – and that coalesced into his vision for what McDonald's could become. After all, lots of people had access to the same raw data he had been given.

Everyone who had ever lined up for a hamburger at that San Bernardino operation, even the McDonald brothers themselves, had been staring at the future of the food-service industry. It was right in front of their noses – a revolution in waiting, to say nothing of an opportunity to make a very great deal of money.

There it was. A small, white, octagonal building, with a grill, a fryer, and eight Multimixers. A modest place. It had two windows, a few stools, a sign that advertised the fifteen-cent price-tag and said, "McDonald's Famous Hamburgers, Buy 'Em By the Bag." And line-ups of customers. Always line-ups. Crystal clear, we all think now. A no-brainer. But Ray Kroc was the only one who saw it. He was the Newton who understood the meaning of the potato that had just hit him in the head.

Demographers could say that the boom in the food-service industry should have been obvious. By the time I was a teenager – playing high school football, working as a Fuller Brush salesman, going out on my first awkward dates – the baby-boom generation was in its infancy, but even by then it had already moved to front and centre of the North American experience. The focus of everything was becoming babies, children, young families. The sheer size of this new generation's demographic bulge was going to have an enormous impact. The world would become more youthful – which would mean more relaxed, less formal – and faster. It would give way to youthful appetites.

For instance, when my parents went out to dinner, which was not very often, it was a big event. They got dressed up. They spent some money. They took their time. It was an occasion. Other than diners and coffee shops and dairy bars, there were no other kinds of restaurants. My parents would never have dreamed of taking their kids with them when they went out to eat. But that attitude changed for the new, upcoming families. In later years, it would change even more as women entered the workforce.

When it came to food – and with a young, fast-moving, and energetic generation it frequently did – the shifting demographics of North America were pointing toward exactly the kind of place Ray Kroc had in mind.

Sociologists could say that the food-service boom should have been obvious. Parents with young families wanted to spend time with their kids – play time, fun time, together time – to do things that the whole family could enjoy. Holidays and outings were no longer simply periods of time when you stopped going to work and sat at home watching the grass grow. They became occasions when families did things together, and these young families were very quickly becoming the biggest and the most influential consumer sector of the population. And it was as if Ray Kroc had seen that all he had to do was open his doors to them – and that there would be, quite literally, no end to their line-ups.

Economists could say that the boom in the food-service industry should have been obvious. Wages were rising, disposable income was increasing. By 1955, the average American was earning 50 per cent more a year than he had a decade earlier. And all sectors of this expanding economy – clothing, appliances, housing and real estate – were being steadily drawn to a single point on the commercial compass: the new spending capacity of the young families giving birth to the baby-boomers. This was no passing phenomenon, for when the parents stopped paying their children's way, the children – the baby-boomers – began spending even more themselves. And then, of course, the baby-boomers would start having their own families. This generation quickly became the pole of the commercial compass, and no sector felt this magnetic tug more strongly than the food service industry.

It seems obvious now – obvious with hindsight. It was there, staring everybody in the face. Those millions upon millions of Dr. Spock babies were going to grow quickly to children, and from children to teenagers, and from teenagers to young adults with fast-paced lives and with children of their own. And how would hamburgers fit into this picture? Perfectly.

There are people who, through intelligence, through intuition, through genius, can take a dizzying amount of information and somehow see exactly what it means – when everyone else sees only the confusion and uncertainty of the present. They are visionaries – people such as Sam Walton of Wal-Mart and Robert Woodruff of Coca-Cola. Ray Kroc was one of these.

I was lucky enough to do my military service in a period between two wars. Had I been a little older I might have served in Korea. Had I been born a decade later, the name of a country that I had barely heard of when I was in basic training would have been on the minds of everyone at Fort Leonard Wood. Vietnam was not yet a place that America cared much about. I was fortunate. I finished my service, and went home to Chicago and to Susan.

If I have ever shown any talent for seeing what was right in front of me, it might have been the night I met Susan Silver. Before my basic training, I had gone to the University of Illinois, but I didn't make grades in my accounting course. This was a huge disappointment – a real brush with failure. I knew I needed a change of scenery. I chose a much smaller school and was very happy at Drake University in Des Moines, Iowa, and from there went to law school at Northwestern. At Northwestern I had a group of buddies. We hung out together, studied together, went to parties together. We were pretty good students, actually. And pretty innocent, really. But we thought of ourselves as a bunch of rakes – ladies' men, mischief-makers, wise guys. We thought of ourselves the way groups of young men have thought of themselves since the beginning of time: We figured we were pretty cool. We gave ourselves the nickname "the Dirty Dozen." Actually, there were thirteen of us, but with my family connections to the bakery business, I had no problems with membership in a baker's dozen.

One of the members of the Dirty Dozen was a guy named Ed Bood. He had played basketball for Northwestern, and Ed and I were pretty good pals. Ed and I were both interested in sports, and we both worked hard at school. I squeaked into Northwestern, and so, in my first year, I felt I had to prove myself. Northwestern was one of the top law schools in the United States, and I was worried that I was in over my head. I really knuckled down and studied as hard as I could. No-one was more surprised than I was when I got the highest grade in criminal law that year. I was asked to write for the *Criminal Law Journal*, which was a big honour. Mom and Dad were very proud.

Still, Ed and I managed to keep some time open for fun. And we shared one enthusiasm that sometimes over-shadowed the others: We both devoted a good deal of time to girls. We often set up double dates together, and I have to admit that we did pretty well. Ed was a smooth talker. He was a real operator when it came to setting up dates – a talent from which I benefited and that I really appreciated. Some of the girls Ed and I went out with were knockouts.

Ed was also from the South Side of Chicago, and often, when my dad was driving in to work in the mornings, he would give us both a lift into the city. It was around this time that Dad sold the bakery and went back into law, and so, of course, he always wanted to know about this class and that professor. We talked law during those drives into the city, and Dad and Ed became pretty friendly. Friendly enough that one day – so I later learned – my father took Ed aside.

"You and George are good buddies," he said to Ed. "You double date all the time."

"Yessir," said Ed, not sure where this was leading.

"You're from a Swedish and Lutheran background, aren't you, Ed?"

"Yessir."

"Now, I don't want to give you the impression that there's anything wrong with that. There isn't. It's a fine background to have. But we're Jewish. I don't want to force anything, and I don't want to interfere. But I've noticed that George is meeting lovely girls. He's meeting very nice girls." My father gave Ed a meaningful look. "I've noticed that George is meeting lots of girls – just not many Jewish girls."

Ed got the point. His expertise in meeting girls was not limited by religious or cultural distinctions. He said, "Leave it to me, Mr. Cohon."

Not long after his conversation with my father, Ed mentioned to me that a sorority in Evanston was having an open house. He said, "Why don't we go up and have a look?"

"Do you know anyone there?" I asked.

"No. Not a soul."

This was a little unusual. Ed was customarily a little more focused when it came to this kind of thing. He usually had some connection with the girls he wanted to date that would give him his opening line. "Say, isn't your brother's best friend's cousin the assistant coach of the basketball team?" – that kind of thing. There seemed to be no connection here that I could see. Still, Ed's success rate in setting up dates was impressive. I was inclined to trust his instincts in such matters.

We got to the sorority at about eight in the evening. The open house ended at eight-thirty – which seemed to me to be a pretty small window of opportunity. This did not appear to trouble Ed. He seemed to be enjoying himself, and when I looked around the room it was easy to see why: The girls were very pretty.

It was a Jewish sorority, and before long I found myself talking to the president.

She was as smart as she was beautiful. She had a spark to her that I liked immediately. And here, I suppose, was an instance where I saw very clearly what was right in front of me. We talked for a few minutes. I learned that she had grown up in Buffalo. She was attending the Evanston Campus of Northwestern and studying political science.

I asked Susan for a date on the spot. We were engaged three months later. Within a year we were married.

But not before I met her father. Not before I went to work for the Democrats in Chicago. And not before I fell out of a tree.

In those days, Richard Daley was mayor of Chicago. He was a legendary, almost mythic figure. He had first been elected in 1955 and he ruled the city until 1976. Under Daley, Chicago was a Democratic town, and the Daley machine made sure that it stayed that way. The Daley people knew how important grass-roots community work was. Like all successful local politicians, Daley made certain that his name stayed front and centre with the voters – with every voter. And so, when I was in first-year law and I volunteered to work for the Democrats in my parents' precinct, I was given an assignment that made it clear to me why Mayor Daley was as powerful a figure and as successful a politician as he was. There was a municipal election coming up, and my job was to canvass a particular ward. The party official who took me on explained things this way: "As things stand now, we expect to get 70 per cent of committed Democrats out to the polls. We'd like to do a little better – about 30 per cent better. That's your goal."

So, leading up to election day I knocked on doors, rang doorbells, talked to people, handed out pamphlets. I threw myself into things, and I managed, in the end, to move the voter turn-out from the 70 per cent mark to something like 87 per cent. I did a pretty good job for the Daley machine, and the way things worked in those days was exactly the way everyone said they worked.

A few days after the election, the party official who had hired me gave me $100 to help cover my expenses. "Thanks for your good work," he said. "Is there anything else I can do for you?"

I told him that I would be going into second-year law in the coming September. I told him I was planning to get married. I told him that I needed a summer job.

"Do you care what you do?"

"No. I'll do anything."

He said, "How would you like to be a tree trimmer?"

I had no idea what a tree trimmer does. I didn't know that trees were trimmed. I thought they came that way. I'm no naturalist. Susan still laughs about how, when the boys were small and used to do a little fishing when we were on holidays, I'd take a handkerchief from my pocket so that I could hold the fish to get the hook out. But I wasn't going to let the Democratic Party know about my lack of outdoorsmanship. "What a coincidence," I said. "You know, I've always wanted to be a tree trimmer."

So I had a summer job lined up by the time Susan's parents learned that we were serious and by the time her father decided it was time that he met me. Susan was an only child, and so, of course, she was the apple of her father's eye. He had an important job as a merchandising manager for Sattler's, a well-known department store in Buffalo. Her parents were on their way to Mexico for a holiday, and they stopped in Chicago so that they could see Susan, and so that Mr. Silver could meet with me.

We met at a restaurant. Was I nervous? Oh, just a little.

I notice things in people. I keep an eye open for telling details. You'd be surprised what you can see if you look closely. Had I been Mr. Silver I would have noticed that there were little beads of sweat on the brow of young Mr. Cohon.

My nerves did not improve when Mr. Silver pulled a piece of yellow paper and a pen from his pocket. "I'd appreciate it," he said, "if you would list your assets and your liabilities here. You seem like a nice enough fellow, but I want to make sure that you are going to be able to support my daughter and a family."

I took the pen and the paper. I gulped. Done for, I thought. In the assets column I was able to write "$953" – the sum total of my bank account. The liabilities column remained blank. I returned the paper to Mr. Silver.

He looked at what must have been the briefest financial statement he had ever seen. "My God, you don't have any money."

"Well, nine hundred and fifty-three dollars," I said with a sheepish grin.

He didn't see the humour in this. "You don't have any money."

"It's enough," I said. "For the moment. And I have a summer job lined up. I've always worked. I've always paid my own way."

"But what happens if you get sick?"

"I don't intend to get sick," I said. "It's not my game plan to get sick."

Mr. Silver looked at me sternly. "It's no-one's game plan to get sick." I really thought I was sunk, but then he seemed to soften a little. A kindly expression crossed his face. Perhaps he was thinking about what Susan had said to him about me. Perhaps he was thinking about how it had been when he and Susan's mom had first thought of getting married. Love isn't always the most practical thing in the world – but it is the most important. Nothing else works if it isn't there, and Mr. Silver could see pretty clearly that Susan and I were head over heels. By the time he asked the next question, his tone had shifted. There was something that sounded a little fatherly in his voice. "So tell me," he said, "what's this summer job you have lined up?"

"I'm going to be a tree-trimmer," I said.

"A tree-trimmer? What happens if you fall out of a tree?"

"Oh, don't worry, Mr. Silver. I don't intend to fall out of a tree."

He didn't say it, but he could have: Nobody intends to fall out of a tree.

When you are a tree-trimmer and you are way up in a tree and a branch breaks – as branches occasionally do – there are all sorts of things you're supposed to do and not do. The harnesses and the boots and the safety catches are pretty sophisticated, and if you do what you're supposed to do, everything clicks and tugs and holds and you don't actually fall, you just dangle there for a while until your fellow workers can get you sorted out.

Above all, what you don't do is to forget all your training and just make a grab for a branch. Which, more or less, is what I did when I heard the branch below my safety boots start to crack. I was a long way up – or, as things looked from my point of view, it was a long way down. A very long way. Twenty-five feet, anyway. And down, pretty spectacularly, I went.

There were enough branches in the way, and there was enough drag on my support rope, to break my fall somewhat. Still, it wasn't a very soft landing. I broke my heel, thereby ending my career as a tree-trimmer. I was paid compensation by the city for an on-the-job injury. And that sum, more or less, was the total of my bank account the day that I married Susan.

September 4, 1960. The bride looked radiantly beautiful. And the groom was very, very happy – even if he did walk with a slight limp.

If I believed in palm reading I would say that it was around this time that my two most important lifelines began to converge. I was practising corporate law with my father and brother-in-law at Cohon, Raizes, and Regal on LaSalle Street, and Susan and I settled down in North Chicago. We were blissfully happy – still are, as a matter of fact. Craig was born in 1963; Mark in 1966. Family was our first priority – still is, as a matter of fact. During my travels for McDonald's in Canada and throughout my negotiations in Russia, I always insisted on returning home for most weekends.

I remember how upset I was when, one day at work in Chicago, I was in a meeting with another lawyer, and his secretary interrupted us to say that his son was on the phone. "Tell him I'm busy," this guy said. I couldn't believe it. It really bothered me – in fact it skewed my relationship with that guy from then on. When I went home that day I said to Susan, "We have to make sure that our children know that if ever they really need to reach us, we will be there for them. They have to know that nothing is more important to us than they are."

If I paid any attention to things like the lines on the palm of my hand, I would say that family is my first and strongest lifeline.

What would become my second began really to establish itself around the time that Susan and I were first settling down to family life in North Chicago. Ray Kroc had acquired from the McDonald brothers in 1954 the exclusive national development and franchise rights for McDonald's; seven years later, he had bought out the McDonald brothers for $2.7 million. By 1963 – the year that Susan and I became parents – McDonald's had grown from the original, small but relatively successful, 8-restaurant chain established by the two brothers to 550 restaurants throughout the United States. That year, in Elk Grove Village in Illinois, the five hundredth student graduated from McDonald's training program, Hamburger University – a very real symbol of the company's insistence on the importance of quality and good service. McDonald's was selling hamburgers at a rate of one million a day, and Ray Kroc proudly served the billionth in front of a national television audience on *The Art Linkletter Show*. The company was well on its way to becoming a household name by 1963. That same year, in Washington, D.C., a funny and endearing clown named Ronald McDonald – played by a funny and endearing fellow named Willard Scott – made his first televised appearance.

Still, this development was not exactly at the forefront of my consciousness. I was a young lawyer, struggling to establish a corporate practice. We had been to McDonald's, of course. The "Golden Arches" had been introduced as the company's official logo in 1961, and like most Americans I recognized them. But I had never thought of McDonald's in any kind of business context until one summer evening in 1966.

Susie and I were pushing Craig around the block in his stroller when we started talking with one of our neighbours. Stan Silver (no relation to Susie) lived about a block from us, and as we chatted, he mentioned that he was interested in acquiring a McDonald's franchise. He had Hawaii in mind – and, since I was always on the lookout for new clients, I asked if I could act for him. He agreed.

The very next day, I called McDonald's and started to negotiate on his behalf. My friend from law school, Ed Bood, was working in the franchise department, which gave me a bit of an in. The negotiations went on for the better part of a year – during which time I travelled frequently with Stan to California to meet with Ray Kroc, and from there on to Hawaii.

By about the tenth month of our negotiations, I was pretty sure we had things in the bag. I had developed a good relationship with Ray Kroc; we understood one another, we trusted one another, and we liked one another. I didn't see how he could possibly turn us down. But Ray, being Ray, did exactly that.

Ray had his own way of doing things. He put great store in his instincts – instincts that had, by the way, served him very well. By 1965, Ray was an enormously wealthy man. And it was Ray's instincts that were at work when he was on a flight one day and found himself sitting beside a bright, energetic Hawaiian resident who seemed to have everything Ray was looking for in a franchisee. They hit it off, and before the plane touched down the Hawaiian franchise was gone.

Ray called my office. "Sorry about Hawaii," he said. "But the rights to most of Eastern Canada are open."

I was a little stunned. I told Ray that I would talk to Stan.

Stan was more than a little stunned. He had had his heart set on Hawaii. I told him of Ray's offer. He discussed it with his wife. They made their decision. They would pass.

So I put in a call to Ray Kroc. I figured it would probably be my last conversation with him. Based on my track record, I couldn't see that a lot of new clients would be flocking to my door so that I could help them acquire McDonald's franchises. I told Ray that Stan had decided against the Eastern Canada licence. "I see," Ray said. He seemed a little quiet on the phone, as if he was pondering something else. I thought that his mind was elsewhere – he was a busy man – and so I was about to say goodbye. But Ray – being Ray – surprised me. Shocked the hell out of me, actually.

He said, "George, you don't want to be a lawyer for the rest of your life. Why don't you get involved?"

I had never mentioned to Ray Kroc any of the misgivings I'd been having about being a lawyer. Opening business discussions by admitting that you're not really happy being a lawyer is not a particularly strong negotiating position. I'd kept my doubts to myself. In fact, I'm not sure that at that stage of my life I had ever admitted any misgivings to anyone – not to Susan, not even to myself. I had too many responsibilities by then to allow myself any doubts about my choice of career. There was a family to raise. There were bills to be paid. But as soon as Ray spoke, I knew that what he said was true. He could see things clearly, even if I couldn't. He knew what the answer was for me, even if I hadn't yet screwed up the courage to ask the question. I didn't want to be a corporate lawyer for the rest of my life. Somehow Ray knew. He could see what was staring me in the face. He was the one who pointed it out.

McDonald's. Canada. I turned the two words over in my mind on my way home that day to talk things over with Susan. We sat up late into the night. Susan has never been afraid of risk or adventure, so long as the will to succeed is there. And it was; the more we talked, the more excited by the possibilities we became. By the time we went to bed, the answer seemed perfectly clear. It was there, right in front of us – as bright and as promising as our future.

· 5 ·

BURGER DIPLOMACY

In 1948, Mac and Dick McDonald closed their San Bernardino drive-in restaurant for renovations. Actually, it would be more accurate to say that they closed their restaurant for a revolution. They made many alterations to their already successful operation, but underlying all the tinkering were several basic changes that would have far-reaching effects – two of which were more far-reaching than the McDonald brothers could have ever possibly imagined.

Nineteen forty-eight was the time of the Truman Doctrine – America's policy of containing Soviet expansion. Stalin was still alive. In 1948, the Berlin Airlift was under way. A year later, NATO would be formed and the Soviets would detonate their first atomic device. In short, this was probably the period of the greatest tension between the West and the East, and the greatest suspicion between the United States and the Soviet Union. It was, perhaps, the most dangerous, most unstable period of the Cold War. And if you had told Mac and Dick McDonald that the changes they were instituting at their little all-American hamburger stand in sunny San Bernardino, California, would someday have an impact on life in Moscow, St. Petersburg, and cities such as Nizhni Novgorod, they would have had a pretty good laugh – and then they would have booked you a room at the local mental hospital.

The first of their basic renovations was to change the operation from a drive-in with car-hops to a restaurant of self-service. In 1948, girls were just beginning to catch my eye. I was going on twelve, and I can still remember my first crush: Her name was Patsy Cavalier and she was in my class at O'Keeffe Elementary School. Had I been living in San Bernardino, I would probably have been disappointed that the McDonalds were getting rid of the cute, long-legged waitresses who always had such an appealing way of leaning into an open car window. In fact, much of the McDonalds' young clientele felt exactly that way, and when the modified McDonald's re-opened in 1948, the teenagers stayed away in droves – at first.

The McDonald brothers had nothing against teenagers and pretty waitresses. What they didn't like was how slow and inefficient the car-hop system was. A drive-in seemed very modern, but in some ways it was just like a traditional restaurant, only with longer distances for waitresses to walk. The McDonald brothers felt sure there was a better, faster way. The system they came up with – customers coming to one of the service windows, placing an order at the counter, and then taking the filled order away themselves – became the basis of the self-service system that McDonald's (and McDonald's many imitators) use today.

The logo of the "new" McDonald's was a zippy little cartoon figure. Speedee the fast-order chef remained the symbol of the brothers' restaurants until 1961 – the year that Ray Kroc bought out the McDonalds and changed the logo to the now world-famous golden arches. It was Ray who took matters a step further: disposable packaging, no cutlery, no tipping, year-round operation, limited menu. All things we take for granted now; radical thinking then.

But the McDonalds' shift from car-hop to "Speedee" self-service was not an immediate hit back in 1948. In fact, it looked for a while as if the decision had been a disaster. Overnight their business fell to one-fifth of what it had been. But the brothers trusted their intuition. They decided to hang tough. Which, as a businessman, I have to say is a tough way to hang when you've just seen your sales plummet 80 per cent. We had a similar, if not nearly so dramatic, experience in Canada in 1977 when we introduced our breakfast. It was a success everywhere – except in Quebec. Our Operations people kept saying Quebeckers just didn't eat breakfast out. But we hung in, adjusted our menu, and our breakfast sales rose from less than 2 per cent of our total Quebec restaurant sales to as high as 25 per cent. Sometimes you have to go by gut instincts – but the uncertainty can be very difficult.

They were low-key and soft-spoken, those two New Englanders. But the McDonalds had the strength of their convictions.

And they were right. The system was better, and faster, and gradually the numbers began to climb – but there was one huge, all-important difference from their pre-conversion clientele. Typically, drive-in restaurants were teenage hang-outs: carloads of kids out for an evening's fun, with radios turned up and convertible tops pulled down. They weren't really dangerous places – compared to the kinds of things teenagers routinely encounter today, they were actually pretty innocent – but they did have a bit of an edge to them. Not many people stopped at a drive-in for a meal after bridge club, or a PTA meeting, or church. You didn't quite fit in if you didn't have a slicked-back ducktail and a comb in your back pocket, or a bouncy pony-tail and a pair of saddle shoes.

When the McDonalds moved their car-hops inside the restaurant to other jobs, the teenagers stopped coming – for a while. But the customers who eventually replaced them came from a much broader spectrum of the population. Inadvertently, the McDonalds had transformed their restaurant into a place where families felt comfortable, and they did it at exactly the point in North America's demographic history when young families were about to dominate the commercial landscape. McDonald's became a place where young mothers and fathers could happily bring their young children. It was a place where working families could afford to eat out, and where grandparents could bring their grandchildren. Single women could eat there without feeling threatened. It became a place where somebody coming home from the office, or a shift at a factory, or a movie, or on their way to a college library could pick up a quick meal without feeling as if they had driven onto the set of a James Dean movie.

The motivation behind this basic change had been speed of service. And speed, the McDonalds got. The new system was infinitely more efficient; the delay between placing an order and getting your food had been measured in minutes with car-hops, and often quite a few minutes at that. Now seconds were what mattered. The McDonalds had invented fast food, and their customers were clearly pleased with the invention. The volume of customers rose to the former level, and then just kept climbing. In three years annual sales jumped 40 per cent. The McDonalds had stumbled onto something very big. By the time Ray Kroc came to have a look in 1954, the first thing he noticed was the line-up.

The brothers had happened upon what would become the very foundation of McDonald's success. By accident, they had discovered what was immediately apparent to Ray Kroc: the virtually unlimited commercial potential of attracting the broadest possible customer base. Their restaurant had become a place for everyone.

And there's a lot of everyone in this world.

Throughout the 1980s, when we were continuing our negotiations with Soviet officials to open McDonald's in Moscow, it was this same fundamental that kept us going. Setback after setback, meaningless protocol after meaningless protocol, trans-Atlantic flight after trans-Atlantic flight, hotel room after hotel room, our team kept making the all-important point that what we were proposing was not a Hard Rock Café – a place for teenagers and tourists – and not a Maxim's – a place for wealthy foreign travellers, expense-account executives, and high-level Soviet officials. McDonald's was a place for everyone.

This message was at the heart of our pitch to the Soviets in the uncertain years before *perestroika* and *glasnost*. Our negotiating team was nicknamed the Wolf Pack by the Soviets. Its membership varied somewhat from year to year, even from trip to trip. But there were usually about six of us in the core group, and we kept circling every government office we thought would be helpful, kept tracking every official who seemed even faintly encouraging, kept hounding every bureaucrat who appeared to have even the most remote connection to a decision maker.

One of the benefits to us of the reforms of *perestroika* was that they clarified our lines of communication. By 1986, we were picking up reports from a variety of sources to the effect that the Soviets were about to authorize joint ventures of some sort. The government agencies that would likely be touched by these new ideas became the focus of our attention. In particular, we concentrated on Glavobshchepit, and on a bright, energetic, newly appointed official there named Vladimir Malyshkov. This, we hoped, looked as if it might just be the light at the end of the tunnel.

Prior to Gorbachev's reforms, however, the Wolf Pack took a somewhat less focused approach. We had to. We were beginning discussions with the Sovincentr – a Moscow hotel and convention complex – but its head, Deputy General Manager Rodkin, kept postponing meetings with us. We shifted our attention to an internal organization called Interservice. This agency was in charge of food at the Mezhdunarodnaya Hotel, and eventually we wore them down. They agreed to meet with us and we showed them a movie we had put together about McDonald's. We gave them all kinds of brochures and information packages. They were polite but completely non-committal. I had the distinct impression that they were going to go home and tell their friends and family about the crazy Canadians they had met. Crazy Canadians with this really, really crazy idea. . . .

Jeff Hertzfeld, our astute lawyer, business confidante, and a fellow member of the Wolf Pack, recalls that in several of these meetings – at the Ministry of (Internal) Trade of the Russian Federation, at the City of Moscow administration, at the USSR Chamber of Commerce and Industry – our presentations were met with stares even more blank than the stares we were accustomed to getting from Soviet officials. In these instances, we eventually realized there was a serious problem of communication. We had to stop and explain what a hamburger was.

George Mencke, our chief financial officer and another Wolf Pack member, recalls that we often spent as much time tracking down Xerox machines that worked as we did tracking down Soviet officials. Signing a deal often seemed a remote possibility, so we had to take our successes where we could find them. There were days when getting our hands on a functioning stapler seemed a real triumph.

I dictated so many letters to so many Soviet officials, I found myself composing them in my sleep:

"Thank you for the courtesies extended during our recent trip to Moscow. We had productive meetings with both Mossoviet and Intourist. . . ."

"We are pleased to report that we are continuing our discussions with Intourist in the city of Sochi where the idea of a test restaurant is being considered. . . ."

"At the present time, we are preparing materials for a joint economic feasibility study with Mossoviet and are likewise preparing certain technical information requested by Intourist. . . ."

"You will be interested to learn that we have received an affirmative reply from Deputy Minister Anslan of the Estonian SSR to our invitation to send a delegation to Canada for technical discussions. . . ."

We showed our McDonald's promotional film to everyone. We handed out McDonald's promotional pamphlets to everyone. We gave away Ronald McDonald watches by the dozen. We wined and dined the head of this department and the deputy head of that. We made toasts. We discussed partnerships; we toured possible sites. We made proposals, and counter-proposals, and counter-counter-proposals. We explained ourselves until we were blue in the face. And always, our pitch was the same. All the literature we distributed and all the visual presentations we gave made this basic point: There was nothing exclusive about what we were proposing. Grandmothers would come; children would come; workers would sit down beside tourists; government officials would share a table with teenagers. The key to the McDonald brothers' success in San Bernardino in 1948 would be the key to the success of McDonald's in Moscow four decades later. Everyone was welcome.

This brings two stories to mind: one about South Africa, the other about our difficulties with the ruble.

Susan and I visited South Africa in the early 1970s. Often you read the "Foreign News" pages in *The New York Times* or *The Globe and Mail*, and you see the news on television, you hear it on the radio, but it's not until you visit a place that you really understand it – it hits you right between the eyes. This happened with us in South Africa. Apartheid seemed pretty nasty from a distance. But it was truly shocking when it was there, right in front of us: signs that said, "Whites Only." Different washrooms, different buses, different beaches, different everything for blacks and "coloureds." We came back to our hotel in Johannesburg after a walk, and we were stunned by what we had seen. Just stunned. In South Africa, at that time, there was no confusing blur between right and wrong – as there often is in difficult and complex political situations. This was – if you'll pardon the expression – absolutely black and white. I said to Susie, "This is God-awful," and I got on the phone right away to Fred Turner in the United States. I knew that McDonald's International was working on a deal in South Africa. Steve Barnes, who was the head of International, had been putting it together. But when Fred got on the line I didn't beat around the bush. I knew that it would have been a big mistake for McDonald's – a company whose success has always been based on welcoming everyone who comes through a restaurant's doors – to give legitimacy to apartheid.

"Fred, this is lunacy. I know the company has been working toward a deal, but Fred, I have to tell you, do not go into this country now. Do not go in. I am here. I am looking at it. I have seen it with my own eyes. And it's wrong. Absolutely wrong. This is an evil system. It's just not a country that's right for us. Not us. Not now."

I was adamant. I suppose that in the Soviet Union I thought that the presence of McDonald's would somehow affect their policies. But South Africa seemed different to me. I couldn't see that McDonald's being there would do anything other than legitimize apartheid. So I talked Fred Turner into backing off South Africa. This ruffled a few feathers – South Africa was a potentially lucrative market – and it particularly upset Steve Barnes. He felt I was meddling in his sandbox, and I suppose I was. But I was certain that this was the right thing to do – and years later I got my reward. In June 1990, after Nelson Mandela had been released from prison and before he became president of his country, he came to Toronto. I met him at a breakfast meeting, and I told him this story. Now, like a lot of business executives, I have all kinds of plaques, and citations, and lots of photographs of me shaking hands with important politicians and VIPs. But one of the things I am most proud of is my memory of that breakfast meeting in Toronto. Mandela has an extraordinary presence, and he listened to me intently. He gave a little nod when I was finished. He turned to me slowly. All he said was "Thank you. Thank you, George." He simply looked at me and said thanks, and the sincerity of his expression and the solemnity of his voice made me feel truly honoured. Today, apartheid is over, and since 1995 seventeen McDonald's restaurants have opened in South Africa.

In the Soviet Union, one of the issues that ran throughout our interminable negotiations in the early 1980s – an issue that gave us a lot of trouble, actually – was the question of hard currency versus rubles. Although there was a thriving black market in American dollars, it was illegal for Soviet citizens to own hard currency. There were very serious penalties for any Soviet who was caught trying to use American dollars or German marks in a sales transaction. Peter Beresford, a young, energetic vice president and a frequent member of the Wolf Pack in those days, has a vivid memory of seeing two young Soviets arrested for trying to buy some boxes of TicTac mints and Mars bars with a U.S. $20 bill. They were being held, outside a shop, surrounded by Army cars, at about four o'clock in the afternoon. They were still there at eleven p.m. being interrogated. For a few breath mints and some chocolate bars!

Then, there were the state-owned *Beriozka* shops that sold all kinds of food and quality items – the kinds of things that few Soviet citizens could ever dream of finding – and these shops would accept *only* hard currency. They all had identical, very distinctive, government-issued brass signs beside their front doors that said "*Magazin obsluzhivaet tol'ko na valyutu*" – "Hard Currency Only." Often these stores had windows that were covered with white paper so that passersby could not see all the luxury items inside.

Needless to say, the *Beriozka* shops were hated by Soviet citizens. They were perfectly clear symbols of the advantages of the West and the disadvantages of the East – and they sat there, almost taunting the people who trudged by in their crummy, Russian-made shoes. A wonderful woman named Julietta worked as translator with us. She was Russian and had never been in a *Beriozka* until some McDonald's people took her into one. She took a look around at all the things that she and her family and her friends had thought were completely unattainable – fresh fruits, imported vegetables, Western goods – and burst into tears.

What currency to charge at our restaurant was a problem for us – largely because rubles could not be converted. Until January 1992 you couldn't buy any other currency with rubles; nor could you invest them. This meant that there was no way for us to do anything with the capital that we hoped to make inside the Soviet Union – not a problem the communist bureaucrats had much sympathy for, naturally enough. On the other hand, for us to insist on hard currency would have effectively cut out almost the entire Soviet population from our restaurants.

It was the Wolf Pack's custom, during our long stints of negotiations, to meet in my suite for a drink at the end of the day before going out to dinner. As the negotiations had gone on, I had been coming to the conclusion that, as tricky as it was going to be to pull off, the restaurant would have to charge rubles only. It seemed to me that the hard-currency route just flew in the face of what McDonald's was all about. It felt wrong – just as South African apartheid had felt wrong. I also thought that it was very important that we send a strong signal to say that we were not carpetbaggers, that we weren't coming in for a quick kill. I wanted to make it clear to the Soviet bureaucracy and to the Soviet people that we intended to be in the USSR for the long haul, and that it was our plan to reinvest our rubles in more restaurants in the Soviet Union.

One evening, Ron Cohen, our executive vice president, and Peter Beresford, our vice president of marketing, were in my suite when I made this pitch. Ron picked up a napkin, took out his pen, and, as a joke, drew a circle with a dollar sign in the middle of it. He drew a diagonal line across the circle. "Here," he said, "we could hang this on our front doors."

Ron was an absolutely critical member of the Wolf Pack. The two of us have always had a great relationship – a kind of shared energy. During our negotiations with the Soviets, we often played off one another – bouncing ideas back and forth until the right one emerged.

We laughed at Ronnie's suggestion. But something went off in my head, and I knew it was absolutely right the second it came to me. I said, "That's it! I want to make a real statement to the Soviets that this is *their* restaurant. I want us to make exact duplicates of the brass plaques that are on the doors of the *Beriozka* shops. They have to be identical, in every detail. Except that in English and in Russian they'll say "Rubles Only."

That's exactly what we did when we finally did open. And there were few things that got more attention. Every newspaper wrote about it. *The Baltimore Sun* called it a "proud slap at the growing number of shops and restaurants in Moscow catering only to tourists, foreign residents, and a handful of Soviet citizens who have freely convertible foreign currency."

Long before the *Beriozka* brainwave, in fact, from the very beginning of our negotiations with the Soviets, I sensed that the McDonald's all-inclusive, everybody-welcome, egalitarian approach would have an appeal in a communist country. This kept me going: the belief that underneath the radical disparities between my political point of view and the beliefs of the officials who sat across the table from me, there was firm common ground. Although it often seemed as if they were doing their maddening, bureaucratic best to do so, I couldn't see how Soviet officials could argue against a restaurant that offered good food at affordable prices and where all Soviet citizens would be treated with equal respect and equal hospitality. So when, a few years later, *Pravda* called me "The Hero of Capitalist Labour," I was amused, but not particularly surprised. The *Pravda* article even quoted the famous Communist Party dictum: "Everything for the sake of Man." And then went on to say, "This quotation, familiar to every Soviet, as applied to McDonald's means the following. The company does as much as possible for its employees, i.e. working conditions, wages, uniforms, breaks, psychological atmosphere, traditions, a bonus system, etc. For their part, the employees do as much as possible for the customers, i.e. food quality, prompt service, friendliness and cleanliness which means doing everything for the prosperity of the company. Simple? Just like all brilliant ideas. And, believe me, it works without a hitch."

I was perfectly happy being "a hero of capitalist labour" – although the word that I tried to keep front and centre with our Soviet friends during our negotiations in the 1980s was "capitalist." We like to say that you need to have ketchup in your blood to work at McDonald's – meaning that we don't want absentee owner-operators; we want people who are going to roll up their sleeves, mop floors, make french fries, welcome customers, and be a real, visible, working presence at the restaurant they are running. I once turned down the hockey legend Bobby Hull when he wanted a McDonald's franchise; he had too much going on in his life, too many other interests and concerns, to be able to devote himself to running a restaurant. Absolutely, ketchup in the blood is a necessary ingredient at McDonald's – but there is another ingredient, one that I had taken for granted in North America, but that I had cause to reflect on often during our negotiations with the Soviets. Let me put it this way: If you need ketchup in your veins to work at McDonald's, you also need the air of free enterprise in your lungs. The philosophy of McDonald's is based on rewarding excellence. As Ray Kroc always used to say, "Free Enterprise works if you do."

Free enterprise had certainly rewarded me. As well as my energy, pride, and professional ambitions, almost all of my savings were invested in McDonald's. I had become a major shareholder in 1971, and from that time the company has prospered. Throughout the 1980s, McDonald's international presence grew from twenty-seven to fifty-three countries. The decade began with the sale of the 35 billionth hamburger and ended with someone, somewhere in the world, biting into the 80 billionth. McDonald's first public stock offering took place in 1965. Twenty years later the company became one of the thirty "blue-chip" stocks that make up the Dow Jones Industrial Average. By the latter half of the 1980s, during the time that the Wolf Pack was beginning to close in on what looked like a deal in the Soviet Union, one hundred shares of McDonald's stock purchased in 1967 for $2,250 had increased to a value of close to over $500,000.

In Russia, this success story sometimes left me in a slightly awkward position. It wasn't something I was ashamed of; in fact, I am immensely proud of the company's success, and proud of the role I played in it. I make no apologies and feel no guilt for the rewards of the free enterprise system. I wasn't going to deny anything about my personal situation – I just didn't think it was politic to talk much about wealth in a place where life was often so difficult and where the communist revolution was still *the* central fact. This sometimes made things a little tricky for a successful capitalist. It definitely made things a little tricky the time I was interviewed on Channel One on Soviet television.

Part of our strategy during the 1980s was to make our pitch through Soviet media whenever possible. I have usually – not always – had fun in my encounters with the press and I could see no reason why Soviet reporters and journalists would be any different. We thought that the more we could raise our profile, the more we could make our presence known, the better. So, I was interviewed by Soviet newspapers, television, and radio. There were not many Western businessmen in Moscow who were as accessible as I was. McDonald's intrigued Soviet reporters. If we called a press conference, a hundred journalists would routinely show up.

I was invited to be interviewed on the six o'clock evening show on Channel One. This was a great opportunity; the six o'clock show was absolutely prime time, and across the Soviet Union there would probably be at least a hundred million people watching. More than likely, some of the officials whom we had been seeing or trying to see would be tuned in. It seemed to me to be an excellent way to establish our credentials and to get our message across.

Anyone who had ever been in a television studio in the United States or in Canada would have been taken aback by a Soviet studio in the 1980s. They sort of slapped some make-up on me in the hallway, and then ushered me into a cold, cavernous space that looked more like an old airplane hangar than the pride of the Soviet network.

The host was waiting for me. He was a slightly soft, overly handsome man with a meticulously coiffed head of white hair. Through the interpreter, he said, "This will just be a little chat, really. Just some easy questions. Nothing too serious. Just enough for us to have a pleasant conversation for seven or eight minutes on air."

"Wonderful," I said. Seven or eight minutes of free publicity. What could be better?

I sat in the rickety, well-worn guest chair, and the technicians scurried around, and the floor director counted down, and the green light went on, and *Whammo!* the first question was, "Mr. Cohon, is it true that you are a millionaire?"

What a question! More than one hundred million people watching – one hundred million people who have been told all their lives about greedy, untrustworthy, money-grubbing, capitalist businessmen, and I'm asked if I'm a millionaire.

I tried to look cool and unruffled, but I was thinking as fast as I am able to think. What to say?

"Well," I said. "I wake up in the morning, and I brush my teeth and I wash my face. . . ."

I could see the host's face tighten a little. He didn't like the approach I was taking.

I continued. "Then I comb my hair." I smiled. I patted my thinning top and gave his thick, splendidly cared-for silver hair a long, mischievous once-over. "That's when I probably gain a few minutes on you. I mean, I guess you have to spend a lot of time on your hair in the mornings to get it so perfect."

The host did not look happy.

"Then, maybe, I exercise a bit. And I might play with the dog. Then, after a while, I have breakfast with my wife. Our sons are at university now, so, probably, after breakfast, I give them a call to see how they're doing."

He had a polite smile sort of frozen on his pudgy face, but his eyes were getting harder, and smaller.

"I'm doing a lot of travelling these days. You know, we're very hopeful that we can open a McDonald's someday, here in Moscow. So, often, when I'm at home, I have to pack my suitcase for a trip, and call a taxi, and wait in a line-up at the check-in counter at the airport. When the plane lands, I have to wait for my luggage like everyone else, and go through customs like everyone else, and go to work like everyone else. And when I'm away I miss my wife and my children just like everyone else. And so. . . . What was the original question?"

He gave me a dirty look. He was about to speak.

"Oh yes. Am I a millionaire? Well, yes, as a matter of fact, I am a millionaire. I started with nothing and I made a million dollars – that's the way our system can work. But is that money the most important thing in my life? Was that your real question? Well, if it was, the answer is no. No, it isn't. I don't dwell on it. I have the same concerns as everyone. The same concerns that people have whether they live in the United States, or in Canada, or in the Soviet Union. There are many things that are much more important to me than my money."

I thought I had dodged the bullet, but I didn't know how well I had dodged it until the next day. I was on my way home, flying out of Moscow, and I usually dreaded going through customs. Not that I ever had anything that I shouldn't have had, but Soviet customs officials seemed to enjoy spreading the contents of my luggage all over the counter – looking for smuggled icons or caviar or defence secrets.

The day after my interview on Channel One, I had a woman customs officer. I had learned from experience that women were often the most rigorous luggage searchers. She looked at me, and immediately her face lit up with a big smile. "You're Mr. Cohon," she said in English.

"Yes."

"I saw you on television last night. That was the best interview I have ever seen."

What I hadn't known was that the broadcaster was famous throughout the Soviet Union for his vanity – and he was particularly vain when it came to his perfectly groomed, magnificently coiffed white hair. People thought that it was hilarious that I had made fun of his hair on his own show. That was far more interesting to the hundred million viewers than the value of my assets.

Still, I was aware that the presence in the Soviet Union of a prosperous Western company would be more than a curiosity. I didn't want to come across as too evangelical on the subject of free enterprise, particularly when most of the people with whom we were negotiating were dedicated party members. But I was well aware that a McDonald's in Moscow would have a role beyond that of a simple restaurant. It would be an important symbol. I have some notes from a speech I gave in Canada in 1979 that now seem very prophetic.

"In my opinion," I said, "if companies like McDonald's, Coca-Cola, General Motors, Northern Telecom, Exxon, et cetera, deal with the Russians, this, in a certain way, breaks down the ideological barriers that exist between communism and capitalism. It may be the large multi-national corporations that do a better job of easing the tensions that exist. . . ."

Attitudes to free enterprise were changing within the Soviet Union. I was right on that. However, like most people, I had no idea how soon or how fast those changes were going to happen.

I am not by nature a patient man. Just ask Nancy, my assistant of the past twenty-three years; I tend to want things done yesterday. But patience was certainly a pre-requisite for dealing with Soviet officialdom. Our team – Ron Cohen, the executive vice president of McDonald's Restaurants of Canada, Peter Misikowetz, our operational vice president, our Paris-based lawyer, Jeffrey Hertzfeld, Paul Duncan from the legal department of McDonald's International, Mike Gerling, vice president and head of purchasing of McDonald's-Germany, Peter Beresford, vice president of marketing, George Mencke, our chief financial officer, and Helmut Hecher, a vice president of McDonald's-Germany and a top construction expert – came to treat frustration and delay like the force of gravity; they were just things that were always there. Negotiations, agreements, protocols, meetings – all moved at glacial speed. Throughout the 1980s, the levels of bureaucracy with which we had to deal were Byzantine, to say the least.

On the Soviet side, there was very little real understanding of what was involved in establishing or operating a chain of McDonald's restaurants, and indeed, not everyone we were dealing with was enthusiastic about the idea. In 1985, during our talks with Aleksandr Khlystov, the Deputy General Director of the Sovincentr, he told us that in Russia people thought of McDonald's as a place where hoodlums hung out. We wasted no time in correcting him on that score, but I don't think he ever had a very clear image of what a McDonald's restaurant really was. For our part, we had to identify suitable sites (the Soviets' instincts seemed to be to put us behind the elevator shafts in hotels or somewhere on the outskirts of Moscow; our instincts, naturally, were pretty much the reverse). We had to satisfy ourselves that it would be possible to source raw materials in Russia, and work out detailed feasibility studies to demonstrate the financial viability of our proposals. We visited existing food-processing plants – an experience that sometimes left us reeling at the conditions we found. These visits confirmed to us that the idea Fred Turner and I had discussed of building our own plant was going to be both a necessity and a compelling signing incentive to the Soviets. We knew that they would never be able to admit officially that there was anything inadequate about their plants, but we also knew that the distinction between what we had in mind and what, at that time, existed, would be too striking for even the most faithful communist official to ignore.

But we had to find our own way. It was the absence of guidelines that made things so difficult. But we gradually learned the ropes. We slowly learned about the codes and the intrigues and the subtleties and the secret signs. We never cracked the Soviet bureaucratic code entirely, but at least we came to realize that things were not always what they seemed. For instance, you could meet with one official who would tell you to your face that he was eager to help you. In fact, all he wanted to do was to get rid of you. He would hurry you out of his office by writing a letter to be shown to some other Soviet official who was on your list of important people to see. The letter would say, "Please give all assistance to these wonderful people." Which was great – except that if he signed it on, say, the left side of the page, instead of the right, the letter would actually tell the official who read it to do exactly the opposite of what the letter said.

As well, every official had a collection of rubber stamps. The stamps had all kinds of complicated meanings, and officials seemed to take particular delight in using them. I got the impression from many of the more junior bureaucrats with whom we had to deal that as long as they stamped a document – a letter, or a memorandum, or an agreement to try to reach an agreement – with their personal stamp, they felt as if they had done something.

Eventually, I became so annoyed with these rubber stamps that I decided to get one of my own. I wanted to have some fun with the system, and I had a stamp made that said "*Chush'*" – "Nonsense." I used to stamp all sorts of things "George Cohon, *Chush'*." When I got frustrated with the Soviet documents that seemed to be piling steadily upward but were getting us exactly nowhere, I'd sit at the vast desk in my suite at the Metropol – a desk, so I'd been told, that Lenin had used – and stamp things. Whap! Nonsense. Whap! Nonsense. It was excellent therapy.

I thought this was a harmless way of venting my frustrations until years later when, during one of what became my fairly regular meetings with Mikhail Gorbachev, I brought up the subject of these crazy stamps.

On this subject – as, indeed, on quite a few of the subjects we discussed over the years – Gorbachev and I were in agreement. He also thought people were getting a little carried away with the stamp thing.

I said, "I decided, if you can't beat them, join them. I had my own stamp made."

Gorbachev seemed amused by this. "*Dayte mne posmotret' na Vashu pechat'*." "Let me see your stamp."

Fortunately, I had it with me, in my briefcase. Gorbachev had his own ink pad on his desk. So, whappo! I stamped a piece of paper lying in front of him.

He looked a little startled. Then, after he'd peered a little more closely at what my stamp said, he looked amazed. "Dzhordzh, *otkuda Vy eto znaete?*" "George, how do you know this?"

"Know what, Mr. President?"

"How did you know about this word *Chush'* – nonsense?"

"I beg your pardon?"

"How did you know that *Chush'* means highest priority?"

There have not been many times in my life when I have been totally at a loss for words. This was one of them.

Gorbachev explained. "At one point, this word *Chush'* was used internally in the Kremlin to designate a matter of the highest priority. People who did not know the code thought it meant nothing. Such an imprint would attract little attention. But, in fact, it meant that this document" – he held up the blank piece of paper I had just stamped – "was of the utmost importance."

With intrigues such as these, and with the subtleties of bureaucratic communication so complex, it was no wonder that we often felt that we were moving one step forward to every two steps back. Despite our allies – Aleksandr Yakovlev, Vsevolod Shimansky, the Minister of (Internal) Trade of the Russian Federation, Valerii Zharov, deputy chairman of the Executive Committee of the Moscow City Council, and Vladimir Malyshkov of Glavobshchepit – we accepted setbacks as the norm. And as the negotiations continued, as the uncertain decade of the 1980s unfolded, I comforted myself with the thought that no setback could possibly be so disappointing as our setback in 1979. That would have taken the wind out of most people's sails – it almost took them out of mine – and yet, here we were, the Wolf Pack, back for more.

Our bid to provide food services for the 1980 Olympic Games had fallen through in spectacular fashion. Flamed out, people would say today. So had the Games themselves, more or less. The Soviet invasion of Afghanistan in 1979 had resulted in the West's boycott of the Moscow Games – a turn of political events that left me with profoundly mixed feelings. It looked as if the Soviets were intent on repeating the same kind of tragic mistake the Americans had made in Vietnam – and my heart went out to the Afghan people, as well as to the frightened young Soviet soldiers who were the pawns of their country's misguided foreign policy. The unsatisfactory conclusion of our negotiations with the Soviets for the 1980 Games had been a major disappointment for me. The Olympic boycott was the only thing that could have possibly made me feel that our failure had actually been a lucky break.

You may recall that I said there were *two* fundamental changes that underlay the renovations the McDonald brothers made at their San Bernardino restaurant in 1948. So far, I have only discussed one: the shift from a teenage drive-in to a more inclusive "family" restaurant. However, the second basic change was to have far-reaching effects, as well. These were effects which I often thought about – and thought about with considerable envy – during our efforts to strike a deal in the Soviet Union in the 1980s.

The McDonalds were intent on improving the speed of their service. For this reason, they stripped their menu down to what they considered their core strengths – hamburgers, french fries, pop, and milkshakes. Naturally, this simplification sped things up. It allowed the kitchen tasks to be broken down into manageable, clearly defined routines. As well, it allowed the McDonalds to focus much more clearly on the quality of the food they served – they would concentrate on doing what they did well, and on finding new ways to do it even better. This was a considerable improvement from their point of view; it was also a change they had expected. But there was another result of their shift to a more simplified menu that the McDonalds discovered more through experience than advance planning.

What quickly became apparent at the new restaurant was that there were clear and discernible patterns to the comings and goings of clientele. The McDonald brothers had so simplified their menu, they discovered that they could anticipate with considerable accuracy the demands of a given week, day, or even hour. They began to see that, say, between eight o'clock and eight-thirty on one Saturday night, the number of cheeseburgers sold would be very similar to the numbers sold during the same half-hour on another Saturday night. They began to see how local events – a baseball game, a fireworks display, a parade – affected their business. They realized that they could "read" the community of their customers. This observation, coupled with the brothers' desire for ever-speedier service, led to a re-alignment of their kitchen's approach which would have enormous implications – implications that are apparent in every McDonald's around the world today. Instead of simply responding to an order, the McDonalds' kitchen began preparing and wrapping food *in anticipation* of predicted demand. The key here was – and still is – timing.

This anticipation is a very fine balance to strike – our customers want things fast, but they also want things fresh and hot. No-one wants a hamburger that's been sitting for fifteen minutes. Quality is key. This is why we have such strict standards regarding how long we will keep, say, a Quarter-Pounder in the transfer area before discarding it. It's either fresh off the grill and piping hot – or it's gone. But we don't like waste either – which is why our managers and owner-operators are trained to be such careful observers. We want them to get a feel for the rhythms of their restaurants. We want them to be constantly taking stock of things. And that is why you can often see them "reading" their clientele:

How deep are the line-ups? How full is the parking lot? How many cars are coming into the drive-thru? How many empty tables are there? How many minutes until the local school has its lunch break? How on the ball is the crew? There are myriad factors that come into play. As well, our computer system shows us precisely how sales at any given moment are stacking up against previously established patterns.

This emphasis on anticipation is something that runs through our entire corporate history, from the present day all the way back to what Ray Kroc saw at the McDonalds' little San Bernardino operation. It is a combination of knowledge, experience, observation, and intuition. All of these elements enable a good manager to know, with some degree of accuracy, what is going to happen next. At a corporate level, as well, we pay close attention to the communities where we are going to open a new restaurant – in part because we feel that it is our responsibility to do so, and in part because it's useful to have some sense of how a restaurant is going to do when it opens in a new market. Whether in the kitchen or in the boardroom, we like to know – or at least have a pretty good idea – what is going to happen next.

I often thought of McDonald's famous ability to gauge what lies ahead with considerable envy while we were so deeply involved in negotiations with the Soviets. I used to long for a computer screen like the ones behind our counters that I could look up at and be told what I could reasonably expect to happen in our negotiations with the Soviets in the next hour, week, month, year. Many of the Soviet officials with whom we were negotiating preferred to keep us in the dark; their negotiating position would always be better than ours if we, consistently, had no idea what was around the corner. As well, the ground beneath all of us at that particular moment in history was constantly shifting. The communist system, the Soviet Union, and indeed the world, were being transformed during this remarkable decade. Things were definitely changing – just as Aleksandr Yakovlev had predicted to me years before. But I'm not sure that even Yakovlev had anticipated the extent of the changes that were under way. We had no idea what was going to happen next for a very simple and altogether breathtaking reason: No-one did.

It is hard, even now, to take stock of the changes that took place during that period. The Wolf Pack was focused on striking our deal, but, like most businesspeople who find themselves on new and unknown terrain, we tried to learn as much as we could about the Soviet Union – the more we knew, the better equipped we thought we would be. We followed the intricate ins and outs of Soviet politics in the papers and on the news. And – this has always been my particular specialty – we talked to Soviet citizens: on the street, in the cavernous passages of GUM, the state department store, at the markets, in cafés, in the parks. We became what the foreign services used to call "Russia hands."

Andropov succeeded Brezhnev. Then came Chernenko. These were the last of the old-style leaders. Frail and ineffective, Chernenko was General Secretary of the Communist Party for only thirteen months before his death. Dorothy Parker's old joke about Calvin Coolidge seemed cruelly appropriate at the time: When the news came that Chernenko was dead, I remember thinking, how could they tell? Andropov had seemed only slightly more vigorous. Their age and infirmity made both men seem hold-overs from what was quickly becoming a bygone age – especially when compared to the energy and vitality of the man who was clearly going to be Chernenko's successor.

By 1985 – with the Sovincentr still a possibility for us and several Intourist sites within our reach – it was beginning to look as if, finally, almost ten years after my initial encounter with a busload of Soviet officials in Montreal, we were beginning to get somewhere. And it was at that moment that the fifty-four-year-old Mikhail S. Gorbachev arrived on the scene. He was a Communist, it was true. He had been a party official since he graduated from Moscow State University. But he seemed cut from a different cloth than his predecessors – and we watched with a growing sense of excitement as he swiftly and deftly consolidated his power at the Central Committee and in the Politburo. This was obviously a breath of fresh air.

It was clear to me that Soviet citizens were desperate for strong leadership and for dynamic change. You didn't have to visit many little grocery stores or stand in many line-ups in Moscow to understand how powerful a force this desperation was. There was a bakery I liked going to next to the Moscow main telegraph office. It reminded me of my grandfather and my father's business, but the weariness, hopelessness, and unhappiness was all too clear on the faces of the customers I saw there. Gorbachev seemed to know this, too. Indeed, he seemed driven by the need for change. He spoke of "grandiose domestic plans" and "a historic reconstruction of the economy." If not, quite, music to our ears yet, this was certainly a very promising opening chord.

The world probably realized that things had changed dramatically when Gorbachev removed Andrei Gromyko. Amazingly, Gromyko had been the Soviet Union's foreign minister since 1957. Gorbachev replaced him with Eduard Shevardnadze – a Georgian party official who came to Moscow to take control of the foreign office at Stalin's famous "wedding-cake" office tower on Smolenskaya Square. With this appointment, Gorbachev seemed to be saying that the old ways were not going to be his ways – and the world took note. But this was not news to us.

I've been lucky enough to encounter rising stars in Soviet politics. Recently, in February 1997, I met the young governor of

Nizhni Novgorod, Boris Nemtsov. I'm not entirely sure why, but I decided immediately that he was someone to watch. It may have been that I saw in him the same will to succeed as I once heard in Silken Laumann's voice. It may have been the same confidence and determination that I sensed in Rick Hansen and the celebrated Russian athlete and adventurer Dmitrii Shparo. I don't know – it's difficult to explain intuition. At any rate, I knew that he was going to be a player – and one month after I met him, Boris Yeltsin surprised the world by making Nemtsov one of his chief lieutenants – appointing him First Deputy Prime Minister.

Although I had no personal contact with Mikhail Gorbachev prior to his becoming president, I was well aware of his dynamism. His rising star was not difficult to spot. Gorbachev had become friendly with Aleksandr Yakovlev, the Soviet ambassador to Canada, whom I had come to know and respect. My connection with Yakovlev made me feel that I was not nearly so distant from the centre of Soviet power and influence as I had been during the regimes of Chernenko, Andropov, and Brezhnev. Long before Gorbachev became president he was talking about the need for drastic agricultural reform in the Soviet Union – exactly the kind of reform on which McDonald's would have to depend were we ever to establish a Soviet network of suppliers for the restaurants we hoped to open. Suppliers are the very foundation of our business; without a reliable network in place, the most modern kitchen facilities and the best-trained crews in the world are completely useless. This was one of the biggest problems we had to overcome. To many observers, the Soviet agricultural and distribution system was beyond repair. But importing everything struck me as a clumsy, perhaps even unworkable proposition – at the very least it would be an ongoing logistical nightmare to channel in bread, meat, and potatoes from all over Europe through a distribution point in

Duisburg, West Germany. Because our demands on the system were going to be so great, and because it would be clearly advantageous for us to source products within the Soviet Union, we believed that the presence of McDonald's would help re-energize their agricultural infrastructure. The kinds of reforms that Gorbachev had long been proposing made me optimistic that we would be able to do that – that we could find the products we needed in the Soviet Union.

As things have turned out, agricultural reform remains a huge problem in Russia. Recently, the Russian Agriculture Minister, Viktor Khlystun, acknowledged that 70 per cent of Russia's farms are on the verge of collapse. Still, I believe that the role of McDonald's in the Russian agricultural system will prove to be part of the solution for which the country has so long been searching.

In 1986, Gorbachev added five new members to the Central Committee Secretariat. The Politburo was, essentially, the cabinet of the Soviet government, and the Secretariat was the Politburo's administrative arm. This was very close to the heartbeat of Soviet policy – and one of the five new members, recalled from his posting in Canada, was Aleksandr Yakovlev, my friend and the man who had assured me, six years before, that the ideology would change.

Yakovlev's prediction, while encouraging, had seemed a long shot in 1979. How could an ideology that was so carved in stone ever change? There were not many signs visible to an outside observer that the ideology was even shifting – but Yakovlev was no outsider. Gorbachev would put great stock in his advice; indeed, Yakovlev is thought by many to be the architect of what became known as *perestroika*. By the latter half of the 1980s, while the Wolf Pack continued to pursue our deal, we could only watch in complete astonishment at what was unfolding directly in front of us.

Stalin criticized in public? Khrushchev had managed it in 1956, but Khrushchev's voice had long been silenced by the time I began my negotiations with the Soviets in the 1970s. By 1987, however, Mikhail Gorbachev was not only allowing people to express such an opinion, he was doing so himself. In a speech marking the seventieth anniversary of the Bolshevik Revolution, he said that Stalin had been guilty of "enormous and unforgivable crimes."

Pravda demanding that the Soviet government speed up the process of Jewish emigration applications? Inconceivable – even at the time when we were picking ourselves up after losing our bid for the 1980 Olympics and starting a new round of negotiations with the Soviets. But by 1987 – while we were continuing our discussions with Glavobshchepit – the restrictions on emigration had begun to loosen, and some nine thousand Jews were allowed to leave the country.

A Soviet proposal to eliminate all nuclear weapons by the year 2000? Soviet withdrawal from Afghanistan? The return of Andrei Sakharov to Moscow? The Russian publication of *Dr. Zhivago*? Of *The Gulag Archipelago*? It is difficult to convey the impact of these changes; it felt to those of us who were spending a fair amount of time in the Soviet Union as if the law of gravity had been repealed. The Cold War was over; the threat of a nuclear confrontation between the superpowers evaporated. Everything was changing. Kids appeared on skateboards, rock 'n' roll was in the air. It was, to put it mildly, an absolutely electrifying time to be doing business – or, at least, to be trying to do business – in the Soviet Union.

Of course, there were setbacks. The Soviet Union lurched between a new role on the world stage and its old, Cold War adversarial position vis-à-vis the West. There was constant tension between Gorbachev's faith in communism and the direction in which his internal reforms were leading. This tension would eventually prove to be Gorbachev's domestic downfall – the man who, literally, changed the world could not convince his own people to support him. And, inevitably, there were tragedies born of a failing system, Chernobyl being the most appalling example. The dimensions of this catastrophe, particularly among the affected children of the Ukraine and Belarus, remain incalculable.

Still, from the very micro, very focused point of view of the Wolf Pack, we could see possibilities suddenly arising that had never been there before. Doors began to open. Suggestions began to be made. Partnerships were proposed. It was as if someone had changed the light bulbs, and we were suddenly revealed, not as hustlers with an eccentric, whimsical notion, but as businessmen with a proposal of exactly the kind that the new Soviet Union understood it had to entertain seriously – very seriously. As unlikely as it had once seemed, my friendship with Aleksandr Yakovlev would prove fortuitous in Russia. The health of the new, reformed economy that Mikhail Gorbachev and his colleagues had in mind would depend, it suddenly became apparent, in large part on ventures such as the one we were proposing. Overnight, we were no longer an oddity. We were no longer the lonely and isolated Wolf Pack. Instead, we had become, as Gorbachev himself would later describe us, "a symbol of the good will of international business, which would be important in helping us build a democratic society." Our allies and supporters were now in the inner circles of power, and we felt, not unreasonably, that our ideas and proposals had gone there with them. This, as you can imagine, was an astonishing transformation to undergo. We felt ourselves on the brink of something big – big, but unknown. For the fact was, at that time, no-one knew what was going to happen next. Anything was possible. It might have been nice to have as confident and as clear a view of the future as Ray Kroc had at the San Bernardino restaurant in 1954 – but it would not have been nearly so exciting. From the time of our opening negotiations with the Soviets we had been flying by the seat of our pants. Now the world was doing the same. Who could tell what was around the corner? All bets were off. Perhaps Solidarity would win free elections in Poland. Perhaps the Berlin Wall would fall. In a world such as this, it was not unreasonable to think that perhaps – just perhaps – a McDonald's restaurant might open someday in Moscow.

• 6 •

O Canada

One. Nine. Fourteen. Ten. It sounds like a quarterback calling signals, but those numbers represent the reality of my professional life from 1968 to 1971 – the years that things were really beginning in Canada. Those are the numbers of restaurants we opened in each of our first four years – one at a time, restaurant by restaurant, manager by manager, staff by staff, hamburger by hamburger, clawing our way into the market. Those numbers represent God knows how many flights all over Ontario, how many miles behind the wheel of a car, how many meetings, how many tours of possible real estate sites, how many lunches with mayors, how many speeches to Rotary and Kiwanis clubs, how many interviews with prospective owner-operators. And how many long-distance phone calls home to Susan and our two young boys from a tired, lonely guy sitting in yet another motel room. I always tried to get home for weekends, and Susan and I tried to duck as many social engagements as we could in order that our family spend as much time as possible together. But on weekdays, and on weeknights, the road sometimes seemed pretty long.

I was putting 110 per cent of my energy into this venture, and I loved it: cutting ribbons at new restaurants, having dinners with employees, establishing campaigns and advertising co-operatives, talking on local radio and appearing on local television, presenting service awards, going to a Restaurant Managers' Convention, an Assistant Managers' Convention. I was always taking hard looks at the competition – Red Barn, in those days; A&W; Harvey's. From the beginning, we did everything we could to make each McDonald's a part of the community. This meant getting actively involved with local charities, and I was going on bike-a-thons, walk-a-thons, ski-a-thons. You name it, I did it. I loved it – but that doesn't mean it was easy.

It was a fascinating time – even if not very much of it was spent sitting still. That period of my life affected me the way a baby, waking constantly in the middle of the night, can permanently alter the sleep patterns of its parents; I know people who, long after their children have grown, still find themselves reading, or working, or wandering the house in the middle of the night. In the same way, the constant attention, effort, and energy that went into starting McDonald's in Canada left its mark on me. To this day, I have trouble staying in one place for very long. I am not by nature very reflective, and I still have to make use of travel time – frequent flights to Russia or to the States; the drives out to Variety Village in Toronto, or to visit a new restaurant, or to our place in the country – to slow down, to focus, to sort issues out, to think things through. The rest of the time, I'm mentally on the move, from this idea to that, from one project to the next.

It was this restlessness that Ray Kroc sensed in me when he advised me to change careers. And he was right – in the early days in Canada there was something in me that fed off the excitement of establishing a business and then helping it grow and expand; it was the perfect job for someone with lots of energy, lots of ideas, lots of dreams, lots of ambition – and relatively little patience. I wanted everything done yesterday; still do. When I moved to Toronto and first met some of the fine old families who, for generations, had been presiding over the city, I had the distinct impression that either they were in dignified and confident slow motion or I was in fast forward – I wasn't sure which.

In my first few months in Canada, I was networking like crazy; I was making every connection I could. Even though it was expensive and even though I didn't care about having little glasses of champagne poured for me as soon as I sat down, I always flew first class in those days – just because the chances were greater that I would find myself sitting beside somebody who knew somebody who could help me out with some land, with a supplier, with a town council, with an advertising agency. I met our first Canadian banker on a plane.

Hustle? It was nothing but. As I mentioned earlier, Ray used to say, "When you're green you're growing, and when you're ripe you rot." Well, we were a pretty green company – which suited me fine. I was still young myself. We were growing like crazy, which suited me even better. I often wonder about people who end up spending their lives doing something they don't really love, and I remind myself how lucky I've been. I don't believe I would have been a very happy corporate lawyer.

Today, McDonald's is such an established presence, people forget that in Canada, in the late 1960s and early 1970s, it was one among a number of very tough competitors. Even in the United States, things were only just beginning to really gel: In 1970, in Waikiki, a McDonald's served its first breakfast; in 1971 the "You Deserve a Break Today" jingle was introduced. And in Canada, to an outside observer, the field looked wide open. There was a time when, for instance, if you were betting on who was going to emerge from the pack, you might have put your money on Harvey's. There was a time when they might have really run with it.

Obviously, I thought McDonald's had an edge over the competition. I felt it had superior systems – both in its kitchens and in its franchising and licensing. I thought I had recruited a good team in Canada – good friends such as Ed Garber, who headed up our operations and purchasing in Ontario; Bud Audett, who oversaw construction and equipment; Ron Cohen, who was in charge of our real estate and our licensing, as well as handling the bulk of our legal work. They had a very intense, very focused style to their management, but there was always a great sense of camaraderie, too. We were young, we were ambitious, and (this, I sometimes think, was our secret ingredient) we were having fun.

I believed that in McDonald's Corporation executives such as Ray Kroc, who in 1969 was the chairman and chief executive officer, and Fred Turner, who at that time was the president and chief administrative officer, were marketing geniuses. They had established a system that we were able to implement in Canada. I found that their ambitions for the company, their drive, and their vision were absolutely infectious. You couldn't spend any time with either of these two men without believing that McDonald's was going to go from success to success. And, restaurant by restaurant, partner by partner, supplier by supplier, country by country, this is exactly what is happening. Under the leadership of Mike Quinlan, the current chairman and chief executive officer, McDonald's continues to chart a creative and aggressive course through a complex marketplace. On the international front, Jim Cantalupo, the president and chief executive officer of McDonald's International, has overseen tremendous growth. When Jim became head of the international division in 1987, there were 2,344 restaurants outside the

United States. There are now 8,338, and international sales have surpassed those of the U.S. market.

Still, in those early days, success was by no means guaranteed, which, I have to admit, was part of the kick. People often talk a little glibly about risk, as if it is a kind of fashion accessory to a well-tailored business suit. But real risk – the possibility of real failure when you have real employees to worry about and real debts to repay, to say nothing of a very real and very young family to support – can be quite terrifying. If, however, you happen to thrive on challenge and uncertainty, risk can be quite exhilarating.

There were mornings, in those days, when I woke up and realized that I could no longer distinguish between fear and excitement. I was running on both – as entrepreneurs do. There were mountains to climb up, but there were cliffs to fall down. This was no-fooling risk, and I'm not sure that I've ever felt quite so alive.

Introducing McDonald's to Eastern Canada was not always an easy sell. There were crucial people – municipal officials, potential suppliers, real estate salespeople – who had never heard of us. For instance, when we first approached J. M. Schneider Inc., a big and a very fine meat company, in 1969, about supplying our hamburger in Canada, they turned us down. They were a lot bigger than we were at the time – we had all of ten restaurants – and they weren't at all sure we were going to make it. They didn't like the idea of McDonald's setting their meat specifications – something on which we have always insisted. So they considered our proposal and said thanks, but no thanks. Or, for instance, in Atlantic Canada, when I approached the Sobey family, who controlled a lot of shopping mall property, about renting sites from them, they turned us down, too. In return for their rental property, they wanted control of McDonald's for the entire Atlantic region – something which, of course, we weren't willing to give. They thought we might, just, do all right down East if they were calling the shots, but without their involvement, the Sobeys weren't at all sure that we would make it. We explained that we didn't do things that way – we were interested in individual franchisees. We wanted to develop individual, local entrepreneurs. They showed us the door. The same with Silverwood's Dairy, a very big and very well-established dairy in Ontario. They decided that we weren't worth the trouble – because, again, there were very specific demands that McDonald's insists on making of its dairy supplier. Likewise, the Bank of Nova Scotia – the bank where we took our business in the late 1960s – would not extend our line of credit in the early 1970s when we desperately needed to expand our operations. So we moved our growing business to the Canadian Imperial Bank of Commerce, where, along with the Royal Bank, we have been ever since.

Do these families, companies, and financial institutions regret their decisions? Well, let's put it this way. In 1969, in our few footholds in the Ontario market, McDonald's had yet to turn a profit. Thirty years later, our projected Canada-wide sales for 1999 are over $2 billion. So, I'm sure they do have their regrets. But do I hold a grudge against these people for their decisions? Not in the least. There were others who took their place: Caravelle Foods became our meat supplier; Hospital and Kitchen (now called H & K Canada Inc.) took on our equipment contract. These companies, and several others, have done very well by us – and we by them. But hindsight, as they say, is twenty-twenty. And one of the things you learn about taking risks is that, if the risk is real, not everyone is going to be willing to take it with you.

In 1967, the year of Canada's Centennial celebrations, there were only two McDonald's in Canada – both of them in the West. George Tidball, a bright, rugged, Western Canadian who was also a Harvard MBA graduate, had acquired the rights to Western Canada before I bought the rights to most of the East.

Tidball had opened his first restaurant in Richmond, British Columbia, in 1967. The McDonald's licences basically divided Canada in two. George controlled everything to the west of the Manitoba–Ontario border. My licence extended throughout most of what lay to the east, and we opened our first restaurant in London, Ontario, in 1968 – the same year that the Big Mac, developed by an owner-operator named Jim Delligatti in Pittsburgh, was introduced in restaurants throughout the United States. In the eastern franchise we opened nine new restaurants the next year, and fourteen the year after that. In 1971, while McDonald's was opening its first restaurants in Guam, Japan, the Netherlands, Panama, Germany, and Australia, our total number of restaurants in the Eastern Canadian licence area – both company restaurants and franchise operations – was thirty-four. Across all of Canada, McDonald's annual sales were almost ninety times greater than they had been in that first, nervous year of operations.

For me, everything began very modestly, very uncertainly, but very hopefully when Susan and I, with two young boys in tow, moved to Toronto in 1967. This, in itself, was not easy. Moves never are – particularly moves to a new country.

We didn't know a soul. My family was all in Chicago. Susie's was in Buffalo, which made things a little less difficult. Her parents were only a couple of hours away, down the Queen Elizabeth Way – but we had left many good friends behind in Chicago. It was a tough decision to leave the United States, and it wasn't as if there was a welcoming committee to meet us when we landed in Toronto. We were on our own.

Don't get me wrong. We love Toronto; in the thirty years we've been living here we've watched it evolve into an absolutely extraordinary city. It's been exciting to play a part in that growth, and I can't think of a better place to raise a family. But it was not such an exciting place in 1967 as it is now. Today there are single blocks that have more good restaurants than the entire city did back then. The winters were a shock – they're brutal, even by Chicago standards. We were too busy at first to concern ourselves very much with Toronto society, but whenever we did get a glimpse of it – the Royal Winter Fair, the Santa Claus Parade, the Canadian National Exhibition, the cottage life in Muskoka and Georgian Bay, the Canadian Club, the Empire Club, the York Club – it all seemed new, and foreign, and impenetrable. As things turned out, I would end up playing a part in saving the Santa Claus Parade, serving as the chairman of the CNE for three years, and introducing Mikhail Gorbachev when he spoke to a standing-room-only crowd at the Royal York Hotel – but no one, least of all Susan and I, could have predicted any of this. We didn't have time to make wild guesses about the future. We had our hands full with the present.

There must have been times when Susan felt we had made a mistake – but if there were, she never mentioned them. She stuck to the decision we had made in Chicago. This was a new career for me, and a new country, new opportunities, and a new life for all of us. So what if Canadians pronounced "out" and "about" a funny way, appeared actually to obey red lights at crosswalks, and seemed oddly quiet at sporting events. So what if zee was zed, if Thanksgiving came early, if there were three downs, not four, if "neighbor" was spelled "neighbour." So what if the words Conservative, Liberal, and New Democrat would replace Republican and Democrat in the political discussions at our dinner table. This was going to be our home. We were moving ahead; there would be no looking back.

My discussions with McDonald's regarding rights were with Pete Crow, who was an executive vice president of McDonald's at the time – and although I was still too much of an American to realize it, I was the beneficiary of what many Canadians believe to be the chief American attitude to Canada: amiable indifference. There is a line across the top of the United States beyond which exists a cold, unpopulated void as far as many Americans are concerned. That's changing now – now that we've won the World Series a couple of times, now that we have exported Wayne Gretzky, Jim Carrey, Céline Dion, Shania Twain, and *The English Patient*, now that Laurent Beaudoin of Bombardier has taken on the world, and now that Canadians have taken the Big Mac to Moscow. But in the late sixties, Canada was never a very big blip on the American radar screen – and, to be frank, I think the potential of the Canadian market was under-estimated by Pete Crow. I was awarded exclusive and perpetual rights to most of Eastern Canada – which, I think, as far as Pete Crow was concerned, was like awarding me exclusive and perpetual rights to the North Pole. For this, I was required to come up with pre-payment of $70,000 – $10,000 per restaurant for the first seven we opened.

This was a good deal. A very good deal. Except for one problem: I was about $60,000 short.

I went to my bank, the Northern Trust in Chicago. They stretched my line of credit to $10,000. That gave me $20,000. My Dad came in for another $10,000. Then I got a couple of my cousins in for $10,000 each, and a few clients at the law office, including my good friend Joe Kellman, for the last $20,000. I had my $70,000 pre-payment. I was heading off to Canada with stars in my eyes and about $60,000 worth of debt.

I made the first few trips on my own. I took a room at the Sutton Place Hotel and I formed a company called McDonald's Restaurants of Ontario Limited. I had a little cubicle in the new Toronto-Dominion Centre in an office called Nationwide Business Centre – the kind of outfit where one receptionist answers the phone for about thirty different companies. We were an unlikely bunch. About the only common denominator we had was that none of us could afford our own receptionist: "Hello, ABC Construction." "Hello, Acme Travel." "Hello, Maple Leaf Printing Supplies." "Hello, McDonald's."

To say the least, I was under-capitalized. Recently, I came across an interview I did a while ago in which I was asked why it had been so difficult to find the site for the first restaurant. "Oh," I said, as if it was the most natural thing on earth, "because I had no money." When I re-read this, I just had to laugh. There I was, in a new country, living out of a suitcase, with an office that consisted of a phone line, a shared receptionist, and a Rolodex. I didn't have much more than two nickels to rub together, and I was running around to shopping malls and plazas and commercial strips trying to find a site for our first restaurant. Some people might call it chutzpah; others might think of it as naivety. Whatever it was, it worked.

On one of my trips back to Chicago, before bringing Susan and the kids up to Toronto, I ended up chatting with a young lawyer who worked in a law firm down the hall from where I had worked with my dad and brother-in-law on LaSalle Street. Ted Tannebaum had a very successful practice. He was doing very well for himself, and his ears perked up when I told him that I had acquired exclusive and perpetual rights for McDonald's for most of Eastern Canada. He knew that McDonald's was a comer, he knew that the licence I had acquired had enormous potential, and he also knew that there was more than vacant, drifting snowbanks north of the forty-ninth parallel. He also guessed correctly that I was finding things pretty tight because I was trying to get started with extremely limited resources. He asked if I could do with some backing.

Could a fish do with some water?

I asked him on what conditions.

What followed was one of the most straightforward and welcome proposals I have ever heard. He said, "I'll provide you with the money you need. You treat me fairly."

That was it. The sum total of our deal. I said, "Sounds reasonable to me" – which was the understatement of the century.

Over the next little while, Ted wrote me a series of cheques that totalled $240,000.

Ted's money eased a lot of pressure. Susan and the kids moved up from Chicago. I knew I needed a car, and I called Ted.

"What kind?" was all he wanted to know.

"I'm thinking of an Olds convertible."

"Fine," Ted said. "Go buy it."

We found a house on Lowther Avenue – a street of Victorian townhouses that is right in the heart of downtown Toronto. One of the things that distinguishes Toronto from many cities in the world is that its downtown has remained vibrant and liveable throughout its growth and expansion. At the time of our arrival, skyscrapers were going up, stores and restaurants were opening, new businesses were being established. It was clear to us that the city was really on the move – and yet, we were raising a young family in a nice house on a quiet street that was only a few blocks away from Toronto's busiest and most established commercial districts. If I wanted to, I could walk to meetings at Toronto's biggest hotels and office towers; the volunteer work that Susan began quickly to get involved in at Mount Sinai Hospital and her night class in art history at the University of Toronto were only a short distance from our home. And it wasn't as if we were alone; we were living in what was actually a lovely residential neighbourhood called the Annex. It was reminiscent, in some ways, of the neighbourhood I had grown up in. There are cities today where people who have a choice would never dream of living – and of raising a family – right in the downtown core. Toronto isn't one of them. We felt perfectly at home.

In my little cubicle in the T-D Centre, I began to put a team in place. It was all Ted Tannebaum's doing that we came together. Bud Audett had been doing some construction work for Ted before he joined McDonald's. Ron Cohen had been a young lawyer in Ted's firm. And Ed Garber, who became head of operations and purchasing, was Ted Tannebaum's brother-in-law. The more I saw these guys in action, the more I came to realize that Bud, Ron, and Ed were going to be as valuable as Ted's investment and his expertise in helping me put together the financial side of the company – and believe me, in those early days, that was really saying something.

We started opening restaurants. Our first was in London, Ontario, on a site at Oxford Street and Hutton Side Road. For years afterward, people used to tell me how brilliant I had been to open first in London. The demographics of the city are such that it is frequently used, along with Kingston, as a test market for products. Everyone knew that – everyone, that is, except me. For a while I didn't contradict the people who kept telling me how brilliant I had been – but eventually I felt I had to come clean. It hadn't exactly taken an MBA to choose London. We opened there for a pretty straightforward reason: It was the only deal we could make.

The site was commercial property owned by the Bennett family, and our first landlord was a young man named Avie Bennett. He was a little worried about my lack of collateral. Who wouldn't be? But, in the end, he was willing to go along with my ambitions, my dreams, and what guarantees I could muster. We became friends, and over the years our paths would cross again.

Avie went from a successful career in real estate into a distinguished career in publishing. He publishes prominent, world-renowned writers such as Margaret Atwood, Alice Munro, and Michael Ondaatje and moves in lofty literary circles now. But I like to remember beginnings. I like to remember the people who believed in me when there was not a whole lot to go on. So I take care to keep my Canadian publisher supplied with business cards that are good, at any McDonald's, for a Big Mac, and that read "Avie Bennett, First Landlord and Special Representative."

There was, as there always is, trepidation and anxiety surrounding a first opening. People who think I'm hyper now should have seen me then. I worked myself into a high gear of worry and activity. Was the crew trained properly? Was the kitchen properly set up? Were suppliers on side? Was the product up to McDonald's standards? I drove back and forth between Toronto and London I-don't-know-how-many times. I got to know that stretch of the 401 extremely well. In the end, the restaurant opened to fanfare and celebration – and, almost immediately, to line-ups. We invited several of the University of Western Ontario's fraternities to take part in a hamburger-eating contest. Dr. Robert Carroll, who is now a dental surgeon in Orillia, wrote to remind me of this titanic struggle. Two enormous frat brothers named Moose and Ox looked as if, between the two of them, they were going to force us to change the "Number of Hamburgers Served" sign out front. But, as Bob Carroll wrote, "the star of the day was some skinny 140 pound guy from another house who consumed what appeared to be more than his body weight."

Our first manager, Nick Misikowetz, was exhausted at the end of opening day, but still he could hardly contain his excitement. Our first day sales were $2,635. Who knows what they would have been if we had charged the fraternities!

Ray Kroc came up to Canada for the celebrations, and that, I think, was when the penny dropped. Ray was an extremely astute judge of market potential, and it didn't take him long to realize that the weather might have been a little chillier, the gas a little more expensive, the beer stronger, and hockey a bigger deal, but that there was one thing that Canada had very much in common with the United States: an appetite for hamburgers and the money to spend on them. He could see what I had seen – the economy was growing, the population was on the rise, the same favourable demographics were at work as in the U.S.A., and, because the Canadian population is stretched out along the southern edge of the country, there was huge cross-border advertising and media spill-over. I remember Ray Kroc looking out of the window of my car – surveying the expanding downtowns and the new suburban developments around Toronto, Hamilton, Windsor, Niagara Falls, and London – and I knew what he was thinking.

My suspicions were confirmed at the party we held in Toronto to celebrate our opening. We had booked a room in a restaurant in a grand old house on Jarvis Street, Julie's Mansion, and we invited many of our first employees, as well as people from McDonald's in the U.S.A. Friends came – both new ones from Toronto and old ones from Chicago – and our families were with us, too. It was a terrific evening. Ray, who had once been a professional musician, played the piano, and we all sang, and, of course, all kinds of toasts and speeches were made. When it finally came to Ray's turn to speak, everyone quietened down. There was something about his manner when he stood up that seemed to signal that he had something important to say.

He began by saying that he had never really had a chance to assess the Eastern Canadian market. He said that he was quite surprised by what he had seen. He congratulated our team on our

London opening. He said he looked forward to seeing what we could do in Toronto. And then he said, "You know, I like this place. I like the looks of Toronto. And of Niagara Falls. And Windsor, and all the rest. I think there's a real market here." Then he turned to me. "George. You were a young lawyer in Chicago, and you took a bit of a gamble to come here to see if you could do well. And it looks as if you're doing fine." Everyone laughed. I smiled, a little nervously; I wasn't quite sure where this was going. "Now," Ray said, "for most people doing fine would mean – well, what would it mean, George? Becoming a millionaire?" Again, everyone laughed. Again, an uncertain smile crossed my face. "Sure," Ray said, "everyone wants to be a millionaire. And so –" Ray glanced around the room; he was obviously enjoying the drama of the moment. "– so, if you want to sell this market back to me, right now, I have a cheque for a million dollars that I will hand to you tomorrow morning."

My dad was sitting beside me at the time. He almost fell off his chair. He dug his elbow into my ribs and he whispered, "Is he serious? Is he serious?"

But it wasn't much of a whisper. Dad's voice carried clear across the hushed room. "I'm absolutely serious, Mr. Cohon," Ray said. "I've got my chequebook right here." He patted his jacket pocket. "It's entirely up to your son."

Think about it. You're thirty-one years old. You have a wife, two young children, a house, a pretty hefty debt load. And someone offers you a million dollars. What do you do? Obvious, isn't it?

You turn the money down.

Ray's offer was absolutely for real. I later found out that he had made a phone call to one of the company's financial officers before the party, and had arranged to have the money transferred from the States the following day. But Ray didn't really expect me to bite. And I knew perfectly well that he'd have been surprised if I had. Delighted, probably – but surprised. He felt he couldn't afford not to make the offer, but he wasn't holding his breath. I knew Ray too well by then to think that he'd be offended if I said no. He'd have done exactly the same thing were he in my shoes. I thought, "I can't sell back now. I didn't come up here to open one restaurant and then sell the whole thing back. And anyway, if Ray's willing to put a million dollars on the table now, he must see something in this market that leads him to believe that we're onto something really good here."

The next day, Ray went back to the United States and we returned to the business of buying land, leasing land, and building new restaurants. The job then was the same as it is now: training crew and management, establishing relations with reliable suppliers, building advertising campaigns and marketing strategies, and maintaining the strict standards originally set by Ray Kroc. Quality, Service, Cleanliness, and Value. QSC & V. This credo, I knew, would be the key to our success in Canada. I compromised on all kinds of things: how much sleep I got, how many meals I ate. I can't count how many days at home I gave up because there was just one more potential site to see, one more licence applicant to interview, one more journalist to meet. But I was not willing to compromise on McDonald's standards. And, restaurant by restaurant, customer by customer, hamburger by hamburger, I was proven to be correct. One. Nine. Fourteen. Ten.

We were off and running, and I spent a lot of time, in those days, talking with the press. I'm good at that – probably because I'm a pretty straight shooter. I came to realize that the press spent so much time dealing with BS, and with egos the size of the SkyDome, that they found my direct, down-to-earth approach refreshing. I always enjoyed talking, and I always enjoyed taking them on – not attacking them if they disagreed with me, just debating with them. For instance, it was around this time that the term "junk food" started being bandied about, and it was a term that always bothered me. I didn't think of myself as being in the junk food business. So if someone wrote an article and equated McDonald's with the term "junk food" I'd just call them up. Not my secretary. Not a public relations person. Me. I'd pick up the phone and call, and say, "Hi. It's George Cohon."

"Uh, hello, Mr. Cohon."

"George. Call me George."

"Okay, George. What can I do for you?"

"I'm curious," I'd say. "What do you mean by junk food?"

"Huh?"

"Junk food. You called McDonald's junk food in your article. So, tell me. I want to understand your thinking. Is meat junk food?"

"Well, no."

"Is bread? Is that junk food?"

"No."

"Potatoes? You eat potatoes. Is that junk food? What about cheese? What about whole milk? Are all these things junk?"

"No."

"Well, then, how do you say that McDonald's, which serves meat, bread, potatoes, and milk of the highest quality, is junk food?"

"Well, if you were to eat at McDonald's every day . . ."

Here, I jump in. With both feet. Fast. "Who says you should eat at McDonald's every day? Do we say that? Do you see ads anywhere that say, 'For a properly balanced and complete nutritional diet you should eat at McDonald's seven days a week?' Do I go around saying, 'Don't eat vegetables? Don't eat fruit? Don't drink lots of water?' Does the company say that? Do our advertisers say that? Do the people who work in our restaurants say that? Of course we don't. Of course, you shouldn't eat at a limited-menu restaurant every day. Don't be ridiculous. But that doesn't mean it's junk."

I liked this kind of direct communication. I liked making my case as plainly, as forcefully, but as politely as I could.

Recently, I had much the same kind of encounter with a writer for a Toronto newspaper about the Santa Claus Parade. The Santa Claus parade is a ninety-two-year-old Toronto tradition, the longest-running parade in the world. It takes place every year in November, and every year it had been Eaton's – the famous Canadian department store – that ran it. In 1982 Eaton's decided they could no longer afford to carry the parade. Paul Godfrey, who was the chairman of the Metropolitan Toronto government, happened to be sitting in my office when the call came through from the Eatons telling him of the family's decision. He was stunned. "What are we going to do?" he asked. "We can't let such a grand old tradition just go up in smoke." I agreed.

Almost immediately, I got together with an old friend, Ron Barbaro, a respected Canadian insurance executive, and within a very short time the two of us put together a small, hands-on board, which went out and lined up twenty sponsors. The parade carried on, without missing a single year. I have always been extremely proud of this – and one of the annual events I most look forward to is getting on my clown make-up and my top hat, and marching along crowd-lined Toronto streets with Ron, my fellow co-chair of the parade. It's a special day – a day that always reminds young and old alike that "Smiles Are Free."

Toronto wouldn't be Toronto without the Santa Claus Parade, and I was thrilled to be able to help save it. But not long ago, I was talking at a press conference about our plans for the upcoming parade, and a journalist stood up and took me to task. She accused me – and McDonald's – of ruining the parade. She told me that when she had been a child she had loved the parade, but that now she found it one long advertisement for its sponsors. Crass, she said. Commercial. Vulgar.

This really upset me. I simply didn't think it was true. And so I arranged to spend the next day with her at my office. Not twenty minutes. Not an hour. I thought that this was important. I wanted to talk this through – one on one. The cost of running the parade, the difficulty in finding sponsors, the requirements of the parade's television broadcasters – these were all facts of life that I thought she should know. If she sincerely wanted to discuss the Santa Claus Parade, I wasn't going to tell her I didn't have time. I made time. And, in the end, partly because she recognized that I was sincere, and partly because I had discovered – to my delight, I have to admit – several files of old photographs that showed that the Santa Claus Parade of the late 1950s and early 1960s was, if anything, *more* commercial than the modern version, she came around in her assessment of the parade. She published a story the next day – a profile of me and of my involvement in the parade. It was a front- page story, with a nice photograph of me taken on a float at the Santa Claus parade warehouse. The story was highly complimentary.

Encounters such as this have been part of my job since the beginning at McDonald's. Without anyone ever really deciding that I should take on such a role, I became a kind of spokesperson for the company in Canada – mostly because I am not in the least shy about speaking. It's an important job; in the early days, media exposure helped to raise McDonald's profile in Canada. But I took a lot of ribbing at the office and in the boardroom for playing so prominent a role. I kept popping up on television, on radio, in magazine articles, in books. When Peter Newman wrote his celebrated book about Canadian business, *The Canadian Establishment: The Acquisitors*, there I was, telling my famous story about our security system. Didn't we have a security system at our house? Sure,

I told Newman. Every night I hang a sign on my front door. It says, "Eatons. Two doors south."

There was a standing joke around the company – among people such as Ed Garber, Ron Cohen, and Bud Audett, all of whom tend to keep a low, business-like profile, all of whom were going full-out for the company, all of whom were doing a super job, and all of whom take great delight in pulling my leg whenever they can. They said the deal was this: They did the work, I took the credit.

Well, I said, it's a tough job. But somebody has to do it.

Actually, it *was* tough. In Canada, now, McDonald's has its infrastructure in place. We have ongoing education programs for crew and management. We have quality control systems, and inspection teams, and carefully defined job descriptions. Our people still work very hard, but our years of experience have helped to smooth things out. The wheels are well oiled, the procedures in place. But in the early days, as we expanded in Eastern Canada from one restaurant in 1968 to fifty-seven in 1972, it often felt as if we were re-inventing the wheel every time we opened a new restaurant. McDonald's isn't a chain – it is a linkage of independent and inter-dependent owner-operators and managers, all of whom are licensed and supported by the McDonald's system. Fred Turner calls this the three-legged stool – a triad of owner-operators, suppliers, and company employees. But this system is a chain insofar as it is only as strong as its weakest link. And it was our job to keep the links strong.

London. Brampton. Bathurst and Steeles in Toronto. Keele Street. Islington. Every opening had its own challenges and its own difficulties – but, in the end, its rewards. We were clearly doing something right – and, after a faltering and slightly tricky start on the financial side, things started looking promising. Our volumes were climbing. Our profile was improving. And, if we were not quite in the black, we were at least aimed pretty unmistakeably toward that side of the ledger.

Our great strength, in those early days, didn't lie in the present. The future was our biggest asset, and there wasn't much doubt that our future in Canada looked pretty good. The corporate account didn't look so hot – but fortunately our fiscal stature was not measured by the birds we had in the hand in those days. The birds we were counting on were the ones in the bush – the ones we were certain we could see in the future. This sort of projection is a kind of financial wishful thinking that accountants call a multiple of losses – but in our case I thought there was good reason to multiply. Our start-up costs kept us in the red, but our positioning was good. Our marketing was strong. Our management team was sound, creative, and energetic. And, most important, our product was good. It was clear to even the most conservative analysts that once we got things going, we'd be hard to stop.

Fred Turner, who took over from Ray Kroc as president of the McDonald's Corporation in 1968, and who had become, in many ways, my mentor, was under no illusions about our potential. He knew – as Ray Kroc had known – that a mistake had been made when Pete Crow had given me an exclusive and perpetual licence to a territory. (A mistake, by the way, the company never repeated.) Immediately he became very anxious to re-acquire my licence. His offers were always tempting, but I wasn't keen to give up such a good hand. Sales in the United States were climbing at an extraordinary rate – they would break the $1 billion mark in 1972 – and I could see no reason why Canadian sales wouldn't climb just as dramatically. However, I was still carrying my huge debts, and so I agreed to sell back bits and pieces of my licence to McDonald's. Through these transactions, I was able to pay back the various people who had helped me out with their $10,000 loans – repaying them at a rate of 300 per cent. Which pleased them. I paid Ted Tannebaum back as well, although our arrangement had been different. His involvement was not simply a loan; it was an investment in the company. For three years Ted had been actively involved in the financial side – and we would, I knew, have to sort out the specifics of our arrangement. All that he had ever asked for was that I be fair.

My arrangement with Ted had been on my mind for a while, but the first time we spoke about it was when we were on a flight together in 1970. I said, "Teddy, it's time we decided who owns what. You've been great. You gave me the $240,000, which I have repaid, with interest. I'm grateful. But I think it's time we started counting our beans."

"Fine," Ted said. "What do you think would be fair?"

"Sixty per cent of the action for me. Forty per cent for you. That's what I think would be fair."

Ted was as difficult as ever. He said, "If that's what you think is fair, George."

"That's what I think is fair."

"Then it's fair by me." So we shook hands.

Around this time, we were thinking of taking the company public. The idea had enormous appeal. Expansion is everything in our business, and if you're going to expand properly – maintaining control of standards and overseeing quality – solid financial backing is a pre-requisite. We knew that we would be seen as a solid and promising investment, and the infusion of capital that would come from a public issue would be a tremendous boost. There were lots of underwriters who were as keen on us as we were on them. We might have actually gone this route had Fred Turner not made me an offer I couldn't refuse.

"George," he said. "My advice is, don't go public. You'll end up spending all your time talking to security analysts instead of focusing on selling hamburgers. Believe me, it will be terrible for business."

"So what do you suggest I do?"

"Well, go ahead and talk to the underwriters if you want. It'll help you get some idea of the value of the company. Then we'll negotiate, and I'll try to sell you on the idea of our buying it back and paying you in McDonald's shares."

In 1969, Ray Kroc remarried, and shortly after that he invited Susan and me to his ranch in southern California to meet Joan, his wife. Ray was extremely anxious to close the deal Fred had outlined to me, and one of the complicating factors was Ted Tannebaum's involvement. Third parties always bothered Ray, as they ran counter to his most fundamental management philosophy that his people should have "ketchup in their blood." From restaurant managers up to company executives, Ray wanted McDonald's people to be directly involved. He didn't like the lack of focus and intensity that sometimes comes with outside investors. I knew that Ted had been playing a hands-on role, and that his financial expertise has been invaluable, but I also knew that McDonald's was not an exclusive interest for him. So, in the end, I had to admit I agreed with Ray's take on things.

"I want Teddy out of the company," Ray said to me on our first evening at his ranch. We had walked off alone to have a word together. "What's the deal you have with him?"

I told him, "A sixty-forty split."

Ray considered this. "In writing?" he asked.

"No," I said. "It's not in writing."

Ray thought a bit more. "Maybe it's not a deal."

I stopped. I turned to Ray. I made a point of looking him straight in the eye. And I said, "Ted and I looked one another straight in the eye. We said, 'That's the deal.' And we shook hands on it."

Ray gave me a little smile. To this day I'm not really sure if he was testing me. Then he said, "George. I've built my entire business on trusting people. Trusting people and on making handshake deals. If you and Ted shook hands on it, then it's a deal. And, as far as I'm concerned, the deal holds."

And hold it did. In 1971, Ted and I formally took Fred Turner up on his offer. We sold back the licence for Eastern Canada to McDonald's and we were paid in company shares. I stayed on as chairman, president, and CEO of McDonald's of Eastern Canada Limited. Overnight, still in my early thirties, I became the second-largest company-employed McDonald's shareholder in the world. Only Ray Kroc had a larger chunk of the company than I did.

I suppose that at this startling point of my career I could have retired, but I was enjoying myself too much to contemplate stopping. Fred Turner had promised me that nothing would change; I'd be able to run the company as if I still owned it. And he was true to his word – that's exactly how it worked. Anyway, my energy level would have driven Susie, the boys, and all our family and friends crazy were I not able to direct it into my work. Our team was really hitting its stride. In fact, I ended up working harder than ever – devoting myself to the establishment of McDonald's in the Canadian market and delighting in the company's steady growth. I won't pretend that it wasn't amazing to suddenly have more money than I had ever dreamed of having – but money also brought new anxieties, and it brought new lessons to be learned. Susan and I wanted to keep our two boys on an even keel; we didn't want them to be brought up as spoiled rich kids. They had their chores and their obligations. We wanted them to learn about work and about responsibility. From time to time, I had to try to keep myself on an even keel, too. Well do I remember one day, in the early 1970s, when McDonald's stock dropped eight dollars. I was still shaken when I put a call in to Ray Kroc. I asked him how he was doing.

"Fine, George. Feeling pretty good. Just getting ready to go out to dinner with some friends tonight."

There was nothing in his voice that indicated that he was upset. I couldn't imagine that the news had passed him by. After all, by my rough estimate, on paper he'd lost about $60 million in a day. "Uh, Ray. You saw today's closing?"

"Yeah. We took a bit of a tumble."

"You don't seem very concerned."

"Well," Ray said, "now that you mention it, I guess I better let my friends pick up the tab."

He laughed. And then Ray taught me an important lesson. He told me not to get too worried about what happened on the market with the stock. "George. We're in it for the long haul. We're not buying and selling. We're not playing the market. So what if the stock drops one day? It will go back up. Just focus on running the restaurants. Just concentrate on making hamburgers. Just keep your eye on the customer. That's what's important. If you do that, everything else will fall into place."

I took his lesson to heart. A little while later, when the stock did bounce back, Ray called me. "So, George, how are you doing?"

"Great, Ray. Just great. We've got a new restaurant opening today, and we've got a couple of really interesting projects I'd like to talk to you about . . ."

"But what about the stock?"

"What about it?"

"You see how it's doing today?"

"Actually, I haven't been paying it too much attention lately. It's been a little busy. We've got a lot going on here at the moment."

Ray just laughed. "See, George. You're learning."

And I was. Every day was another lesson, another bit of experience, another piece of the puzzle put into place. It was exhausting. It was demanding. It was on-the-job training. But it was also exhilarating. The work suited me – to be frank, I thought I was pretty good at it – and when, later, in 1971, Fred Turner, the president of McDonald's, and George Tidball, who controlled the Western Canada licence, had a pretty spectacular falling out, I was there, ready to step in, to join East and West into a single company – McDonald's-Canada.

The trouble had been brewing for quite a while. There had never been particularly good chemistry between Turner and Tidball. Fred was creative and innovative, but he was also a company guy – he knew that McDonald's success came from sticking to Ray Kroc's philosophy and management style. Fred has always been very focused and very clear on how McDonald's should and should not do things. George, on the other hand, was more inclined to go his own way. He was under-capitalized, and he was selling bits of his licence back to McDonald's in order to keep afloat. But he was also unloading master franchises – selling off Calgary and Edmonton, for instance. He was also not particularly concerned with telling any of his associates what, exactly, he was up to. This steady diminishment of control was frustrating the head office in the States. And it was frustrating Fred Turner. At a meeting in Winnipeg in 1971, the two men finally had a showdown that at one point I thought was actually going to come to blows.

The discussion had been going from bad to worse, and Turner had finally had it with Tidball's position. "Damn it. You forget we're a partner of yours. We're not spectators. We've got a stake in your company. And you've got to tell us what you're doing. You've got to give us some financial statements. You've got to keep us in the loop."

Western Canadians have a reputation for not mincing words. George Tidball lived up to it. "Screw that. I'm the majority owner. I'll tell you what I want to tell you."

It went downhill from there.

For a while they were spitting nails, eyeball to eyeball. We all sat there – all our people from the East and all George's from the West, and the people who had come up from the U.S. with Fred – watching this confrontation. We were stunned. It was like a movie. At the point when I thought the two of them were going to start throwing punches, George stood up and stormed out of the room. Slam!

No-one said a word. One by one, everyone cleared the room, until Fred Turner and I were alone. Neither of us spoke for quite a while. Finally Fred said, "Well, what do you think?"

"I think you guys just had a hell of a fight."

"But what do you think?"

"I think the situation is intolerable. You better do something."

It was clear that Tidball had had enough – he came to my room and told me so himself, early the next morning. "It's just no fun any more," he admitted.

"You want me to tell Fred?"

"Tell him whatever the hell you want to tell him. This is serious."

I told Fred that George wanted out – and Fred complied. He called Don Lubin, a McDonald's Corporation director who was a lawyer for the company and a key advisor. Turner told Lubin what had taken place. The situation had to change.

The company put together an offer not unlike the one it had made to me: It would buy back George's licence and pay him in McDonald's stock. It was a good offer – a far better offer than any of us realized at the time – but George didn't see it that way. He was certain that the company had peaked. He didn't think it could grow any more than it already had. He insisted on cash. And cash, in the end, was all George got. Whether his judgment was clouded by his ill feeling toward Fred Turner or whether too much of his MBA training and not enough of his street smarts were coming into play, George Tidball's decision would prove to be a costly mistake for him. I'm sure he's replayed it thousands of times since.

One question remained: Who was going to take George's place? I was having breakfast with Fred Turner when I asked him.

He said, "I don't know."

There are times in life when, rather than being subtle, or clever, or modest, the best thing to do is to put your cards on the table. Sometimes, if you want something, you have to ask for it. I said, "I think I should be president of the whole thing." I meant McDonald's in Canada.

Fred looked a little startled by so direct an approach. "That's a big step. I'm not sure you're ready, George."

One of Ray Kroc's sayings was, "None of us is as good as all of us," and it was that idea – the notion of putting together a really amazing team – that kept me pressing Turner.

"I know I'm ready," I said. "To do it any other way doesn't make sense. We should consolidate East and West. We've got great people in the East – Ed Garber and Ronnie Cohen are building a terrific company. And, in the West, Ron Marcoux has been doing the same. We should bring them together – combine their talents. And I should be president and CEO of McDonald's-Canada."

Which is, of course, exactly what happened. I wanted in – and so I stayed in, even after my fortune had been made. Selling the licence for most of Eastern Canada back to McDonald's in 1971 turned out to be a beginning for me, not an end. In a way, it was a beginning for Ted Tannebaum, too. Unlike George Tidball, Ted didn't think that McDonald's had peaked. Ted had other interests he wanted to pursue, and he decided to leave the company (a company in which he had always been far more than a passive investor), but he held on to his stock. It proved to be the right decision for Ted because he went on to be extremely successful in many other ventures. In the meantime, the stock continued its spectacular rise. In 1989, the stock split two for one – the tenth split since the company had gone public in 1965. By 1991, the service industry's revolution was complete; McDonald's became one of the twenty stocks that make up the "blue chip" index of the U.S. stock exchange. Ted Tannebaum made tens of millions of dollars on his original $240,000 investment. And you know what? I think that's fair.

· 7 ·

Doves of Perestroika

January 31, 1990. I remember the day well. I also remember the previous night. I had one of the worst sleeps of my life.

It was the night before our opening day in Moscow – the night before the big moment for which all of us had been working so hard. The Wolf Pack had grown from a little band of four or five to a team of several hundred: Canadians, Russians, Americans, Germans. And the team was going flat out. The schedule had been gruelling; the deadline had been a killer. Opening a restaurant is never easy. Opening a restaurant *and* a processing plant, *and* establishing reliable supply lines in the Soviet Union in the late 1980s was . . . Impossible? Well, not quite. It's not a word I like to use. But there were times, I have to admit, when impossible was the word that came to mind.

No-one on our team was doing much sight-seeing. By the time we had established our restaurant site in late 1988, found the location for our processing plant, McComplex, and had set our opening date, it was a race against the clock. We brought in suppliers from around the world to help us design the processing plant. This was new for us; we had never been so vertically integrated. It was new to McDonald's; nowhere in the world had anyone done anything like this. In Canada, for instance, we go to an independent meat supplier for our meat. We give them our standards and specifications, and they deliver the product. The same for baked goods – we deal with independent bakers. And dairies – cheese, milk, and shake mix all come to us from our independent suppliers.

But in Moscow, we had explored all sorts of meat plants, and dairies, and bakeries, and had found that they weren't up to our standards. So, we decided to develop our own processing centre in Solntsevo by the Moscow Ring Road; a 100,000-square-foot plant, its construction cost began at an estimated $10 million U.S. but was closer to $21 million U.S. by the time we had finished. On top of that we would have to pay for a meat line, bakery line, potato line, dairy line, dry storage, freezer storage. It would have a liquid facility for the production of ketchup, mustard, and Big Mac sauce. It would employ four hundred people – all of whom had to be trained. It was a massive undertaking. Today, our McComplex processes fifty-seven tons of food a day. And it doesn't only supply what we need at McDonald's; at any number of Moscow's finest restaurants and hotels, as well as foreign embassies, chances are that the food – the meat for the filet mignon, the cream in the *crème caramel* – comes from our plant.

Nothing was easy. In the USSR of the late 1980s, the simplest things became logistical headaches. Could we get our bags from the Soviet Union? Could we get our napkins? Could we get our drinking straws?

Even – could we get enough sand and gravel for construction? Could we get enough electric power?

These were enormous problems – partly because some of the City authorities with whom we were dealing never quite understood the scale of what we were trying to do. They seemed to think that sand and gravel would just materialize somehow. Their attitude seemed to be: Electricity? What's the problem with the electricity? Just take your appliances and plug them in. That's what everyone else does.

But we weren't everyone else – which was, after all, the point. Fortunately, we had seasoned professionals, such as Mike Gerling, who oversaw purchasing, and Helmut Hecher, who oversaw construction. Still, we were going to need hundreds of tons of sand and gravel. Once our restaurant was operational, we were going to need five times the power used by the café that had been there before. In order for that kind of juice to be consistently available to us, a new transformer substation was going to have to be built. No-one at the City of Moscow disputed this, but no-one seemed to be doing much substation building, either. And, as opening day drew closer, I became increasingly anxious about the lack of progress. Days often began with me cajoling and pleading with civic engineers. But not even my Big Mac cards and my McDonald's watches seemed to be getting me anywhere.

Finally, by sheer chance, I ended up at a dinner, sitting beside the Soviet Ambassador to the United States, Yurii Dubinin. This was at a McDonald's–Coca-Cola conference in California, and Dubinin was one of the speakers. Naturally, he was very interested in how things were proceeding in Moscow. We chatted, and he asked if there was anything he could do to help. I didn't want to concern him with our problems, and so, at first, I said we were working things out. But he kept pressing. Finally, I told him about the sand and the gravel and about our little electrical glitch.

His face darkened as I described to him our futile attempts to get the City moving. When I had finished, he nodded gravely.

"Thank you for bringing this matter to my attention," he said. "Please leave it with me."

Shortly thereafter I returned to Moscow. When I got off the plane at Sheremetyevo-2, I was met by one of the City's deputy chairmen. I could tell something was up. He was quite agitated. He said that matters had become complicated.

I wasn't interested in how complicated matters were. I only wanted to know, do we have the sand and the gravel? Do we have the power?

His answer was a little strange. We were hurrying through the airport. He told me that everyone was mad at me.

"Who's mad?"

"Everybody."

"But do we have what we need?"

He explained: Dubinin had sent an official cable from Washington, "requesting" that all necessary assistance be provided to McDonald's. This "request" was like a hand grenade that had been passed from department to department within the City administration. Yurii Dubinin was a pretty heavy hitter. His cable had scared everyone who saw it, and finally it ended up in engineering – the department of the people who should have done the job in the first place. They got really scared – as well as getting really mad at me for getting Dubinin involved. They looked at the cable, and then they looked at the calendar, and the next thing anyone knew there were sand and gravel trucks lined up at the processing site as far as you could see, and *the Soviet Army* was digging trenches to lay the massive electrical cables required by the substation.

Apparently, hundreds of soldiers were at work with picks and shovels. "I guess we're going to have our power," I said to the deputy mayor. "I wonder if I should have let Ambassador Dubinin know about some of the problems our farmers are having getting their potato fields irrigated."

The deputy chairman did not appreciate the joke. In the car, on our way from the airport into the city, I smiled at him. He squirmed uncomfortably.

And so, one of the first things I did on that trip was to go see Ambassador Dubinin's miracle at first hand. We drove out to the site. Sergei Tsivunin, my interpreter, and I trudged through a long, muddy trench to the substation. There were four or five Russian soldiers there, more than a little surprised to see us. We were covered in mud, and had come, it seemed, out of nowhere. But we started chatting. They told me about how much pressure there was, about the long hours they were working.

"Well," I said, "you should know that I'm the guy who's applying all this pressure. And I want you to know how much we appreciate your efforts." I shook their hands and gave them Big Mac cards. Then Sergei and I disappeared back down the trench.

All in a day's work in Moscow. Everyone with whom we were working – the suppliers, tradespeople, labourers, soldiers, architects, and designers – might have been left with the impression that all McDonald's employees were unhappy, driven, sleep-deprived, time-line-obsessed workaholics, were it not for the fact that we all appeared to be having so much fun being driven, sleep-deprived, time-line-obsessed workaholics.

It had been a long journey – from a chance encounter in Montreal in 1976, through round after round of negotiations with Soviet officials, through the failure of our deal for the 1980 Olympics, and on to the hopeful pursuit of other possibilities throughout the early 1980s. It was during this latter period that we formulated the idea of the processing plant – partly to help solve our supply problems (the existing Soviet abattoirs and processing facilities were, as George Mencke said at the time, "like something out of Upton Sinclair") and partly to offer a signing incentive to the Soviets. At the same time, we were pursuing a number of potential sites: Would we open in Estonia first? Would we open in the Sovincentr? Would we form a partnership with Intourist and set up in Soviet hotels?

Then, finally, in April 1988, we made a deal – a partnership with Glavobshchepit, the food services agency of the City of Moscow. During the previous year or so, Glavobshchepit had become the primary focus of our efforts; we dropped our scattergun approach and concentrated on this agency, and, as a result, we felt things finally begin to budge. What Glavobshchepit brought to the table was the real estate we required in the city and the permission that we needed to operate in Moscow. What we brought was our system – our expertise in building, operating, managing, and training – and our capital. A lot of our capital. Our early estimations of our investment were in the $25 million range; by the time we opened, $50 million was closer to the mark.

But we signed – finally – after a last, intense week of negotiations that April. In a small room in the City's administration building, the Soviet team of a half-dozen government officials, lawyers, and accountants hammered out a deal with our team – Ron Cohen; Jeff Hertzfeld; Bob Hissink, a vice president; George Mencke; Marc Winer, and me. Under the terms of the original agreement, McDonald's Restaurants of Canada, Ltd. owned a 49 per cent share of one food-processing plant and an eventual twenty McDonald's restaurants in Moscow. Soviet law at that time required that the Soviet partner have majority control.

As Aleksandr Yakovlev had predicted, the ideology was changing. But even so, none of us expected it to change as radically or as quickly as it was. We talked about some of these changes with

On the dotted line: I'm glad there were no video cameras when I signed my original contract with Ray Kroc in 1966. Everyone would be able to see how much my hand was shaking.

Real Canajun, eh? Our first restaurant: London, Ontario, 1967.

Hands-on executives: President Fred Turner and Chairman Ray Kroc knew what these things were for. Both men had worked their way to the top.

Early days in Canada: "Are you serious about that million dollars, Ray?" Ray Kroc, Susan, and I discuss an interesting business proposition.

I was lucky enough to have Ray Kroc as both mentor and friend. The bus in the background is the same one we loaned to the Soviet delegation for their visit to the Montreal Olympics in 1976.

Tough work but somebody's got to do it: A meeting with the Miss Grey Cup contestants in 1976. For some reason, nobody ever notices the photographs, taken by me, on the wall.

East meets West: My friend and arch-rival, Den Fujita, at a Toronto McDonald's in 1976.

Competitive? Who me? An example of the lengths our people went to when they wanted quietly to draw Fujita's attention to an apparent Canadian victory in the battle of the restaurants.

The McDonald's Canada top management team – (left to right) Gary Reinblatt, Ed Garber, George Mencke, Ron Cohen, me, Ron Marcoux, and Bud Audett – hard at work in 1986.

Workaholics Anonymous: The officers of McDonald's Canada, shown here with their noses to the grindstone, as usual.

The Busted Bust: At McDonald's Canada headquarters in 1985, in Toronto, Ed Garber unveiled a beautiful statue of me, just moments before he shattered my ego completely. Mike Quinlan, Doug Creighton, and Ken McGowen look on.

This won't hurt a bit: In 1986, Fred Turner passed the torch to the new president and CEO, Mike Quinlan.

Jim Cantalupo: The driving force behind McDonald's International's astonishing growth. There are now over 21,000 restaurants in 103 countries worldwide.

Pierre Trudeau, Susan, and I arrive at the fundraising dinner I chaired for the prime minister in 1982.

A Canadian Hero: A chance to talk with Rick Hansen during the Toronto stop-over of his 1987 Man in Motion tour.

An early McHappy Day: Presenting a cheque for $689,453.37 to Whipper Billy Watson and the twins Peter and Paul Settle for the Crippled Children of Canada.

Clowning Around: The co-chairs of the Santa Claus Parade, Ron Barbaro and I, share a solemn moment.

The company I keep: I'm thrilled to be part of Variety Village. The celebrated athlete Jeff Adams, former lieutenant-governor Lincoln Alexander, and Premier Mike Harris look on as two great kids – Raffi Shirian and Kaley McLean – ring the bell to start the Sunshine Games.

Home away from home: When a child is sick and sent away to a hospital, the last thing many parents can afford is a long stay in a nearby hotel. Ronald McDonald Houses, like this one in Hamilton, Ontario, do their best to help families through difficult times.

Play Ball: At the 1989 opening of SkyDome, in Toronto, with a few of my close friends.

our Soviet counterparts during the final stages of our negotiations, and I remember one of them saying, "They may put the crosses back on the churches, but don't ever think that Communism will be replaced."

But Yakovlev – a wise and circumspect man – understood the implications of *perestroika* on both the large and the small scales. His attention to the smaller scale was by no means an afterthought – in some ways, it is the small scale that has proven to be the most important. In 1997, more than 220,000 enterprises made up the burgeoning small-business sector of the Moscow economy. In 1996, almost every third ruble earned in Russia was earned in Moscow, and 40 per cent of the city's taxes came from small businesses. As Mayor Yuri Luzhkov has said, "Small entrepreneurship is a mass demonstration of the economic initiative of individuals, and in this sense one can say that small business is the philosophy and ideology for building a socially oriented democratic state with a market economy."

This came as no surprise to Aleksandr Yakovlev. One observer has noted that "if Gorbachev was the evangelist of *perestroika*, Yakovlev was its theologian" – and although, during the period when they were implementing their reforms, the two men were wrestling every day with issues infinitely bigger than our concerns, Yakovlev was able to see where my notion of McDonald's in the USSR fit into his complex equation. "I personally liked Cohon's idea," he wrote. "Both from the political viewpoint – the wall of distrust to everything capitalist as the source of all the troubles in the world had to be broken down; and from the practical point of view – to show in reality to all Muscovites that there can be service with a smile, without rudeness."

We had started off as the most unlikely suitors. I remember how utterly implausible the old-guard Soviet bureaucrats, such as

Viktor Bychkov, Deputy Minister of (Internal) Trade (USSR), Vladimir Promyslov, chairman of the Executive Committee of Moscow City Council, and Mikhail Suslov, the Soviet Union's chief ideologist, had found our proposals. It is hard to convey how alien our ideas were to these officials. Imagine, for instance, someone suggesting to the stock exchanges across North America that a chain of socialist bookstores be installed on their floors. That will give you some idea of the stone-faced, unamused, and profoundly unimpressed expression I encountered on Viktor Bychkov's face when in the early 1980s, in his office on Razina Street, I tried to explain to him what McDonald's was and why it made sense for us to open in Moscow.

But by January 30, 1990 – my sleepless night in Moscow – everything had changed, or was in the process of changing. Fourteen years after I had first had the idea of bringing McDonald's to the Soviet Union, we were – as surprising as it was to our incredulous hard-line communist and capitalist friends – absolutely in the right place at the right time.

It had been Yakovlev who really broke the log jam for us. He helped us to establish a link with the City of Moscow – the connection that led to the deal. He did this, in part, because what we wanted to do in the USSR accorded with his view of the future of his country. But also, I think, he did it because by then we had become friends.

I met Yakovlev in the late 1970s and our relationship had always been cordial and warm. He is only thirteen years my senior, but he played a kind of avuncular role. Slowly, through him, I came to some understanding of the intricacies of the Soviet bureaucracy as well as the difficulties the Soviet people faced. He was posted in Ottawa as the Soviet ambassador during this period. He was the dean of the diplomatic corps in Canada, and I used to visit him frequently – to seek his advice, but also, I must admit, to enjoy his company.

Our relationship intensified, however, in 1982, during one of our semi-regular meetings. We were in the Soviet Embassy in Ottawa – a place that I always assumed was bugged, and that may well have been. I had several people from McDonald's with me, and he had his people from the embassy. McDonald's was, at that point, still pursuing various alternative proposals in the USSR, and Yakovlev was, within the constraints his position imposed, doing his best to help us. Suddenly, though, he turned to me. "I'd like to talk to you – privately."

His people vanished almost as quickly as mine did. We sat, alone in his office, facing one another across his desk.

He reached into his drawer. He pulled out a brown folder. "This," he said, "is your file."

I must have looked a little stunned. It was naive of me, I know, but I'd never imagined I had a file. I thought this sort of thing happened only in spy movies.

He opened the folder in front of him, and began flipping through its pages.

He said, "I see you were recently honoured by the State of Israel Bond organization and that you received the Israel Prime Minister's Medal."

"Uh-huh."

"Do you know leaders in Israel?"

"I've known several of them, yes."

"Such as?"

"Well. Golda Meir, Menachem Begin, Moshe Dayan, Chaim Herzog, Yitzhak Rabin."

"And you have made generous contributions to Israel."

"Yes, but . . ."

"And you are Jewish, yes?"

Throughout all my negotiations with the Soviets, this was actually the first time I'd been asked this question. I thought, where is all this leading?

"Yes," I said. "I am very proud of being Jewish."

Yakovlev peered at me intently. "And you visit Israel a lot?"

"Quite often, yes."

Yakovlev leaned back in his chair. Sometimes I thought that Aleksandr also worried that his office was bugged. Just because he was the ambassador didn't mean that he necessarily had any idea what was going on behind the light fixtures and under the lamps of the Soviet Embassy. He dropped his voice. He said, "We have a very serious problem between the Soviet Union and Israel right now."

"I'm aware of that."

"People are trying to get out. Many want to get to Israel. They are applying for exit permits. And this, as you know, is a very contentious issue."

"Yes it is," I said flatly.

Then, as is Aleksandr's custom, he seemed suddenly to send the conversation veering in a new direction. He asked me, "Do you think that when there is a problem, people should try to solve it with dialogue?"

"I think that's the only way to solve a problem."

He nodded and then appeared to get lost in thought for a few seconds. "I'd be prepared to come to your house in Toronto. I haven't been to Toronto for a long time. If you could put together a responsible group of people from the Jewish community, I'd like to come to discuss this matter. I'd like to hear people's thoughts."

"Of course."

"I don't want to meet with people who are only going to yell and scream and attack me because I'm the Soviet ambassador. That would not be useful."

When I got back to Toronto, I went to see Ray Wolfe. Ray was the head of The Oshawa Group, a parent company that manages stores like IGA, Knechtel, and other food retailers. He was also very involved in the Jewish community. I had often sought his advice. When I told him what Yakovlev had asked me to do, he knew immediately how important this was. He wasted no time. He put in a call to the Israeli ambassador in Ottawa.

The Israeli ambassador didn't waste any time, either. He said, "I'll be on the first plane to Toronto. Let's not talk on the phone about this." By the time he arrived he had learned that similar overtures had been made to members of the Jewish community by the Soviet ambassadors in many different countries. This was, obviously, a feeler – and a very important one. In 1979, under pressure from the United States, Jewish emigration from the Soviet Union had reached a high of 51,300. But by the early 1980s, in the wake of the Soviet invasion of Afghanistan and a new chill in Soviet–U.S. relations, that figure had dropped below a thousand. Now, apparently, the USSR was beginning to re-think its policy.

The Israeli ambassador encouraged Susan and me to convene the dinner for Yakovlev – and so, of course, we did. We invited Harvey Fields, the rabbi at Holy Blossom Temple, and his wife, Sybil; Ray and Rose Wolfe, and other leaders from the Jewish community both in Toronto and across Canada. Aleksandr and his wife, Nina, arrived – along with a driver whom I took to be a KGB operative.

It turned out to be a fascinating evening. The discussion was informed, passionate, sometimes pleading, occasionally angry – but, in the end, civil and articulate. I think we all sensed that we had a sympathetic ear. I remember watching how intently Yakovlev listened to what people were saying. I was struck with the realization that, unlike most dinner table conversations, this one was going to have some real influence. Some of the guests may have thought that it was a long way from our dining room in Forest Hill to the decision makers in Moscow. They may have felt that Aleksandr Yakovlev was too far out of the Kremlin's loop to have much clout. But that was going to change soon enough.

By 1987, the trend that had so alarmed Jewish communities throughout the world had begun to change. That year, an official predicted that between ten and twelve thousand Jews would leave the country. In 1989, 100,000 Jews left for Israel and for the West.

What role did Aleksandr Yakovlev play in changing Soviet emigration policy? What effect did our dinner in Toronto have? It's difficult to say. The reforms of *glasnost* unmuffled many voices of morality – Andrei Sakharov's being the clearest and most authoritative – and the injustices of the old regime could not long stand against them. Certainly I know that Yakovlev viewed this change with great satisfaction. It marked the shift from a policy of lies to one that began the struggle for the truth – and truth, for Yakovlev, as for so many Russians today, is a matter of almost religious fervour. Deprived of it for so long, they are now uncompromising in holding on to it – on small issues as well as big. For instance, I recently asked Yakovlev whether he thought I should include, in this book, the story of my buying my neighbour's house after I heard the words "dirty Jew" through their open window. I told Aleksandr that some people who had read the manuscript were offended by the story; they thought it reflected poorly on me. Some friends worried that it made me seem so aggressive and prickly that I – and not the anti-Semite – came across as the least likeable character in the anecdote. Yakovlev didn't hesitate. "No, you must tell it. Once you start hiding these stories – that is when the trouble begins. People must know that they cannot act this way. They cannot speak this way. They must know there are repercussions.

People must know what happens. It is very important that you tell the truth."

He spoke intently, and as he spoke, I remembered how intently he had listened to our dinner guests on that evening in Toronto.

Yakovlev's ten-year sojourn in Ottawa ended in 1983. Not long before he returned to the Soviet Union, I invited him on a fishing trip to a secluded river in Northern Quebec.

It was a beautiful spot, and its beauty made me wonder why Canada and Russia – two nations that share the landscape and the climate and the spirit of a vast, northern space – are not closer than they are.

I remember how quiet and pensive Yakovlev was. Brooding would probably be an accurate description. He went for walks by himself in the woods; he picked mushrooms; he often seemed lost in thought. Trips like these are often arranged for the purposes of discussing business, but my instincts told me not to bring any business up. Something else was going on. "What struck me most," Yakovlev later said, "was the absolute silence in that area, as if you are turning deaf."

I didn't know it at the time, but of course he was contemplating the enormous challenges that would await him when he returned to Moscow. Mikhail Gorbachev became General Secretary of the Communist Party of the Soviet Union in 1985, and he had enlisted Yakovlev's support. Yakovlev was going from the outer reaches of political influence to the very centre, and he must have had an inkling of what the future would bring. It seems quite remarkable when I think of it now: The affable, courtly gentleman who was fishing a few yards upstream from me on a river in Northern Quebec was as quiet as he was because his mind was elsewhere. He looked as if he was just casting his fly line. He appeared to be simply concentrating on landing a fifteen-pound salmon. But he was actually mulling over the beginnings of what eventually became known to the world as *perestroika*.

So when, in 1986, I had another meeting with my friend Aleksandr Yakovlev, it was not in Ottawa. It was not at our house in Toronto. It was not on the shore of a river in Quebec. He was now ensconced in the Central Committee as the Chief of Ideology. I called him and requested an appointment. Our meeting took place, late one night, in his office. In the Kremlin.

I said, "Aleksandr, you know, I met you in Canada in 1976. It is now 1986. That's ten years of my life. You told me once that the ideology would change. Don't you think it's time for McDonald's to come into your country?"

He looked at me long and hard. "George," he said. "You're right."

He had a battery of telephones behind his desk. He picked one up, gave a few orders, and in no time at all he was talking to Valerii Saikin, the Chairman of the Executive Committee of the Moscow City Council. Saikin was at his dacha, sitting in a sauna, when Yakovlev reached him. I was really struck by this. In a Moscow hotel, you couldn't expect to get an answer if you called the front desk. But when Yakovlev wanted to get in touch with Saikin, the call got through – to the sauna if necessary.

Yakovlev didn't beat around the bush. He told the Chairman, "I'm here with Mr. Cohon of McDonald's." I pictured Saikin wrapped in a towel, dripping all over the receiver. "I would like you to meet him tomorrow morning at eight o'clock."

And that was that.

Or, to be absolutely precise, that was almost that.

Meeting me at eight o'clock in the morning was not exactly what Chairman Saikin had had in mind for the following day. But since Aleksandr Yakovlev had instructed him to, he did. He was at his desk in the elegant red building on Gorky Street which housed the warren of offices of the Moscow City Council when I arrived. He was also in an extremely foul mood.

Saikin is a huge man. He had been an Olympic wrestler for the USSR. When I was ushered into his office, I said hello and thanked him for making the time to see me at such short notice. He growled back. I tried a few more conversational pleasantries. He snarled. Had he been any less friendly, he probably would have pinned me to the floor.

I began my pitch. As usual, I had to begin by explaining what McDonald's was. But Saikin interrupted.

He said, "Yes, yes. You are in the food business. Fine. I understand. Well, Mr. Cohon, we are having some trouble with the schools in the city. We have hundreds of schools, and we are having trouble feeding the children. So, you. You build one of your warehouses and every day you bring some food out for lunch for the children. *Da?*"

His concept of a market economy seemed to have a step or two missing. I said, "That's not exactly how it works, Mr. Chairman."

And so I continued my explanation – an explanation that Saikin grudgingly endured. It was not one of my most successful pitches. I felt as if I was giving a lecture: Capitalism 101. He stared at me sullenly. When I left his office I had the impression that this awkward confrontation – Adam Smith in one corner; Karl Marx in the other – had ended without a decision.

Saikin might not have noticed, but the wheels had begun to turn – even within his own City administration. The ideology had begun to change. By 1988, Vladimir Malyshkov, the head of Glavobshchepit, and Valerii Zharov, a deputy chairman, were our principal contacts. Here, at last, was a breakthrough. Both were bright and energetic men. Malyshkov, in particular, really grasped what it was we were proposing. He understood the implications of what we wanted to do. He knew the effect it would have on the food-service system, and he had a strong sense of how this fit into the plans that were, at that moment, being formulated in the Kremlin by Gorbachev, Yakovlev, and Shevardnadze. Malyshkov trusted us: Years before, he had worked for Vsevolod Shimansky in the Ministry of (Internal) Trade for the Russian federation – Shimansky, for whom I had played my rigged balalaika in the early eighties – and he remembered Shimansky saying that the McDonald's people were honest and that their proposals were good. This little coincidence always makes me smile. There were people who had told me that I was wasting my time with Vsevolod Shimansky, that he was not influential enough, that his line into the Kremlin was not direct. (In much the same way that people thought I was wasting my time with Yakovlev when he was in Ottawa.) But I had liked Shimansky – just as I had liked Yakovlev – and so I had developed a friendship with him. I don't choose my friends on the basis of what they can do for me. But sometimes – especially if you trust your instincts – you get lucky.

Years after I played my balalaika for him, Shimansky's endorsement paid off. Almost a decade after I first met Aleksandr Yakovlev, his intervention finally came through for us. Until then it was as if we had been caught in the back eddies of a river. Now we were in the mainstream.

The night before the Moscow opening we were staying at the Hotel Oktyabrskaya. I had moved from my usual rooms at the Metropol because we had invited hundreds of guests from all over the world for the gala opening celebrations, and we had made arrangements for almost everyone to stay at the Oktyabrskaya. The group included top McDonald's executives – Mike Quinlan, Fred Turner – as well as an interesting and varied gathering of good friends, including John Cleghorn, president and chief operating officer of the Royal Bank of Canada; Doug Creighton, the founder and driving force behind *The Toronto Sun*; Rick Hansen, the athlete; and the comedian Buddy Hackett. How's that for varied?

The Oktyabrskaya is a huge hotel near the Kremlin, previously used exclusively by Party officials. Its name commemorates the October Revolution of 1917. Visiting dignitaries from other communist regimes often stayed here: Castro, Ho Chi Minh, Tito. Although people often mistake the Oktyabrskaya for an office building because of its nondescript appearance, its interior is actually quite luxurious. The main hallway is dominated by an enormous central staircase; at the top of the stairs, back in 1990, a massive statue of Lenin looked down on the lobby. The ironies that were soon going to abound in the last days of the USSR – kids in baggy jeans and Chicago Bulls windbreakers lounging on the grassy slopes in front of the Kremlin – were beginning to appear. (Not the least of these being a McDonald's about to open in Pushkin Square.) The day before our opening, it was amusing to see so many free-enterprisers checking in under Lenin's stern gaze. It was difficult to know, at that strange moment in history, which of the two was more out of place.

As I've said, I had a terrible night – tossing and turning and waking constantly from anxious and fitful dreams.

I was probably over-tired. The run-up to the opening had been quite a marathon. In 1988 – a year after one of Gorbachev's most important reforms allowed foreign investors up to 49 per cent partnerships with Soviet partners – we finally entered into our joint venture with Glavobshchepit. But it hadn't been easy. In the final week of our negotiations in April that year, the biggest stumbling block had been trying to place a value on the real estate the Soviet authorities were using as the principal component of their investment in the partnership. Naturally, there would be differences of opinion on both sides of the table – but at that particular moment in history, Moscow real estate values were almost impossible to establish. There was, essentially, no market to prove or disprove whatever value the Soviets gave the property. Their system of evaluation was based on an arbitrary application of zones: Concentric circles were drawn out from the centre of Moscow, and anything within a certain zone was given an automatic, and apparently indisputable, price tag. The Soviet negotiators would simply announce what a parcel of land was worth, and with the Pushkin Square site very close to the absolute centre of Moscow, they weren't exactly giving it away. At the table, George Mencke always had his calculator at hand, and he would quickly convert from rubles to dollars.

"What do you think, George?" I asked.

"F — ing ridiculous," Mencke said – a reply that we didn't bother to translate for our friends across the table.

In negotiations there are feints and counter-feints. There are positions and fall-back positions. For instance, there was a lot of back and forth on the royalty fee that McDonald's-Moscow would have to pay the Canadian company. These discussions became, at times, quite heated, but eventually we found common ground. We were able to conclude that McDonald's-Moscow would pay the Canadian company 5 per cent of sales – an agreement that left the Canadian company with a pretty hefty receivable until the ruble became convertible in January 1992.

But there are other instances in negotiations when, if there is no room to move, it's important to make that perfectly clear. We signalled unmistakeably to the Soviets that we weren't anywhere near accepting the value they'd given to the land under discussion.

Everything we said and did during our final week of negotiations conveyed to them that we were not going to budge. And so, little by little, they began to move. Over a period of a few days, their estimations began to accord with what we took to be reality.

By the end of the week, we were, at last, in a position to sign. Then there were a few small details: building the restaurant, finding suppliers, hiring and training crew.

The site, the old Cafe Lyra on Pushkin Square, had probably accommodated 250 customers a day; we needed partly to tear down, and completely renovate, refurbish, rebuild, re-equip, and re-wire a facility to serve 25,000 a day. When we advertised the 630 positions we needed to fill, we received 27,000 written applications. When we began our training, most of our new crew and our Soviet managers had never actually tasted a hamburger, much less made or served one. As well, suppliers of high-quality produce needed to be secured – this in a country that, while facing crises on every social, economic, and political front, faced no problem more complex than the failure of its agricultural policy. It was thought that as much as 25 per cent of the USSR's harvest rotted in the fields every year. We also needed absolutely reliable supply lines – this in a country where no break-down was more complete than that of its food distribution system. Every time I saw a Russian truck stalled or abandoned at the side of a highway – a fairly frequent sight in the USSR in the 1980s – my heart sank. I imagined wilting lettuce, souring milk, rotting potatoes – and disgruntled customers. We had to start from the ground up to ensure that we never suffered from what, by then, were absolutely routine throughout the Soviet Union: unpredictable and seemingly unavoidable food shortages. I had no intention of opening a restaurant that was not going to be able, always, to serve its customers the food that was on the menu. Having crew members say, "Sorry, we're out of Big Macs" was simply not in the cards.

This might seem a modest ambition by North American standards. It was an absolutely revolutionary concept in the Soviet Union of the late 1980s.

My encounter with the stony Valerii Saikin had been difficult, but years later – long after he was out of power – I learned what kind of interference we were up against. Officials such as Malyshkov and Zharov were often working against the intentions of their boss. I learned that Saikin's very specific instructions had been: Placate these McDonald's people, string them along, have fun with them if you like, see what you can get out of them, but whatever you do, get rid of them eventually. We do not want these restaurants in our city.

But, suddenly, Gorbachev's reforms were being felt in the Kremlin, the Politburo, and the Moscow City Council. Suddenly McDonald's was a prominent symbol of momentous change. The once-powerful apparatchiks were now the curiosities. Everything turned topsy-turvy. It would not be very long before Viktor Bychkov, who in 1977 had been so unhelpful, came to *our* office, seeking *our* help. His world, the world of the monolithic state and the all-powerful government official, had crumbled – and what did he want? Well, when revenge comes, it's often more sad than you expect it to be. I didn't feel the satisfaction of victory when I learned that he wanted a job at McDonald's.

We were no longer the hungry wolves to whom bureaucrats could throw scraps of protocols and meaningless agreements. We were . . . well, don't let me get carried away. We were what we always were: a clean, reliable, quick-service restaurant, with a friendly crew and a product of the highest standard. We were people who knew how to make hamburgers and how to sell them. But that's not the way many Soviets and many members of the press saw us. Suddenly, we were the doves of *perestroika*, the heroes of capitalist labour!

As opening day approached, the pressure had steadily mounted. Journalists and TV crews from all over the world had gathered for the event. I'd been giving interviews for days – American, British, Japanese, Italian, Spanish, Finnish, Chinese, and Canadian journalists were all fascinated by the symbolism of McDonald's at the heart of the Soviet Empire. I told them how confident I was. I boasted that the Moscow McDonald's would break all kinds of international records – sales, volume, number of customers. I told them that we weren't worried about the fact that we would be earning profit in what were then non-convertible rubles; we'd sink the money back into further expansion in the USSR. I told them we intended to open twenty restaurants in Moscow. I remember almost bursting with pride when I heard Khamzat Kasbulatov, our Russian manager, say in front of a television crew, "Many people talk about *perestroika*, but for them *perestroika* is an abstraction. Now, me – I can touch my *perestroika*. I can taste my *perestroika*. Big Mac is *perestroika*."

I knew that our team had done an absolutely super job of preparation – both the restaurant itself and the gala opening celebrations were ready to go. The day before, I'd had a chat with a commander of police in Pushkin Square and he'd predicted that "thousands upon thousands" of people would show up for the opening. He said that they would line up all night. I thought of the attending television crews and photographers and journalists. I thought of how much we had at stake. "I hope so," I told him. "I hope so."

The commander's encouraging prediction was a comfort. Still, I was anxious. I was too excited to sleep properly. In spite of all my confidence in our team, I tortured myself with worry upon worry. What if this? What if that? I knew that if something was going to go wrong on opening day, the entire world would be tuned in to see it.

Two a.m. Three. I kept waking from terrible dreams: I dreamed I was being interviewed by Bryant Gumbel on the *Today* show and, for some reason, I was still in my pyjamas; I was showing a Japanese TV crew how I used to trim trees in Chicago and I got stuck in one of the big birches in Gorky Park; Mikhail Gorbachev and I were making Big Macs at the SkyDome in Toronto for a McHappy Day and we couldn't keep up with the orders – terrible dreams! I'd wake up in a sweat. Four. Four-thirty. Finally, at five o'clock I couldn't stand it any longer. I crawled out of bed. I fumbled around in the dark. I looked from the window into cold, black, pre-dawn Moscow. I couldn't resist. I called the restaurant.

"Hi," I whispered. I didn't want to wake Susan. "It's me. How's it going down there?"

"*A Vy – kto?*" a female voice said. "Who is this?"

"It's me," I whispered again. "George. George Cohon."

"Ah, good-mornink, Mr. Cohon."

"George, please. Call me George. How's it going?"

"Is going very good, Mr. Cohon."

"Everything okay?"

"Everythink okay."

"But the line-up? Tell me. How's the line-up?"

"*Chto?* – What you mean, line-up?"

"All the people. Outside the restaurant. The crowds. The police thought they'd be lining up all night. They said there would be thousands."

"Just minute," the young woman said. She put the receiver

down, stepped away from the phone, and then, a few seconds later, picked up the receiver again. "Is nobody."

"What?"

"Is no line-up."

"There has to be."

"Is nobody out front. Was somebody. But he was cleanink the street. Now is gone."

"No. That can't be right. There should be hundreds of people there by now. A thousand. Maybe more."

"Is nobody there, Mr. Cohon."

"Nobody?"

"Nobody."

"No line-up?"

"*Ni dushi.* Is empty, the street."

I couldn't believe it. The nightmares I'd been having all night were nothing compared to this. I could see the world-wide coverage. The London papers. The Hong Kong papers. The New York papers. The papers in Milan, Barcelona, Sydney, Rio. The Toronto papers.

Headlines. "McDonald's opens in Moscow: No-one shows."

"Great," I thought. "Just great."

I sat in our hotel room, stewing and watching a winter dawn break over Moscow. Moscow is an extraordinary place – particularly as it emerges from darkness into soft, early-morning light. The transformation is almost invisible, which seems to suit so mysterious a city. In all my visits I have never ceased to be fascinated by it – to stand in Red Square at midnight and imagine the history that has taken place there is unbelievably thrilling.

But early in the morning of our opening, I was having some difficulty concentrating on the city's haunting beauty. At six I put in another call to the restaurant. I called again at seven. But the answer was the same: no people, no line-up. Susan was awake by now. I told her, "I can't stand it. I've got to get over there." I picked up the phone again. I woke up our sons.

Craig, who was twenty-six, and Mark, who was twenty-three, had come with Susan and me to Moscow for the opening celebrations, and although they had been almost as excited as I was, I don't think a wake-up call quite that early had been part of their plan. There had been a party for staff the night before. We had taken our invited guests to the Moscow Circus and then to a restaurant on the lively Arbat. There had been dancing and floor shows and speeches, and none of us had got to bed early.

Craig and Mark met me in the hotel lobby. I was pacing the floor under the stern gaze of Vladimir Ilyich Lenin. I was literally wringing my hands. I almost never drink coffee, but I had a pit of anxiety in my stomach that made me feel as if I'd just had a dozen cups. "We might have a problem," I said. A few minutes later, we were in a taxi, racing through the streets of Moscow, on our way to Pushkin Square.

Ray Kroc used to say, "We have an obligation to give something back to the communities that give us so much." This has always been McDonald's philosophy, and it is the reason why, over the years, we have supported so many charities. In Canada, during the thirty years since we opened our first restaurant, our focus has been children. We have helped establish and have continued to support the thirteen Canadian Ronald McDonald Houses – homes away from home for out-of-town families whose children are being treated in hospitals for cancer or other life-threatening illnesses. Through Ronald McDonald Children's Charities of Canada, we have, since 1984, distributed more than twelve million dollars to hundreds of local children's charities – the Terrace, B.C., Child Development Centre, the Northwest Territories Family Services in

Yellowknife, and the playground in Bowring Park in St. John's, Newfoundland, are just three of the places where we have helped out. Over the years we have raised millions of dollars through our McHappy Day program. We helped raise funds for Terry Fox's Marathon of Hope in 1980 and for Rick Hansen's Man in Motion Tour in 1985–87.

A personal passion of mine is Variety Village – a world-class sports training and fitness centre in Toronto that allows both youngsters with special needs and able-bodied athletes to compete and play together. It is the largest complex of its kind in North America. I'm particularly proud of Susie's involvement with the Village. While she was chairing the board, she came home one day and said that they had come up with a fundraising idea: an annual event of Olympic-style games. She thought that I would make a good chair. I told her that I was extremely busy and that I'd have to think about it. Susie said, "If you want dinner tonight, you won't think about it." I'm now the honorary chair of the Sunshine Games.

Giving back to the communities that have given us so much: This approach very quickly became part of our way of doing things in Russia. At our first opening in Moscow, we gave $1 million to the Soviet Children's Fund. But it has been an important element of who we are from the beginning. I still smile to myself when I remember our first charitable involvement – at our first restaurant in London, Ontario. I didn't want our commitment to local charities to seem like an afterthought. I felt it was important to send a signal that we wanted to be an integral part of the community, and so, well before our opening in London in 1968, I made some inquiries about local philanthropic organizations.

I'm not sure what it is in my background that has always drawn me to crippled kids. There is no particular reason for my involvement in this area. But my heart has always gone out to children who have to deal with physical challenges. I admire their strength, their courage, and their perseverance. I am often amazed by their good humour. No-one more embodies Ray Kroc's belief in "pressing on" than these kids. I don't know how many times I've stood at Variety Village watching some of these kids and have said to myself: "And George, you think you've faced some tough challenges!"

The motto of Ronald McDonald Children's Charities is "Little children shouldn't have to deal with big problems." These words carry a lot of weight with me. When people ask me why I feel as strongly as I do about this, I say it's just nice to be able to help someone. That's about as complicated as it gets.

In London, we decided that we would like to donate our opening-day proceeds to what was then the city's Crippled Children's Treatment Centre. It had been doing terrific work in the London area, and it seemed a natural connection for us to make. It was, however, one of the most established of London's charities, and we were, without question, the least established of London's businesses. When I called the centre to discuss our plan, they said they'd never heard of us.

"Hamburgers," I said.

This, I could tell from the silence over the phone, did not impress them.

"French fries."

Silence.

"We also make excellent milkshakes," I added.

They were not bowled over. They thanked me for calling. They told me they would be pleased to consider my proposal. I realized that they were about to hang up without giving me an answer. I persisted. Finally, they told me that I would have to come to a board meeting to state my case.

The board meeting was held at the London Hunt and Country Club, an extremely upper-crust, extremely exclusive, and extremely conservative club. It was only as I was being ushered into the boardroom that the irony of what I was doing dawned on me. I had been a little overwhelmed by the sweeping drive and the imposing Georgian building. I was a little embarrassed when the board member who met me looked at my striped tie and asked what regiment it was, and I had to reply that I had no idea; it was just a tie that I had bought at Eaton's. This staid, dignified place was making me extremely nervous. After all, who was I? Just a thirty-one-year-old hamburger salesman from South Side Chicago, who barely knew a fox from a hound. I was led through the marble foyer toward the room where the board meeting was to be held and where, in a blue haze of tobacco smoke, the pillars of the London establishment were waiting for me to state my case. The door was opened, and that was when it came to me. I had to smile.

State my case? What case was there to state? I was there to *give* them money.

Still, they were a pretty daunting bunch – not the sort of group that took money from just anybody. I bit down on my smile, and started to . . . well, to state my case. I had a kind of sales pitch I gave in those days. This was a description of McDonald's – our standards, our insistence on quality and good service, our commitment to cleanliness and to value – and a few colourful statistics that would convey the size of the company to people who didn't know us.

It was pretty clear to me that the dignified gentlemen gathered in that boardroom didn't know McDonald's from Adam. I'm not sure that they knew of the existence of restaurants that didn't come with maîtres d', linen tablecloths, wine stewards, and cigar humidors. But after I told them about McDonald's, I gave my spiel: We had sold enough hamburgers that, if they were laid end to end, they would go to the moon and back, twice – that kind of thing.

I told the board, "One hundred and ninety five thousand tons of onions have dressed our products. Eleven million gallons of mustard have been squirted between enough buns to stretch the length of the Great Wall of China, 186 times."

I looked around the room. My audience didn't exactly look fascinated. I continued. "We have poured enough ketchup over our hamburgers and cheeseburgers to fill the Grand Canyon . . ."

At that point there was a loud harrumph from an older gentleman at the table. I'd thought he was asleep. He hadn't said a word all meeting, and, from where I stood, he appeared to be dozing – his chin down on his crisp white shirt collar, his arms folded across his pin-striped vest.

His deep voice had the gravelly, articulate, patrician texture I was coming to recognize as the sound of confident, old-monied Ontario. "Son," he said.

I stopped in mid-sentence.

"Son, have you ever seen the Grand Canyon?"

"Uh. No sir, I haven't."

"Well, there's not enough ketchup in the world to fill the Grand Canyon. I suggest you check your sources."

I said, "Actually, I've got my notes right here." I reached into my jacket pocket and pulled out the crib-sheet that head office had put together. "Let's see. Ketchup, ketchup." Hamburgers to the moon. French fries around the equator. Skyscrapers of pickles. "Ah, here," I said. "Ketchup. Well, what do you know? You're right, sir. Absolutely right. It's not the Grand Canyon at all. It's the Missouri River. Enough ketchup to fill the Missouri River."

"Quite another matter," the gentleman said. "I'm not sure we should accept money from someone like you." And then, as far as I could tell, he went back to sleep.

In the end, the London Crippled Children's Treatment Centre decided that they would indeed take our money – and, to be fair, twenty years later, we all had a laugh about my anxious but successful "sales" pitch to them. As part of our twentieth-anniversary celebrations in London, McDonald's donated $20,000 to the same organization. It had changed its name from the Crippled Children's Treatment Centre to the Thames Valley Children's Centre, but there were some people there who had been involved twenty years earlier. When we presented our cheque to them, one of the longtime board members stood up and told everyone about the time I had come so nervously to the Hunt Club to state my case. He said, "So, Mr. Cohon. We want you to know that you can give us as much money as you want, as often as you want. You don't have to come and sell yourself to us." Which was something. I finally allowed myself the wide smile I'd had to stifle twenty years earlier.

I have never questioned the wisdom of Ray Kroc's notion that we should give something back to our communities. It was part of my upbringing. My parents gave volunteer time to their community and to their synagogue, and they taught us to help those who were less fortunate than we were. The lesson stuck. Corporations – particularly ones with the size and global reach of McDonald's – have enormous capacity to do good, and I think, as corporate citizens, it's important that we try to do just that. Colin Powell's 1997 Presidents' Summit on volunteerism in the United States addressed this issue. So did Joan Kroc's 1997 donation of $15 million to flood victims in North Dakota.

Whatever the business, it doesn't exist in a vacuum; as soon as you start to think of a corporation, or a company, or a partnership, or a cottage industry, or a lemonade stand for that matter, as being something separate from the culture in which it exists, you diminish the long-term prospects of both your business and the community. That's why I've always been a little surprised and, sometimes, angered by people who try to tell me that we use the charities we become involved in as advertising vehicles for us – that we helped with, say, Terry Fox's Marathon of Hope or Rick Hansen's Man in Motion Tour simply because the publicity helps us to sell more hamburgers.

Does our charity work help us sell more hamburgers? Well, I suppose it does – in the same way that Mr. Smith's involvement with the Kiwanis Club might mean that his sales are better at his hardware store because local people know who he is and like to support his business. Or in the same way that Mr. Jones, who always helps out with the Junior League Flower Show, does better at his nursery than the garden-supply place down the road that takes no interest in local concerns. If Mrs. Brown, the woman who owns your local drugstore, is on your doorstep every spring selling daffodils for cancer research, maybe you're more inclined to buy your toothpaste and your cough syrup and your bandages at her shop. I don't think this is such a bad thing. I think this is what makes capitalism really work. Why shouldn't you give your business to your neighbour, to your friend, to your family, to people who demonstrate that they have a real interest in you and in the place where you live?

The real question is, do companies get involved in charity work *primarily* to promote their own products? Obviously, I can't speak for others. But I can offer you proof of McDonald's point of view. Come with me to Variety Village, or to a Ronald McDonald House, or to Camp Oochigeas, a summer camp for kids with cancer, or to the Ronald McDonald Children's Centre in Moscow, and just watch what goes on there. Look at the kids' faces. Listen to their laughter. Watch a game of wheelchair basketball. Or talk to a few anxious parents who are spending their days in a ward at the Hospital for Sick Children in Toronto and who, instead of incurring the expense of an anonymous downtown hotel, are staying at Ronald McDonald House – and then try to tell me that we're only interested in selling more hamburgers. You know what? I just don't buy it.

Cynicism is easy – too easy. Because of our prominence, McDonald's is often a target – people who distrust capitalism, who resent the new, globalized economy, who think that free enterprise and the public good are mutually exclusive, often take aim at us. But it would have been difficult to be cynical in the Soviet Union in the weeks leading up to our opening. The expression on the faces of the passersby who peered through the hoarding and into the new restaurant on Pushkin Square was more than curiosity – although people were indeed extremely, almost uncontainably, curious. In the few years that have passed since, at McDonald's we have become accustomed to having restaurants in Moscow, in St. Petersburg, and in Nizhni Novgorod. By January 1998, there will be at least thirty McDonald's in the former Soviet Union – thirty restaurants, by the way, that in volume of sales will be the rough equivalent of one hundred and fifty restaurants in North America – and the Russians have become more accustomed to us. At the time, however – at the end of 1989 and the beginning of 1990 – the sight of a McDonald's in Pushkin Square was about as astounding as the sight of the airplane of Mathias Rust, the West German kid who landed in Red Square in May 1987. People literally could not believe their eyes. They stopped. And they stared. Their expression was not just of curiosity – it was also, I came to realize, one of hope. Not because of McDonald's per se – we are, after all, only a restaurant. In the end, a hamburger is a hamburger: I don't pretend that it is a philosophy, or a belief – and I don't want to belittle the long and difficult struggles of courageous people inside the Soviet Union who for decades, and often at great risk, had been working toward their freedom. But the expression on people's faces as they stopped and stared at the McDonald's being built in Pushkin Square was unmistakeable, and it was there partly because of what we stood for. Our presence represented an opening – maybe only a little one, but an opening – in what Churchill had called the Iron Curtain. On the one hand, it was just a restaurant. On the other, no less a figure than Mikhail Gorbachev has called it "an extraordinary event."

We represented a system that is by no means perfect: I've seen what South Side Chicago was like during my last visit; I've seen the conditions in which so many Canadian aboriginal people have to live; I know how tough it can be for people who suffer the hardest of circumstances to pull themselves out of the cycle of poverty and welfare, even with the best of intentions. I know the imperfections of our system only too well. Nonetheless, in the USSR, we represented a system that worked, and if there was a single thought that dominated the minds of Soviet citizens in those days, it was that their system did not. At the time of our opening in Moscow, the foreign television crews took a certain delight in comparing our gleaming counters and happy, enthusiastic crew with footage of grim Russian cooks slopping out inedible-looking bowls of stew at typical workers' restaurants in Moscow. This stark visual contrast was certainly not lost on Soviet citizens. I don't think I'm being immodest in saying that McDonald's meant far more to the average Muscovite than we – even after our years of negotiations in the USSR – had ever imagined it would.

To be told that a restaurant would be a clean and friendly place, and then to find that it actually is. To order a Big Mac, and then actually to get a Big Mac. To work, and then actually to get paid for your work. In their way, these were miracles in the Soviet Union of 1990.

In hindsight, the first wave of Soviet liberalization – the reforms of Mikhail Gorbachev – and then, following quickly, the second wave – the elections of 1989 and the ensuing disintegration of communist ideology – seem to have been inevitable. Gorbachev understood the revolutions of technology that were sweeping the globe. He was a modern leader – a distinct break from the elderly, old-fashioned, and unimaginative rulers who preceded him. He remained a faithful communist, but he knew that even if the USSR had not been faced with a grave economic crisis, the improved communications of satellite television and cable-linked computers meant that Soviet authorities were not going to be able to do what they had always done so successfully: keep the Western world at bay.

Far from seeming inevitable, the direction in which the Soviet Union was headed, throughout the first six or seven years of the 1980s, was not really obvious at the time. At one point during that period, when I was returning to Canada after another round of negotiations in Moscow, I found myself racking my brain, trying to understand what was going on. There was an upcoming McDonald's board of directors' meeting in Quebec City – and I knew I would face some very tough questions from some of the directors. How much longer was this going to go on? When was I going to cut a deal? I remember feeling quite frustrated – because I really wasn't sure what I would say. I couldn't help but think that somehow – despite all our hard work – we were not getting it right, that there was a key to the Soviet system that, somehow, we had not yet found.

Consider it this way: If you visited a family you did not know well, and they made a great show of telling you how happy they were and carried on as if all was well, you might never realize, throughout your entire stay, how bad things really were. You'd see the dilapidated furniture, but still not know that the marriage was about to break up, that the bank was about to reclaim the house and the car, that the children were about to run away. It might occur to you that something was a little odd about this family, but if they kept insisting that they were happy, you would perhaps attribute your perception to your unfamiliarity with them. You might decide that they only seemed odd because you didn't know them well enough. You might think: Once I get to know them better, I'll understand. To some degree, our experience in Moscow was like that. We took the delays, the indecision, the confusion, and the bureaucratic run-around that we encountered as simply being the Soviet way of doing things. We thought it was normal.

Even though the signs were everywhere – the line-ups for food, the empty shelves in stores, the broken-down trucks on the highways, the absence of energy, of creativity, of ambition at almost all levels of society – we did not really understand how bad and how chaotic things were. Other than the millions of people who were living it every day, I'm not sure that anyone did.

There was nothing normal about it. This was a system in the final stages of a complete breakdown – which tended to make our negotiations more than a little tricky.

Here, for instance, is the entire text of a telegram I received in May 1986 from V. I. Solodov, the deputy general manager of the Sovincentr in Moscow. We had been involved for several years in negotiations with the Sovincentr. Opening a McDonald's there was one of several possibilities we were pursuing at the time. We felt we were getting close to a deal, and, months earlier, we had set up a May meeting. These meetings were always a little complicated – the concept and principles of our proposal had to be detailed and discussed; we hoped, always, to sign a protocol of mutual intent to pursue the project further, and then to embark on a joint technical and feasibility study; we liked to meet, through the Soviet officials, with possible suppliers at the same time. All this required a good deal of advance planning, and our team, which included Ron Cohen, Bob Hissink, Peter Misikowetz, Marc Winer and myself, always did its homework before meetings of this sort. We wanted our proposal to be as comprehensive as possible. Our lawyer, Jeff Hertzfeld, was always fastidious in his preparations. We came with our graphs and our models and our spreadsheets and our artist's conceptions. Time, money, and effort went into getting ready for these meetings. Calendars were shuffled. Commitments were made. The travel plans alone required more than a little effort on our part. Then, only a few weeks before the scheduled meeting, we got this: "We inform you that in May 1986 we have no possibility to discuss the establishment of the Macdonald's [sic] restaurant . . . When we renew our iniciative [sic] of the saild [sic] establishment we shall no doubt adress [sic] you in due course. Best Regards, Solodov V. I."

That's all he wrote. Was this sudden about-face the result of new and pressing preoccupations? Did it signal an internal shift of power and priorities? Who could say? Jeff Hertzfeld and Marc Winer thought perhaps that in the wake of the 1986 American bombing of Libya, the Kremlin had decreed that a high-profile visit from McDonald's would not be a good idea. Any explanation was possible, from high-level international intrigue to low-level bureaucratic laziness. In any case, we were left cooling our heels.

This was not an isolated incident. Throughout the first half of the 1980s this uncertainty was particularly difficult. There were, simply, no guidelines for doing what we were trying to do, and so we ended up trying everything and everyone: Simultaneously, we had begun to formulate proposals for partnerships with two government agencies and with Tallinn, the capital of Estonia. All roads, it seemed, led to the State Commission for Foreign Economic Relations. The chairman, Vladimir Kamentsev, became the recipient of my usual barrage of faxes and telegrams and communications. This letter, copied to Ron Cohen, Bob Hissink, and Peter Misikowetz – all key members of the Wolf Pack – is typical of the messages Kamentsev received from me on a regular basis:

"Pursuant to our discussions with you in Moscow in February of this year and our meetings at that time with various interested ministries and Soviet organizations, we have now prepared and delivered three separate joint venture proposals for the establishment and operation of McDonald's Restaurants which have been submitted respectively to Mossoviet, Intourist, and the authorities in Tallinn."

But by 1986–87 the ground had begun to shift. We knew that Gorbachev and his inner circle were favouring the idea of joint ventures between foreign companies and Soviet agencies as the best means to upgrade the ailing Soviet economy. We had been saying this all along. For more than a decade, our proposals had always spelled out that McDonald's would provide "its know-how, new developments, techniques and improvements in areas of restaurant management, food preparation, and service. . . ." But until Gorbachev's reforms began to take shape, our offer to pass on our expertise was never treated as the enormous asset that we felt it was.

The Soviet bureaucracy often operated with total unpredictability. It drove us crazy. We felt that somehow there was a code that we had not yet cracked, a pattern to their thought that we had not yet discovered, an underlying rationale that we had not yet perceived. But this was where we were wrong. Until the reforms of Mikhail Gorbachev began to transform everything, we didn't find the key for a simple reason: There was no key for us to find.

It was the official endorsement of joint ventures in 1987 that, at last, unlocked the door. Once this policy became apparent, things began to fall into place. What we had been saying all along – that we would provide jobs and technology, that we would help to improve the food service sector, that our demands would benefit the Soviet agricultural system, that we would provide good, affordable food and clean, reliable restaurants to *Soviet* customers – started to make sense. We were in alignment with the people who had understood us from the beginning – people such as Gorbachev and Yakovlev – and they were able to encourage, cajole, or push the people who didn't understand us.

Looking back, I'm struck by something very odd. Here we were in a new and strange environment, trying to do something that many people said couldn't be done, and that certainly had never been done before. We were, until we finally began to close in on our deal, operating in a system that was extremely difficult to understand when it was working properly, and impossible to comprehend when it wasn't. And it usually wasn't. Yet, fundamentally, we didn't do anything different from the way we do things everywhere. We made no special rules; we changed no basic policies. We did what McDonald's always does – and, in the end, that has proven to be the secret of our success.

We insisted on our standards. Second nature, to us. Not a negotiable item. This insistence was always a stumbling block when we were dealing with the old regime, but when we began to deal with the new one, our standards turned out to be exactly the kind of approach they wanted their joint-venture partners to take. They were looking for associations that would help improve their system, and, clearly, ours was going to go some distance toward that. In the absence of a reliable infrastructure, we were going to have to build one. We were going to have to go right into the countryside and develop a network of suppliers that didn't exist before.

We insisted on good service – again, something we consider to be a given at McDonald's. Everywhere, we expect our staff and crew to be cheerful, friendly, and efficient. Again, this basic requirement addressed an enormous gap in the service sector that the new regime was anxious to fill. It also addressed an enormous gap in the experience of our Soviet customers. One of the great pleasures of our Moscow opening was watching the grim, stony faces of some of our older customers – people who had been scowled at by officials and shopkeepers all their lives – slowly break into a smile simply because one of our crew members was smiling at them.

We insisted that our restaurants be for everyone. Of course, McDonald's always is. We would never dream of opening in Orillia, Ontario, or in Red Deer, Alberta, or in Dartmouth, Nova Scotia, and telling the people there that we would serve only holders of gold credit cards who had college degrees. We don't believe in exclusivity – and so it didn't make sense to open in Moscow and tell people that we would accept only hard currency. This just wasn't the way we did things. As it happened, this policy spoke powerfully to people who were fed up with being told they were allowed to do one thing but not another, allowed to go here, but not somewhere else, allowed to buy something in this shop, but not in that one. We couldn't have predicted this, but in a small way, our "rubles-only" policy was a small revolution – in a country that was on the brink of a very big one.

Last, but not least, we insisted on giving something back to the community. This, to be perfectly modest about it, is simply McDonald's policy. It always has been.

This policy – what many other corporations might think of as a frill or an add-on – turned out to be of absolutely basic importance. We couldn't have known that the Russian market was going to open up as much, and as quickly, as it did. We couldn't have known that it would be crucial for us to distinguish ourselves from the quick-buck artists – "the robbers and pirates," as Gorbachev has described them to me – who came rushing in to take advantage of the confusion of the nation's economic and social transformation. We had been negotiating for too long, trying too hard to establish a real footing, working too carefully toward becoming an integral part of the nation's fabric, to be suddenly lumped in with the carpet-baggers who so greedily attended the dissolution of the Soviet Union and the fall of communism. And, in the midst of this difficult and chaotic period of transition, it was McDonald's support of Russian charities that signalled our long-term commitment to the country. Nothing else could so clearly state what was, after all, simply another example of basic McDonald's philosophy: We believed in our new community, and we were there to stay.

Early in the morning of January 31, 1990, as Craig, Mark, and I, sitting anxiously in the tobacco-stale interior of a Moscow cab, headed toward Pushkin Square, I was formulating all kinds of emergency plans. If – as seemed to be the case – Muscovites were not interested enough in the opening of their first McDonald's to come out to the opening ceremony, perhaps we could . . . Well, what could we do?

"Look," I said, turning to Craig and Mark in the back seat. "We'll go over to the university and hand out free Big Mac coupons. That might work. That will get out a crowd."

My two sons looked at me with the slightly strained patience that the young sometimes reserve for their fretful elders.

"Dad," Craig said, "just relax."

"It'll work out," said Mark. "Don't worry."

Relax? Don't worry? With the international press waiting to record my moment of complete and very public humiliation? Fat chance.

I didn't think it was possible for my heart to sink any farther, but it did – when the taxi turned the corner into Pushkin Square. I'd been told, but now I could see with my own eyes. There were no crowds. Other than a single policeman in the square and the busy crew behind the brightly lit windows of our restaurant, there was hardly a soul in sight.

I think this was when Craig and Mark started to get anxious, too.

I still wasn't quite willing to accept the visual evidence. We approached the policeman. I felt we needed his help. I'm not sure what I expected him to do. Conjure a crowd of thousands out of thin air?

But that, more or less, was what he did.

The policeman explained to us that they had decided to keep the people in a holding pattern around the corner, out of sight.

"Holding pattern? Holding pattern? What do you mean, holding pattern?"

"Uh, Dad," Mark said. He gestured to me to calm down – a little. I think he was worried that I was going to lift the policeman up by the lapels of his jacket.

The policeman explained that they had put barricades up because there were so many people.

"So many people? So many? What does that mean? How many is so many?"

"Lots. Lots and lots."

I said, "Walk us there. Show us."

He was right. Around the corner, behind several rows of police barricades, there were lots of people. Lots and lots. Thousands, in fact, standing in a quiet, orderly line in the grey cold of an early morning in January.

There were other policemen standing at the front of the barricades. We approached them, introduced ourselves, and asked one – very politely, very nicely – when they planned to open the barricades.

He said, "Nine-thirty." His plan was to let people trickle down to the square for the opening at ten.

Trickle? This wasn't quite the scene that I – nor, I think, the international press – had in mind. I looked at my watch.

You never know how Russian police are going to react. Sometimes you can say something or do something, and they'll laugh and slap you on the back. Other times they'll slap you in jail. I could only hope for the best.

I said, "It must be nine-thirty somewhere in the world. Let's open the barricades right now."

Craig, Mark, and I moved toward the barricades.

"*Da?*" I asked. Our hands were on the railings. The people at the front of the line looked at us anxiously.

One policeman shrugged. Then another smiled, and I knew we were all right. "*Da,*" he said. I gave him the thumbs up. And then, in one of the proudest moments of my life, Craig, Mark, and I moved the barricades away. We stepped aside, and the crowd moved forward, in a steady, solid, unbroken line, toward Pushkin Square.

As was well documented by newspapers, television stations, and radio news programs around the world, our opening on January 31, 1990, at Pushkin Square was a great success. The line of people wound around the square until midnight. We served 30,567 customers countless "Beeg Makkov," french fries, and pies. We raised over $1 million for the Soviet Children's Fund. We broke the McDonald's world record for the number of customers served on opening day. Yet it was not the volume, not the numbers, that gave me the greatest satisfaction. It was watching our crew and our customers.

As *The New York Times* reported the next day, "Customers who waited up to two hours to get into the 700-seat restaurant, the largest McDonald's in the world, greatly appreciated the sweet revenge in the sign by the front door: 'For rubles only.' Usually Muscovites can merely salivate outside several richly stocked groceries and restaurants newly opened for Westerners, exclusive marts that want none of the internationally valueless rubles, and so bear the sign: 'For hard currencies only.' Many departing customers proudly took their logo-ridden refuse with them to show they were pioneers. They had seen the future and it works, at least as far as their digestive tract."

For the team who had worked so hard toward this, the opening was an enormous achievement. We felt, I think, the way a theatre company must feel on opening night – nervous, exhilarated, exhausted, energized – all at once. McComplex was running smoothly. The restaurant gleamed – everything finished, everything up and running, everything in its place. The system – the same system you would find in a McDonald's in Toronto, or Tokyo, or Toledo – functioned like clockwork. The four Russian graduates from a training program that is a lot more demanding than its name (the Canadian Institute of Hamburgerology) might imply were in attendance. One of the four, Khamzat Khasbulatov, has gone on to become general director of McDonald's-Moscow. And the entire crew – six hundred Russians – came through with flying colours, as, from the beginning, I had been confident they would.

Today, the Russian operation is extremely profitable, and is starting to make a significant contribution to McDonald's growth worldwide. But perhaps the greatest success on opening day was one that was not readily apparent to the photographers and camera crews gathered in Pushkin Square. As in theatre, a lot of the hardest work had taken place off the stage. Our most significant accomplishment – one that remains a significant challenge, one that we're still working hard on – was establishing our network of suppliers.

From the beginning, we were determined to source as many agricultural products and raw materials as we could in the Soviet Union. This was basic McDonald's philosophy – to integrate as much as possible into the local economy and distribution networks. This was not going to be easy – our standards and the disintegrating Soviet system were not, on the face of things, a very good fit. Our critics had always thought that simply keeping our restaurants supplied would be our greatest stumbling block. They wondered how we thought we could succeed where it seemed the vast powers of the Soviet state had failed.

Our advantage was focus. We didn't have to solve all the problems of Soviet agriculture or crumbling infrastructure. We could concentrate on specifics. We could determine exactly what we needed – what kind of product, in what quantities – and then take very detailed steps toward fulfilling that need.

The first clues were provided by our partner, the food service department of the City of Moscow. Since Mosobshchepit, the successor to Glavobshchepit, provided essentially all the food service for the city, its warehouses were the obvious starting points for our search. Our team could assess the quality and acceptability of various ingredients, products, or raw materials, and then begin to trace them from the warehouses, to shops and markets, to their sources within the Soviet Union. Cocoa powder for our chocolate toppings, for instance; strawberries for our milkshakes; mustard seed for our mustard; vinegar for our pickles – our team often found these kinds of things in products quite different from what we had in mind. But with this discovery made, it then became a matter of leg work and consultation: tracking items from the warehouses back to their sources, and then ascertaining whether the producer had the capacity, the commitment to quality, and the adaptability to work with us.

On the agricultural side, our approach was pretty much the same, if somewhat more complicated. We started with Glavobshchepit, and, through its network of partners and co-operatives, found our way to cattle farms, dairy farms, and to growers of lettuce and potatoes. It was a crash course, for most of us, in the agricultural geography of the USSR. The term "working in the field" became quite literal, as it was in the fields that our team – McDonald's personnel, Canadian agronomists, Soviet agricultural experts, experienced European and North American suppliers – often found some pieces of the puzzle we were trying to put together.

For instance, a farm might have had the capacity that we needed, but not the storage facilities. Or capacity and storage, but not the right equipment. Or, if they were successfully growing lettuce, it wasn't the right kind of lettuce for our purposes. Potatoes presented one of the biggest challenges: We needed farmers to switch from producing the small, round, traditional Russian potatoes to the longer variety that we required for our french fries.

Once we had identified a potential source – once we felt confident that a farmer was willing and able to commit to the quality on which we insisted and was willing and able to work with us to adapt his production to our needs – we stepped in wherever we could. We provided training and assistance. Our team returned to farms frequently to offer advice and consultation. Where equipment upgrades, new storage facilities, improved irrigation, soil improvement, or crop adaptation was required, we helped secure loans and credit for our new partners. We helped set up reliable transportation and distribution networks.

Although they were not the centre of attention to the international press, these suppliers were among the stars of the opening day festivities. Certainly, they were the part of our operation that caught the attention of Mikhail Gorbachev. He understood the ripple effect that our presence would have throughout the Soviet agricultural system. As he has written in his foreword to this book, the suppliers' "co-operation with the company means the inflow of new technologies and new ways of providing service and also challenges them to improve product quality, which in turn contributes to the development of civilized modern markets."

As I've said, on our opening day at Pushkin Square, we served 30,567 people – a new world-wide company record. We were very proud of this – but just as proud of the effort we had made to make sure that those thirty thousand people were consuming as much domestic product as possible.

It is a little odd, perhaps, to have a memory documented so thoroughly. Even the most important events in one's life – wedding days, the births of children, important anniversaries – are often recorded only with snapshots, or bits and pieces of video. Much is left to memory. The opening at our Pushkin Square restaurant – certainly one of the most important events in my life – was, on the other hand, recorded in unbelievable detail. In the archives at our head office in Toronto, we have three full 120-minute video cassettes of nothing other than the international press coverage of the event: everyone from *Canada A.M.*, to *Good Morning America*, the *Today* show to the BBC and Japanese TV covered the story. We also produced our own twenty-nine-minute documentary, *A Taste of the West: Bringing Free Enterprise to the Soviet Union.*

So, if ever I want to relive the excitement of January 31, 1990, it is easy enough to do. It's all there – the faces, the noise, the excitement. When I watch the videos, memories come flooding back: the wintry temperature in Pushkin Square, the clamouring journalists, the musical hubbub of the Russian language. I see children with parents and grandparents. I see students and workers. I see our crew members smiling and waving astonished-looking customers over to the counter. It was a very happy day.

I have a few very fond memories, though, that weren't recorded by cameras. First among these, of course, is moving the barricades with my sons. I cherish that one. The second, I suppose, is watching a junior officer from the American embassy approach one of our young staff outside the restaurant. It was early afternoon and the line-up still looked as if it would go on forever. The man from the embassy asked where the other entrance was. The private one.

"There's only one entrance," was the reply.

He said, "Sorry, you don't understand. I'm from the American Embassy."

"No," said the McDonald's employee respectfully. "You don't understand. There's only one entrance. And this is the line-up that leads to it."

My third fond memory is being stood up by Fred Turner that night at our gala opening party at the Kremlin.

I had got an enormous charge out of negotiations with the Kremlin for our gala – because our negotiations seemed a perfect metaphor for what was going on in the country. I wanted it to be an enormous event – a party, an absolutely tremendous fundraiser, with a silent auction and a cheque presentation to the Soviet Children's Fund. I wanted it to take place in the most prestigious surroundings possible, and so we kept asking for permission to do things that no-one had ever done before. Could we have the ceremonies in the Palace of Congresses? Could the Red Army Orchestra entertain our guests? All the officials we initially approached thought it extremely improbable that the answer to these requests would be yes. But we kept pointing out, forcefully, that we were trying to raise money to help children.

This worked. The answer came back: yes.

Very good. Would it then be possible for our guests to enter the Great Kremlin Palace through the grand staircase to St. George Hall and later gather in the Palace of Congresses?

Few people had ever seen the huge white and gold ballroom in the Czar's palace and the grand staircase that swept away from a huge painting of Lenin speaking to a crowd the day after the Revolution – much less used them for a private party.

"Impossible," said the officials. But we pushed. "It's for the children," we kept saying. Eventually word came back. Again, yes.

Very good. But would it then be possible to serve our guests champagne in the St. George ballroom? The officials stared at us as if we had lost our minds. They laughed. But we pressed. "The children," we said. "It's a fundraiser for the children."

"This is impossible. This is ridiculous. These are sacred rooms that few people are even allowed to view. We are already breaking so many rules, we don't have the nerve to make any more of your requests."

But we pressed them to pass on to their superiors our request. And again the answer eventually came from up top. The officials with whom we were dealing could hardly believe it. Someone up there liked us. The answer: "*Da.*"

The gala party was going to be a once-in-a-lifetime experience. Everything – the food, the surroundings, the wine, the music, the guest list – was exquisite. It was going to be an extraordinary conclusion to an extraordinary day. So I was stunned when, late that afternoon, Fred Turner told me he wasn't going to come.

Throughout the long negotiations that led up to the Moscow opening, Fred Turner's support had been extremely important to me. I admire him. His tenure as chairman and CEO – positions now admirably filled by Mike Quinlan – was a period during which the company expanded aggressively while holding fast to McDonald's basic principles – a strategy that Quinlan has continued. Turner understood why it was important to stick to the path that Ray Kroc had established. He got very uncomfortable whenever the company looked as if it might start to meander. The Canadian company once put together a very slick presentation for him; we had an idea about selling McDonald's cookies in a chain of Canadian grocery stores. We really laid it on – we had lots of our marketing people, several of our vice presidents, and executives from the grocery chain at the meeting. When the presentation was over, everyone was waiting to hear what Turner thought.

He stood up slowly. He looked around the room. He walked over and contemplated the display case we had set up. And then he said, "This is the dumbest f— ing idea I've ever heard."

And he was right. Once we all turned down the glow of our own excitement, we all realized it. He made his point crystal clear. He took a box of our cookies, crumpled it, and dropped it on the floor. Then he gave the display a kick, and a few more boxes crashed to the floor. He pointed out that, as soon as we lost control of distribution, there was no guarantee that our products would meet our standards of presentation. Turner would never support something he didn't believe in, and he had made it just as clear, through the thick and the thin of our long negotiations with the Soviets, that he believed in us.

So, I was very disappointed when Turner told me he wasn't going to attend the gala party. I had looked forward to celebrating with him. Disappointed, that is, until he told me what he wanted to do instead. He said he was going to spend the evening in the restaurant.

"What?"

"I'm just going to stay here and watch," he said.

And that's what he did. While the VIPs drank champagne in the St. George ballroom, and celebrated in grand style in the Palace of Congresses, one of the most important of the VIPs, Fred Turner, senior chairman, sat quietly in the corner of our new restaurant. The line-up was still snaking around Pushkin Square late into the evening. The restaurant was always full. And Fred Turner just watched – watched our new customers and our new crew. He had started his career thirty-four years earlier on the grill at Ray Kroc's first McDonald's in Des Plaines, Illinois. He knew that this – the happy bustle of a busy restaurant – was what it was all about.

That's all he did, all evening. The restaurant, originally scheduled to close at ten, had to stay open until after midnight to accommodate the crowd. Fred Turner never came to the Kremlin party. In his own quiet way, he did his celebrating in Pushkin Square. I don't think he could have paid us a higher compliment.

• 8 •

Roots and Wings

I often speak at universities and business schools. I am often invited to address chamber of commerce meetings across the country. I am frequently the speaker at business awards dinners. And I am often asked about my management style.

It's a difficult concept, style. When you think of it, it's very hard to define your own. The same is true of reputation. You don't set out to establish one; you build it almost imperceptibly, deed by deed. Reputation and style are things you create but never see very accurately for yourself. Style is just the way you are – the way you conduct yourself, the way you act. It's others who think of it as a "style."

Part of the difficulty I have with describing my style is that I have been able to establish it gradually. It's a bit like my sweaters. Susan and my pal Ken McGowen kid me constantly about the number of sweaters I own, and when, recently, I actually counted how many I had, even I was a little shocked. If anyone thinks we have too many bathrooms, or too many telephones, they should get a load of my sweater drawers. And yet, I've never spent a lot of time thinking about sweaters. It's just that over the years I've bought them – one at a time – and they've kind of added up.

In the same way, my management style is something that's accumulated so naturally that I don't think I was even aware of it until people started asking me what it was. In 1968, we started with one store, a management staff of three, and an office that was smaller than some of the hotel rooms I stay in now. As I write, we have more than one thousand company-owned and franchised restaurants in Canada, a management staff of three thousand, and a gleaming new head office building in North Toronto. Our sales are approaching $2 billion; we are one of the largest employers in the country; and we raise millions and millions of dollars for charity every year.

Under the leadership of Ray Kroc, Fred Turner, and Steve Barnes, the company expanded into Canada, Puerto Rico, the Virgin Islands, Costa Rica, Guam, Japan, the Netherlands, Panama, Germany, Australia, France, El Salvador, Sweden, Guatemala, England, Hong Kong, the Bahamas, New Zealand, Switzerland, Ireland, Austria, Belgium, Brazil, Singapore – and that's only up to 1980. That was only the beginning. From the year we opened in Moscow until 1997, McDonald's virtually doubled the international expansion of the preceding thirty years.

In 1961, the year that the "Look for the Golden Arches" theme was introduced, there were no McDonald's outside the United States, and Ray Kroc served the 500 millionth McDonald's hamburger to Charles S. Murphy, the U.S. undersecretary of agriculture. Three decades later – one year after we opened in Pushkin Square – McDonald's was in fifty-nine different countries throughout the world, and had served its 85 *billionth* hamburger.

In Canada, we weren't letting the grass grow beneath our feet either. From 1971, Ron Marcoux, Arnie Nelson, and Pat

Donahue were overseeing the expansion of our operations in Western Canada: Victoria, Vancouver, Calgary, Winnipeg, Brandon. In the East, Ron Cohen, Ed Garber, and Bud Audett were moving just as aggressively into new markets: Etobicoke, Scarborough, Kitchener, Mississauga, Sarnia, Fredericton and Dartmouth. Our growth from the early seventies on into the 1990s was not only staggering, it was also incremental. During the past three decades we have expanded rapidly, but we have expanded one restaurant at a time. We've learned our lessons – and I suppose I've developed my management style – along the way.

So the question always throws me a little. Style? Well, this, I suppose, is my style:

First and foremost, I'm competitive. To tell you the truth, I don't really think of this as a question of style. I think of it as a fact of life, as a condition of existence. It's like air. It's the context in which I function. There are people, particularly my friends on the left of the political spectrum, who find the concept of competition a little disturbing. But I find competition bracing. I find it exciting. I find it exhilarating. I find it almost impossible to be any other way.

For instance: tennis. I love playing tennis, and I take it quite seriously. However, there are times when it would be to my advantage to take a little pace off my game – to slow down for a more social, less competitive match. But I can't. It's not my nature.

One of my tennis partners when I am in Russia is Vadim Bakatin. I met Vadim in the mid-1980s. I was introduced to him by Albert Likhanov, the well-known Russian writer of children's books and the founder of the Soviet Children's Fund. In July 1988, I became the first North American member of the Soviet Children's Fund, and, eventually, the head of the North American chapter. In 1995, we started Ronald McDonald's Children's Charities (Russia), but we remain supportive of the Soviet Children's Fund, now called the International Association of Children's Funds (Russia). As an example of our co-operation, we recently translated into Russian and published *The Diary of Anne Frank*. This is a book that has never appeared in Russian, and it was distributed to 50,000 Russian school children.

Likhanov used to host wonderful dinner parties at his house, a large dacha outside Moscow. It was at one of these dinners that I met Vadim – a very bright, forward-thinking man. I liked him immediately. He had risen through the party ranks, and in 1990 he had been appointed minister of the interior by Mikhail Gorbachev. As it turned out, Bakatin was more liberal in his thinking than Gorbachev. Disagreements arose, and eventually Gorbachev fired him. But in August 1991, Bakatin was among the small group of officials who were sent to bring Gorbachev back from where he and his family were being held hostage during the coup engineered by the communist hard-liners.

I got to know Vadim during the uncertain and difficult period when power was see-sawing back and forth between Gorbachev and Yeltsin. Gorbachev and Yeltsin had different political philosophies, different agendas, and different priorities. Their personalities were oil and water – but the one thing they did agree on was that the KGB had to be dismantled. For this, they turned to Bakatin. He became the head of the KGB – traditionally one of the most powerful positions in Russia.

The first thing Bakatin did in the new job was to look up his grandfather's file. This is typical of him – he is an emotional man, with a big heart – but it was also typical of the search for history that is part of Russia's struggle today. Stories – particularly the stories of the victims of Stalin's purges – are being told now that were hidden for decades, and Vadim was able to reclaim a missing piece of his own family's story. His grandfather, a liberal thinker, had been a school teacher in Siberia. He'd gone out fishing early one morning. Vadim's grandmother had left his breakfast on the table for his return. The food was partly eaten, so the family knew he had come back from his fishing, but that was all they knew. He was never seen again. More than fifty years later, his grandson sat in a large office in the KGB building in Dzerzhinskii Square and pored over the yellowing pages of the long-forgotten file. Vadim learned that his grandfather had been arrested, and that, after who knows what kinds of torture, he had signed a bogus confession. He had admitted to being a spy – which, of course, was ludicrous. He was executed.

Bakatin also had a friend who was a famous entertainer. His friend asked if he could see his file. But once Bakatin saw what was in it, he refused to show it. He knew his friend would have been devastated by the number of colleagues and supposed friends who had been reporting on his activities over the years.

In Russia, these are not uncommon stories.

The more I saw of Vadim Bakatin, the more I liked and respected him. He always surprised me; he has a quick, discerning mind, and he doesn't like to hide his emotions or his beliefs behind meaningless words. I learned quickly that it was not possible to take anything for granted with him. Once when we were talking I referred in passing to my "best friend," Ken McGowen.

Vadim immediately bristled. "Your what?"

"My best friend. Ken and I go back more than twenty-five years.

Vadim listened to this with a stern expression. "What am I, then?"

"What do you mean?" I asked.

"Do you rank your friends?"

I didn't know what to say.

Vadim said, "If Ken is your best friend, what number am I?"

"You? Oh, you're my worst friend."

He laughed – which was a relief. And when, some time later, I told Ken McGowen about this, he immediately wrote to Bakatin – whom he had never met. He said that he was tired of being my best friend and wanted to trade positions. He told Vadim that he was looking forward to being my worst friend, and that all Vadim had to do to be my best friend was to congratulate me constantly on my genius as a businessman and on my full head of hair. As a result of this correspondence, Vadim and Ken soon met. They are now "the best of friends."

Vadim and I got along well together, and soon discovered that we both enjoyed playing tennis. We played at a tennis club at a residential complex where many cosmonauts live – which I thought was quite neat and which was the kind of club I never would have had access to had I not known someone like him.

In tennis, you often hear people use the term "client game." As I understand it, this means that if you're playing with someone with whom you want to do business, you ease up on the throttle. If you're a better player, you let your opponent win, or at least make certain that you don't completely cream him, in order that your business agenda proceed smoothly and without unnecessary animosity once you step off the court.

Now, I had no specific business dealings with Vadim Bakatin. We were friends. We were becoming very good friends. Even so, I always kept in mind the fact that he was extremely well connected, and that even if his purpose was the dismantling of the KGB, he was still the head of an extremely powerful institution. I am a businessman, and businessmen like to stay on the good side of powerful institutions. Even then, in the Soviet Union, it was always good to have powerful friends, and always bad to have powerful enemies.

Which, you would think, was the kind of basic truth I might have considered the day Vadim tried to lob me during a tennis game.

We were both mid-court. I'd anticipated his shot, and I was already backing up by the time he hit it. He tried to lob the ball behind me. But I'm quite tall. I've got a good reach. I was in position. It was going to be a put-away. And – my competitive instincts completely obliterating any notion of a "client game" – I connected. I hit the ball as hard as I could.

Excellent pace. Unbelievable slam. I'd thrown everything into it. There was, however, one problem with the shot. I had him frozen in the middle of the court. I could have gone to his forehand. I could have gone to his backhand. There was plenty of room either way. Instead, I did neither. I went straight down the middle. Hard and fast and dead-square. I hit him right between the legs.

Vadim dropped to his knees. His gasp was not a pleasant sound. I stood there, stunned – although not half as stunned as Vadim was. I thought: My God. Of all the people in the Soviet Union, who is the last person you'd want to do this to? Answer: the head of the KGB. And I'd just done it.

This was not a wise move. This was not how to do business in the Soviet Union.

I ran over to him. He was turning a pretty alarming shade of red. He looked at me helplessly – there are levels of pain that a man just has to go through on occasions such as these. He was riding out the storm. He had my sympathies and my regrets – which I don't think were a big help. And when it seemed as if the worst had passed, I crouched beside him. I said, "And they say the KGB doesn't have balls."

Fortunately, for me, he laughed. Very fortunately. Our friendship survived – a friendship I value highly.

Not long after my ill-aimed overhead slam – and partly as an expression of regret for so aggressive a shot – I put together a gift for Vadim. He was immersed in the complex business of dismantling the secret-police agency. So I had some research done on the different names that have been used for the KGB over the years – OGPU, NKVD, and so forth – and I had tennis shirts, tennis balls, and wrist and head sweatbands made with these names on them, with a diagonal line through the names like a No Smoking sign.

I presented this gift to him, and – as I should have expected by then – his reaction was nothing like I had thought it would be. He immediately took offence. He spoke to me gravely. "George. This is not a laughing matter. This very serious, what we are doing. Don't make light of this."

Of course, I felt badly. It is easy for a foreigner to underestimate the emotions and the passions that underlie Russian history. The KGB might be a source of some amusement to us – a name out of a spy novel – but to Russians it was something very real and very frightening. It was a truly sinister presence, and so I respected Vadim's reaction. I never mentioned the subject again until, some years later, at a birthday dinner for me in Moscow, Vadim rose to give a toast. He had a mischievous twinkle in his eye as he started to tell the story of my gift. I sat there, waiting to be chastised for my insensitivity. But in his toast he said, "The real problem was that George gave me only twenty shirts. Everyone in the office wanted one, and there were not enough to go around."

He also reminded me of our tennis game, and of the pain he endured, but he said that, like many of my friends, he has managed to forgive me the excesses of my competitive instincts.

I'm grateful. There's not much I can do about it. It's just the way I am.

At the moment, in North America, McDonald's is facing some of the stiffest competition the company has ever seen. The service sector of the economy and the quick-service industry has expanded rapidly. At the 1997 shareholders' meeting, McDonald's Chairman and CEO Mike Quinlan said, "The U.S. business is extremely competitive today, and the reason is the classic economic scenario of supply increasing faster than demand. Over the past three years, the number of quick-service restaurants grew at a 21 per cent rate in the U.S., while overall sales for the industry increased only 14 per cent."

Today, in Canada, instead of a few competitors down the street, we've got Burger King, Dairy Queen, Harvey's, KFC, Pizza Hut, Taco Bell, Tim Hortons, and Wendy's (listed alphabetically, and not in any order of importance or lack thereof) on every corner. McDonald's is the target they all share, and they're constantly on the attack with ad campaigns, price wars, promotions, and launches of new products. Even real estate is a battlefield. Instead of a quiet, civilized chat with someone such as Avie Bennett – our first landlord, at our first restaurant in London, Ontario – it's a race, a fast-speed Monopoly game, a constant turf war; our real estate people have to be extremely aggressive in their pursuit of the best sites.

As Mike Quinlan put it in his speech to our shareholders, "In an impulse business, where 70 per cent of all decisions to eat at McDonald's are made on the spur of the moment, it is critically important that our restaurants are located wherever people work, shop, live, visit, learn, and travel. . . . This means identifying and developing the choice locations in each marketplace so that we continue to compete from a strategic position of strength."

In response to this competitive environment, Jack Greenberg, the chairman and CEO of McDonald's U.S.A., has announced a reorganization of the management structure of McDonald's U.S.A. The creation of five new geographic "divisions" is designed to make the company more decisive, flexible, innovative, and responsive in meeting the needs of our customers. This is a major restructuring, aimed at bringing us closer to our customers, which, I believe, will prove to be very successful.

It's a tough world. But am I happy the competition is there? Of course I am. In the former Soviet Union, I saw the result of competition not being there, and it wasn't a pretty picture. You had grocery stores without groceries. You had clothing stores without clothes. You had restaurants without service. You had bureaucrats without energy or vision. If you believe in free enterprise – as I absolutely do – you have to acknowledge that competition is the lifeblood of the system. Recently, in Moscow, a chain of restaurants called Russian Bistro, which specializes in traditional Russian fare – meat pies, potato breads, and kvass (a fermented bread drink) – has moved onto the scene in a big way. It's clear that they've been inspired by McDonald's success, and people often ask if I am worried by their presence. My answer is: not half as worried as I would be if they weren't there.

At all levels of our operation – service, product development, marketing – we have to be as creative and as innovative as possible. The pressure doesn't let up. If we don't find the best way to serve our customers, if we don't earn our customers' trust every time they enter one of our restaurants, someone else will end up serving them.

So, when it comes to my style, here's a key question. Since I'm so pleased that we have such fierce competition, and since I think the existence of competitors is so fundamental to free enterprise, would I hold back if we had one of our chief competitors on the ropes?

Would I ease up on my tennis game if it was my advantage, and my opponent threw up an easy lob?

Not a chance.

Just ask my friend Vadim Bakatin.

In his book *The Acquisitors*, Peter Newman wrote, "The mischievous twinkle that is George Cohon's trademark overlays the glacial glint of a tax assessor's eyes." Or, as my good friend Ken McGowen puts it, "George might seem like an easy-going, laid-back kind of a guy, but that's not the whole story. If you want to understand George there are two things about him that you have to know. The first is that he hates to lose. The second is that he loves to win."

So that's a given – one that I don't want to underplay. When I take up mountain biking, I set distance goals, I set time goals, and I focus my attention (and my legs) on achieving those goals. When I set out to do a book – the book, as a matter of fact, that you have in your hands – in order to tell my story and, at the same time, to raise money for Ronald McDonald Children's Charities, I don't envision a modest book launch. I plan as ambitious a fundraiser as possible. Why hold back? Why modestly tug my forelock (as if I had one), and just hope that a few of my friends show up for launch party? At McDonald's we launch new products with every marketing tool we have at our disposal, and our launches are generally about as quiet and restrained as New Year's Eve in Times Square. I don't see why promoting this book should be any different. I want people to enjoy it. I want to hear what people think about it. But I also want to raise as much money as possible for a cause I think is an important one, and so I set myself to work toward that goal.

Just as, when we were opening twenty-five new restaurants a year across Canada, I always wanted each one to be best. Period.

On that day in the early 1980s, in Moscow, when I stood in the lobby of the Sovincentr beside Pierre Trudeau, and decided that Don Kendall, the imperious and overbearing chairman of PepsiCo, would be eating McDonald's dust before I was through, it was my competitive instinct coming to the fore. He under-estimated us. He dismissed us. And I determined then and there that we were going to try to accomplish everything that he so smugly assumed we wouldn't.

It's a goal toward which we are working steadily. Pizza Hut, which was owned by PepsiCo, has nowhere near the presence in Moscow that McDonald's does. Pepsi, in recent years, has been struggling in Russia. McDonald's, of course, serves Coke.

Not only that – in 1986 my son, Craig, joined Coca-Cola, and in 1990 he moved to Moscow. He spearheaded Coke's drive to open a bottling plant there. His early days in Moscow reminded me of my early days in Toronto. He lived and worked out of a small hotel, and whenever I visited him there I often wondered where he actually slept because the room was always full of files and campaign plans, and the bed was always covered with Coke ads and displays.

Eventually, Craig moved out of his hotel room – but instead of moving into the kind of exclusive foreign enclave that is so popular with many ex-patriates, he found a flat in an ordinary apartment building. Surrounded by Russian neighbours, he set out to learn the language and to improve his understanding of the people and the culture. (In this regard, Craig has not proven to be a chip off the old block. After more than twenty years of regular visits to Russia, here is the sum total of my command of Russian: *spasibo*, thanks; *do svidaniya*, goodbye; *dobryi vecher*, good evening; *khorosho*, good; and *ya ne govoryu po-russki*, I don't speak Russian.)

Craig has been part of the team that has guided Coke to its position of supremacy in the Russian market. A Russian bottling plant was an important part of their game plan, but, for a year and a half, they were getting the kind of run-around that we had experienced at first. So Craig decided to take the bull by the horns. He found out that the first elected mayor of Moscow – Gavriil

Popov – was going to be flying to America. Craig booked himself onto the flight and, during a refuelling stop in Ireland, introduced himself. In a conversation conducted entirely in Russian, he got the mayor's approval for the plant.

When George Bush met Mikhail Gorbachev in the Kremlin in 1991, bottles of Coke were prominently displayed on the negotiating table – a table that of course appeared in almost every newspaper and on every television news show in the world. After the summit, Don Keough, the chief operating officer of the Coca-Cola Company world-wide, sent my son a note attached to a newspaper photo of Bush and Gorbachev with a bottle of Coke between them. It said, "I saw it on the table, and I know who put it there." Craig showed the note to me, and I was so proud that I had it framed. It hangs on the wall of my Toronto office.

And, while I'm on the subject of Coca-Cola, here's another story. A classic.

Not long ago, I was going to buy a new car. I had a dark-blue Jaguar convertible in mind. There is a dealership in Toronto, Grand Touring Automobile, that I like. I'd dropped by their showroom a couple of times and taken various models out for test drives. I like good cars, and I'd pretty much made up my mind to buy a new X-J8. The salesman and I were close to a deal. But when we sat down to do the paperwork, he asked if I'd like a cold drink.

"Sure. A Coke would be great."

"Pepsi okay?"

"I beg your pardon."

"Is Pepsi okay? We only have a Pepsi machine."

"No, actually, it's not."

The salesman looked a little uncomfortable.

I realized that I had some pretty good leverage here. Their sales figures for the day were going to take quite a jump if I put pen to paper.

The salesman said, "I can run across the street and get you a Coke."

He was being very accommodating. I smiled pleasantly and thanked him for the offer. But I said, "Not good enough. You'll have to get a Coke machine."

"Sorry?"

"You have to get rid of the Pepsi machine, and get a Coke machine."

The salesman chuckled.

"Or else I won't buy the car."

He thought I was joking.

I said, "No Coke machine. No deal."

I kept smiling.

He stared at me uncertainly. I toyed with my pen for a few seconds. Then I pointedly slid it back into my jacket pocket.

That was when he realized I wasn't kidding.

He said, "Excuse me for just a second, Mr. Cohon."

"George. Please. Call me George."

"Just a moment, George."

When the salesman returned, he had the owner of Grand Touring with him. They both looked very anxious. The owner was mystified. I knew what he was thinking. Coke, Pepsi, what's the difference? Well, there's a big difference in my books. He wanted to know why I felt as strongly as I did.

I said, "Aside from the fact that Coke is the better drink, McDonald's has a great relationship with Coca-Cola. And I have a son who works for Coke. I just don't think I'd enjoy getting in my beautiful new car every day and being reminded of Pepsi."

The owner said, "But I don't think we can change machines, just like that."

I asked if they had a contract with Pepsi.

"No."

The next step was simple. "May I use your phone, please?" I called my friend Bill Casey, the head of Coca-Cola in Canada.

The next day, Grand Touring Automobile got their Coke machine. And I got my new, dark-blue, convertible Jaguar X-J8.

Now, whenever I get in my car, or whenever I glance at Don Keough's note to my son on my office wall, or whenever I see a nearly empty Pizza Hut on a Moscow street, I smile to myself and I wonder if Don Kendall ever imagined how tough the competition was going to be.

When McDonald's goes toe to toe with a competitor, I enjoy the energy and creativity this rivalry injects into our system, but I never lose sight of the scoreboard – and at the end of the game, I like the results to be unambiguous. The competition loses; we win. Whatever else anyone can say about my style, its most important element is that it has a very clear objective: success.

However, success does not mean you have to be mean, single-minded, driven, and inhuman. It doesn't mean you have to be rude and insensitive. It doesn't mean you have to sit in your office all day and only count beans. It doesn't mean that you don't concern yourself with your community, or with the environment, or with charities. In fact, I've found that exactly the reverse approach is the most effective. And so, when MBA students or the members of a local chamber of commerce ask me about my management style, they are often a little surprised at the word I use in my answer. They expect some kind of elaborate theory of business. They expect flow charts and fiscal analyses. Instead, they hear a word that you don't hear bandied about too much in business schools: fun.

Fun is a much under-estimated activity. In North America we tend to think of it as something trivial, as something that isn't part of the real world. You do your work, which is serious, and then when you want to do nothing, or nothing of any import – when you want to goof off – you have fun.

My philosophy – my management style, I suppose – is that fun is something that shouldn't be taken lightly. It's a force to be reckoned with. It's something to be harnessed. It's energy and focus. Take, for instance, an old, long-established business – something that's gone on for generations and generations, that has met with great success in the past, but that, for reasons that aren't perfectly obvious, has run out of steam. You could look for all kinds of complicated explanations for this – a changing economy, changing demographics, a change in consumer spending patterns – but I think the real explanation of this kind of a failure is often disarmingly simple: The people running the business just aren't having fun any more. By contrast, companies that are growing by leaps and bounds, that are steam-rolling their competitors, that are roaring from success to success, are doing so not because they have some magic formula for blue jeans or computer software, or because they've lucked out in the marketplace. They're winning because, from their executive suites to their mailrooms, they're bursting with people who are having a whole lot of fun working together toward the company's success.

Throughout the 1970s and 1980s, when Ed Garber, Ron Cohen, Ron Marcoux, George Mencke, and an ever-growing officer group and top management team, and I were establishing McDonald's in Canada – when, between 1973 and 1990, we were expanding at an average rate of about twenty-five restaurants a year – if we hadn't been having fun, I don't think we would have found the energy to do what needed to be done. I travelled from coast to coast. I met with more civic politicians, discussed deals with more landlords, attended more conventions of franchisees, talked with more crews than now seems possible. Looking back, I'm astonished at the pace of our growth. I'm astonished at the pace of my life. During those years, energy was a basic requirement of the job.

It sounds strange, perhaps, but I think that what Ray Kroc sensed when he suggested I leave my career in law and start a career with McDonald's was that I was not a person who would have a lot of fun as a lawyer. He had always followed his own instincts and enthusiasms – his own dedicated and focused sense of fun – and he knew that risk was always part of that pursuit. He sensed that I, too, was a risk taker, and he guessed that I was a person who would have a lot of fun running with the McDonald's ball in Canada. He must have also sensed that I was the kind of person for whom having fun was a serious matter. And he was right. I don't think there's anything that I do – my family life, my work in Canada, my work in Russia, my involvement with charitable organizations – that doesn't give me a real kick. I get up early most mornings, not because I have to, or because I feel obliged to, or because someone is telling me to, or because if I don't I'm afraid my world is going to come crashing down around me. I get up and get going – whether my agenda is opening a new restaurant in Russia, or meeting with Rick Hansen in Vancouver or Dmitrii Shparo in Moscow, or helping to build a new YMCA in Toronto, or attending an Israel Bond dinner with Susan in New York, or flying to Montreal for a Royal Bank board of directors' meeting, or sitting on Northwestern University's board of governors, or just going to the office in Toronto – because I can't imagine anything I'd rather be doing.

Here's an example of what I mean. At McDonald's we take the successes of each of our restaurants very seriously. We review sales figures daily. We offer owner-operators and managers advice and ongoing training. (In Canada, 65 per cent of our restaurants are run by independent owner-operators; the others are company-owned, operated by people who have worked their way up from crew, to assistant manager, to manager.) We recommend equipment upgrades that we think will be useful. We remain in constant contact, and we try to ensure that the relationship between the company and the franchisees is strong and productive. We visit our restaurants often and we insist that they attend religiously to our credo – Quality, Service, Cleanliness, and Value. And if a restaurant is not doing as well as we think it should be, we do whatever we can to help get it back on track. Our independent owner-operators pay a service fee to the company, and for that fee we provide all the back-up, all the expertise, and all the cost advantages that come with the kinds of volumes in which we deal. In short, we provide these individual entrepreneurs with the power of the system. We do whatever we can to help them please the customer and thereby increase their market share.

It's a serious matter – but not, necessarily, a solemn one. Our company is made up of all kinds of competitive people – that's the kind of person attracted to an organization such as ours – and so, naturally, there's all kinds of good-natured internal rivalry. The Golden Arch Award is presented every second year to the top licensee. The Best Bets Award is presented for achievements in marketing. There are awards for community relations and for best crew. The President's Award is given to top employees.

This competition is part of what drives us. It's part of what makes what we do so much fun. And there is no rivalry that's ever given me quite as big a charge as the one between me, in Canada, and Den Fujita in Japan.

I got to know Fujita at the regular McDonald's Worldwide owner-operator meetings. McDonald's opened in Japan in 1971 – just about the time we were getting our feet on the ground in Canada. We had sixty-three stores across the country by then, with annual sales of about $18.5 million – I was on the road a lot in those days. I suppose Fujita and I were drawn to one another because we were both going through much the same thing – starting from square one.

Fujita is a good-looking, muscular man – hard-working and fiercely proud of his Japanese heritage. I liked him immediately, and recognized almost as quickly that he was an extremely competitive guy. Takes one to know one, I guess.

At the McDonald's meetings, we started kidding one another. "Cohon-san," he would say, "is not as strong as Fujita-san. McDonald's in Canada is not as good as McDonald's in Japan." That kind of thing.

This banter escalated, and – with two very competitive characters involved in the bantering – it kept escalating. Soon we were making speeches at the Worldwide meetings, debating constantly with one another. We began exchanging letters: How does the average restaurant in Japan stack up against the average restaurant in Canada? It became a running feud.

In fact, what was interesting about our ongoing battle was that it used information, and had fun with information, that in a strictly business sense we took very seriously indeed. We were both in the process of establishing our organizations and trying to analyze our strengths and weaknesses – and our arguments with one another focused on this. We were kidding one another in one sense; in another we were assessing ourselves, holding our operations up and looking at them from different angles. If I said our average volume was higher, he'd say he had more customers, and that, in the long run, it was numbers of customers that counted. I'd say no: If you were running an operation in which a too small number of choices was holding back sales volumes, you weren't really doing your job. You weren't giving the customers what they wanted. Of course, Fujita would come back with a counter-counter-argument.

This debate was fun, but it happened also to be the kind of thinking we were doing all the time during the time of our company's initial growth. What did this statistic reveal about what we are doing? What consumer pattern was apparent in these figures? What lessons could we draw from the failure of products such as Mini-Macs and McDLT? Or from the successes of Chicken McNuggets or McDonald's Breakfast? We analyzed everything, because we wanted to understand the implications of everything we were doing. Fujita was doing the same in Japan. We both wanted to learn how to do things better.

Then Fujita and I started betting one another. Bets that, like our arguments, were never really resolved. Fujita wrote to me in 1986 – the year, incidentally, in which our total Canadian sales topped $1 billion. "Cohon-san. You have 508 restaurants. It is my duty to tell you that we now have 509. Finally we have passed you. Please accept my condolences."

But of course I wrote back: "Fujita-san. Yes, but your sales are nowhere near ours, and so I offer my sympathies to you on the occasion of this terrible embarrassment."

"Cohon-san. You have not taken into account the weaknesses in the yen in your calculations of our performance."

"Fujita-san. Have you checked out the Canadian dollar recently? Don't talk to me about weaknesses."

Then, of course, Japan really did pass us. It has a much bigger population. It's a much bigger market. "Cohon-san. We have more restaurants. We have greater sales. You are defeated."

"Fujita-san. Ah yes. But our average customer spends more than your average customer."

Around and around we went. An endless game of one-upmanship – one that was often played out with flamboyant speeches and presentations at McDonald's Worldwide meetings. Neither one of us ever actually won or lost the various bets, but in the end Fujita sent me an absolutely beautiful antique statue of an ancient Japanese warrior as a kind of acknowledgment of our epic struggle. The statue, which curators at the Royal Ontario

Museum tell me is of museum quality, sits in a place of honour at our country house.

Of course – our relationship being what it was – I had to send him something that was as unusual as his gift, and as Canadian as his was Japanese. Even when it comes to gift-giving, my competitive instincts never quite leave me.

But Fujita had snookered me; it was difficult to compete with such a rare and beautiful object. I racked my brains, until one day I happened to hear somebody talking about the buffalo coats that the RCMP used to wear in Western Canada. They are unbelievably heavy. When a Mountie put one on, his horse must have thought that it had two riders on its back. I thought, who else in Japan would have an RCMP buffalo coat? Who else would be able to say, "This is what the famous, world-renowned Mounties wore when they were tracking down bad guys through the howling blizzards of the prairies"? It would be unique – as was his gift to me. And so, like an RCMP investigator myself, I tracked down one of these coats. It wasn't easy, but I found one, and I sent it to him. He was suitably amazed. We declared a truce. And now, whenever I tell curious guests at our country house the story of Fujita's statue, I smile. I imagine him, at home on the outskirts of Tokyo, telling his curious guests about the massive coat on display there.

Even when I think we're starting to get solemn, I inevitably get my balloon popped. I'm not the only one in the company who thinks fun and business are a good mix.

Here's an example of what I mean. Not long after we'd settled in to our new headquarters in Toronto, everyone was called down to the lobby for some kind of presentation. I didn't know what was going on. We all gathered in front of a mysterious-looking object that was draped with a cloth. Ed Garber gave what, for Ed, was a very serious – I might say, almost solemn – speech about the new building. He pointed out – graciously – that he, along with Ron Cohen, George Mencke, and Ron Marcoux, had been opposed to the idea of the new building, while I had been in favour. But that now that it was completed, they were thrilled with it. I was touched by this, because we'd had some real fireworks over this issue. Against almost everyone's advice (including Fred Turner's), I chose the city over the suburbs for the site. Against the same array of advice, I'd gone ahead and installed a 124-seat auditorium in our new headquarters for meetings with owner-operators, suppliers, and our regional offices, as well as for charity events.

But these battles were behind us. And now, with everyone gathered in the new lobby, Ed unveiled an absolutely beautiful bust of me. It appeared to be bronze. It was an excellent likeness – and it was one of those dignified pieces of statuary that are normally reserved for great statesmen, soldiers, or heroes. It had a rather comic inscription – "The only man among us who would like to die in his own arms" – but even so, it was solid and impressive. It was magnificent. Ed announced that it would always have a place of honour in the front lobby, and as he did I stepped forward. There's something about seeing your own bust that can't help but puff you up a little. You feel that you are in pretty good company once you become a statue. I was giving the ego a bit of a gallop. I was trying to stop myself from thinking: Julius Caesar, Napoleon, Winston Churchill. However, I was thinking: See, they're admitting that I was right about the building, about the site, about the auditorium.

And then Ed, concluding his speech, made a grand, sweeping gesture toward the bust as he presented it to me.

A little too grand. A little too sweeping. He hit the bust with the back of his hand. It flew off its stand.

I rushed forward to catch it. I was seeing my immortality going for a nose-dive before my eyes.

It smashed into a thousand pieces on the floor. My expression must have looked just as broken up. And then, an odd thing. Instead of a gasp of horror and dismay from the crowd, I heard a huge burst of laughter.

I looked down at my shattered head and shoulders. My ego lay in ruins at my feet. The bust had been made of plaster, painted to look like bronze.

They got me.

It was a hilarious moment – and I had to admit, later, once my ego had recovered from the blow, that the idea of a bust of me in the front lobby of our building ran counter to something I've always believed in. It's part of my management philosophy. It's something Ray Kroc always used to say: "None of us is as good as all of us."

You'll often hear people within the company refer to McDonald's as their McFamily, and although some outsiders might find the notion corny, it's true. Recently, I was having lunch in one of our Toronto restaurants, and I ended up chatting with a young first assistant manager named Tony Pinto. It wasn't the quietest conversation I've ever had. I'd gone into the play area to look at some of the new equipment our restaurants were using, and there was a birthday party in full swing. Our play areas were introduced in Chula Vista, California, in 1971. In Canada, we began installing them in 1978. They've evolved over the years – from outdoor, to covered, to covered with seating. They've been a huge hit; their presence usually substantially increases a restaurant's volume.

Tony came over to say hello. We'd met before. He's been with McDonald's since 1982. I asked him about his relationship with the company, and, as we stood there, I was really taken with his observations. I said, "Would you do me a favour?"

"Sure, Mr. Cohon."

"George. Please. Call me George."

"Okay. Sure, George."

I think he was expecting me to ask him to get me my lunch or something – although I never like to do that. I much prefer lining up at the counter like everyone else. And whenever I visit one of our restaurants, I always insist on paying for my meal. I go to be a customer, not a head office big-wig.

I said to Tony, "Would you mind putting some of these thoughts down on paper?"

"Sure," Tony said. He looked a little apprehensive. "Why?"

"Well, I'm working on a book . . ."

Tony gave me the politely skeptical, slightly askew look that people often seemed to give me when I brought this subject up. "You're working on a what?" As if they somehow don't picture me as a literary type.

"A book – about me, and about McDonald's. And I think in these kinds of books – you know, business autobiographies – there's a tendency for big executives to get all hung up on big executive-type things. You know: this deal, that big wheel, this enormous sum of money. But I don't think McDonald's is about big executive-type things."

Tony looked around. We were surrounded by a dozen noisy, happy kids. Behind us, at the counter, the lunch rush was on. He said, "I guess it's about places like this."

"That's why I thought it might be interesting to hear from someone like you in the book."

"You're going to put me in your book?"

"Why not?"

A week later, Tony's letter arrived on my desk. "I am here today," he wrote, "still working for McDonald's for two reasons. First – it's fun; the people I work with make it so. Second – there are no dead-end levels in our company, just many doors to open with many different opportunities." He went on for four pages, concluding: "It seems to me that at McDonald's we are always challenging one another as if almost in a competitive sport. Who can serve the most customers in one hour? What restaurant can raise the most money for Ronald McDonald Children's Charities every McHappy Day? These are prime examples of how the competitive spirit within us brings McDonald's crews and managers together. It is these people that push our company forward and keep it strong. I'm proud to be part of it all."

And here's another example of McFamily. Some years ago, Gary Reinblatt, our senior vice president of marketing, had a bad accident while skiing at Whistler in British Columbia. He took a terrible fall and suffered a serious spinal cord injury. He was in really bad shape. This sort of thing had never happened to us before. What should we do? There were two sides to my thinking at the time. One – let me call it the traditional corporate approach – was: Find out how much will be covered by insurance and then, within that range, do what you can. The other side – the side that easily won my little internal debate, I'm happy to say – was: Forget what is and what isn't covered by insurance, charter a plane, fly him back, get him into the best hospital, with the best doctors, look after him. Do whatever – *whatever* – you can to help.

Why? Because we're a big company. Because we can afford it. Because he's one of our people. Gary is now a motivational speaker. He drives his own car. He has even returned to skiing – even though his doctors originally predicted that he would never be able to do much more than shrug one of his shoulders. His courageous efforts are something of which we all are very proud.

That's why I try, within McDonald's, to avoid the expression "working *for*" someone. I try always to say, "So-and-so works *with* so-and-so." And this isn't just a bit of corporate gobbledegook. I call it controlled casualness. Meaning that you can leave funny messages on your voice mail; you can pull all kinds of office pranks; you can call your boss by his or her first name; you can even laugh uproariously when the bust of your esteemed president is shattered all over the floor – so long as, at the end of the day, McDonald's customers come out on top.

If you are the head of a company, you shouldn't need to have everyone kow-towing to you, and yes-sirring this and no-sirring that. You should have the inner strength that allows you to deal directly with people. So, if someone is not doing his job, you are able to sit down and talk to him about it – directly, no hidden agenda, no power trips, no secrets. This kind of open communication is more like a friendship than like the traditional employer–employee relationship – the sort of understanding that means you can give praise when praise is due, and offer constructive criticism when that's what's needed. (Or, if the situation requires, blow your stack.) In other words, act like a human being – not a creation of a management consulting firm. This is something that's really special, and this is why when someone leaves McDonald's and goes to one of our competitors – something that happens rarely, I'm happy to say – I don't take it personally. I take it very personally.

I'm talking about a direct approach, and I suppose you'd have to say that directness is another aspect of my management philosophy. I like to take things head on.

Recently, at the Sunshine Games at Variety Village, I met Chris Delaney, a twenty-four-year-old, blind cyclist. He's a terrific guy, with crew-cut blond hair and movie-star good looks. Solid muscle. And he plans to ride a tandem bicycle across Canada with a sighted partner to raise money for RP Research Foundation-Fighting Blindness.

It was a bright, beautiful Sunday morning. Scarborough's Variety Village was packed with competitors, and spectators, and Canadian celebrities such as broadcaster Dan Matheson, skating champion Elvis Stojko, and Olympic cyclist Curt Harnett. The Sunshine Games are an annual fundraising event for Variety Village, and companies such as Astral Communications, the Royal Bank, Vickers & Benson, H&K Canada, Caravelle Foods, Lily Cups, Nestlé Canada, Shoppers Drug Mart, and Sears Canada pitch in. It's always a really special day. I love it – it seems to me a shining example of the corporate world putting something really meaningful back into the community.

I was standing a few feet away from a boisterous wheelchair basketball game when someone called me over to meet Chris Delaney. We shook hands. And the first thing I wanted to know – the very first thing – was how much he could see. Could he see my hand? Could he make out that figure a few feet away? Some people might have avoided such questions. Or they might have thought that they should be raised only after a while – after some kind of rapport had been established. But I wanted to know. I'm curious by nature. And my curiosity turned out to be the vehicle that established our rapport. We had a great conversation about the biggest challenge he faces: He was born with vision, but a degenerative disease is steadily stealing his eyesight. Eventually this wonderful, good-looking, athletic kid will be totally blind.

Instead of a meaningless exchange of pleasantries, I felt as if I'd really got to know Chris. I learned something – which, I think, is always the point of talking to someone. That's why, in meetings, I always want to get to the heart of whatever matter is under discussion. That's why in restaurants, I don't only want to know how the manager thinks things are going – but also how the crew thinks things are going, and, most important, how the customer thinks things are going. "How are you enjoying the meal?" "What do you think of our pizza?" "How do you like the restaurant?" – these are the kinds of questions I ask people – complete strangers – I find sitting, eating, in McDonald's.

Not long ago we were trying out a new lid on our soft drinks and milkshakes. I had dropped in on one of our restaurants just outside of Toronto, and I wanted to know how the lids were working out. I asked the manager. I asked the crew. I tried the lid machine myself. And then, customers were surprised to find me poking my head out the drive-thru window. "Hi. I'm George Cohon. I work at McDonald's, and I'd be really interested in hearing what you think of these new lids we're trying out."

The McDonald's system is designed to put as few steps as possible between product and customer. We want our food to be good, but we also want it to be fresh and hot and to get to the counter as quickly as possible.

It seems to me that business executives often take precisely the opposite approach. They like to put as many intermediaries as possible between themselves and the public: publicists, spin doctors, advisors, consultants, strategists, spokespeople. I think this is a mistake. Once at an executive meeting of McDonald's-Canada, we were listening to a presentation from a consultant we had hired. He was very high-powered, very high-tech, very expensive, but as we sat listening to him, I looked around the room. There was Ed Garber. There was Ron Cohen. There was George Mencke – and there were all twenty of the McDonald's-Canada officer group. It occurred to me that they were the experts, they were the ones who knew our business from the ground up. They were the ones with ketchup in their blood. What did this guy know that we didn't? I couldn't contain myself. "Why should we listen to you?" I asked. "You're just another consultant."

He looked a little bit surprised, to say the least.

You have to talk directly to people – whether they are the people with whom you are working or the clients you are serving. You have to stick your head out the drive-thru window and hear what people have to say.

There are questions that people often ask about McDonald's policy, and I'm not in the least shy about answering them. Environmental concerns, for instance. From school children to environmental activists to politicians – I'm always pleased to make our case directly to them. Once, at a meeting of the World Wildlife Fund – an organization I happen to support – H.R.H. The Duke of Edinburgh gave me a rough ride on environmental issues. I don't mind being given a rough ride, if I think we deserve it. That's how we learn. You don't ask people what they think about McDonald's if you're not prepared to listen to what they have to say. If a customer tells me that a washroom is dirty or that his french fries were served cold, I take the criticism as legitimate and try to do something about it. The same is true when it comes to big issues – issues such as recycling, or packaging. We've listened to our critics, to our customers, and to the concerns raised by experts. In the 1980s, when damage to the ozone layer first became an important environmental issue, McDonald's took the industry lead by instructing our packaging suppliers to begin a prompt phase-out of the use of CFCs in the manufacture of foamed polystyrene food containers. In 1990, we switched to paper wraps and phased out all polystyrene clamshell packaging. Today, McDonald's is the largest user of recycled paper in its industry: All tray liners, french fry, hash brown, and pie boxes, serviettes, and drink holders incorporate recycled paper. Carry-out bags are made with 100 per cent recycled content.

On the environmental front, our industry, like most industries, still has a way to go. Of course, I'm concerned about the quality of life of future generations. Energy conservation, waste reduction, and new, even more environmentally friendly forms of packaging remain priorities for us. But I'm proud of our achievements, and I'm proud of our policies. Sam Joseph, a McDonald's vice president, is our point man on environmental affairs, and he takes his responsibilities very seriously – as do we all. We don't for a second think of environmentalists as being a force we work against. They voice their concerns loud and clear – that's what they're supposed to do. I hope they keep doing it. We've learned from them – as have our customers, as have governments – and, in many key areas, we've responded to the issues they have raised.

In the case of Prince Philip, however, I felt his criticisms were based on misinformation. And I could see no reason to be shy about pointing that out.

The way it happened was this: I got a call one day from Sonja Bata. She was the head, in Canada, of the World Wildlife Fund, and she was organizing a big fundraising dinner. She said that Prince Philip, who is the international head of the World Wildlife Fund, was going to attend.

It's a cause I believe in, and so I bought a table – a $10,000 table, but it was money well spent. According to its mandate, the World Wildlife Fund is dedicated to preserving genetic, species, and ecosystem diversity; ensuring that the use of renewable and natural resources is sustainable both now and in the longer term. It also promotes actions to reduce pollution and the consumption of resources and energy. At the time of the dinner, a United States senator, Senator Larry Pressler of South Dakota, was in town. I knew him through a McDonald's owner-operator in his state. Senator Pressler is a very bright guy, a Rhodes Scholar. I invited him to go to the dinner with me. It isn't every day you can say to someone – even to a senator – "Come and meet Prince Philip."

He wasn't travelling with a tuxedo, and so we went over to Yonge Street, the senator and I, and rented him one. And off we went to the dinner. At one point, Sonja Bata brought Prince Philip over to where Susan and I were standing with Senator Pressler. Sonja said, "This is George Cohon of McDonald's."

Prince Philip looked at me with an expression that made it pretty clear which one of us was royalty and which one the commoner. He sniffed, "McDonald's?"

"Yes, uh, your Highness."

"The hamburger people?"

"Well, the french fries are very good, too."

He wasn't in the mood for jokes. He said, "You people are destroying the rainforests of the world by grazing your cheap cattle. You're cutting down trees to graze your cheap cattle to sell your hamburgers."

You can read etiquette books and you can attend comportment classes from here until doomsday and no-one will tell you what to do when the Queen of England's husband accuses you of destroying one of the earth's most precious and important natural resources. His tone was venomous. His voice was a real snarl. I didn't know what to say. So I tried to dodge the bullet. I introduced him to Susan and Senator Pressler.

"How do you do," he said curtly. He gave them both brief nods. And then he returned to me. "You are destroying the rainforests of the world."

I said, "With all due respect, we are not remotely involved in the depletion of the rainforests anywhere in the world. We don't have cattle that graze in rainforests. We don't cut down trees in rainforests."

Prince Philip looked me straight in the eye. "Rubbish," he said. And stormed off.

I was a little shaken. Bewildered. I looked over to Pressler for guidance. After all, he was a U.S. senator. Perhaps he'd understand the nuances and the implications of this kind of situation. He'd probably have a pretty accurate reading.

He said, "A bit of a flake, isn't he, George?"

Later, Tom Bata was working the room with the Prince, and he approached us. "I'd like to introduce George Cohon," Tom said.

The Prince cast a cold eye in my direction. If looks could kill, I'd be six feet under. "We've met," he said.

"Yes," I told Tom, who was trying to figure out why the temperature had dropped so suddenly. "Yes, we had a nice chat."

It was quite an evening.

Still, the accusation got under my skin. This rumour was really starting to haunt us – even though it was only that: a rumour. To this day, many McDonald's offices all over the world still get letters about the rainforest. The subject came up – yet again – at a celebrated libel trial in Britain. And just in case it needed to be said one more time, the judge ruled that claims that McDonald's was involved in the destruction of the rainforest were completely unfounded.

I had no idea where Prince Philip was getting his information; I did know, however, that it was wrong. Absolutely wrong. I also knew that this kind of rumour, however false, was insidious. These things take on a life of their own, however much the facts argue against them. When I told Fred Turner about my encounter with the Prince he was adamant that we correct him. He said, "You've got to get to the bottom of this."

So, I got some people on the case, and they were able to trace the rumour to a British academic. Dr. Norman Myers had written a paper in the environmental journal *Ambio* about cattle grazing on land that had once been rainforest, and in his paper he had simply made the assumption – the incorrect assumption – that since McDonald's is the largest buyer of beef in the world, McDonald's must be cutting down the trees in the rainforest.

I learned that Myers was soon going to be presented with an award in Switzerland from the World Wildlife Fund for his research. I felt that most of his research was important and deserved to be honoured. It was just his mistake about McDonald's that I wanted to correct. He was going to make an acceptance speech at the presentation. And so, I sent him a registered letter, documenting our company's policy and environmental record, and pointing out his error – and in his speech, at the WWF dinner, he did, in fact, say that he had made an incorrect assumption about our company.

I then wrote Prince Philip a respectful, but carefully documented letter. I told him about Myers's error. I clearly stated McDonald's environmental policy. And I included letters from governments around the world attesting to the fact that McDonald's was playing no role in the destruction of the rainforests.

I told him that the preservation of tropical rainforest land is a real concern at McDonald's. McDonald's does not purchase, and has never purchased, beef grown on cleared rainforest land. I pointed out that McDonald's carefully checks the quality and origin of all the beef it purchases. And, everywhere in the world, our suppliers must document that McDonald's products are not derived from rainforest land. This policy is closely monitored and strictly enforced.

I did, eventually, get a letter back. It was not exactly a retraction. But it was, I think, about as close to one as princes ever give.

"I was interested," the Prince wrote, "to read your letter about cattle ranching in Central America. I don't remember accusing McDonald's of being responsible for converting forest into grazing. My recollection is that I mentioned that I had heard a story that cattle raised on those ranches were being used to make hamburgers in the United States. . . . Anyway, as you have now heard from Mrs. Bata, Myers has made it publicly clear at a dinner in Switzerland that McDonald's is exonerated."

I'd come a long way from "Rubbish!"

Another issue is unions. People often ask me about unions, and they're usually surprised that I'm happy to talk. It's my nature to talk, to argue, to debate. It's my nature to engage in dialogue. If I see the well-known Canadian labour leader Bob White in an airport – as I do from time to time – we don't glare at one another from opposite sides of the departure lounge. We don't pretend we haven't seen one another. We inhabit different ends of the political spectrum, but we sit down and chat.

Sometimes Bob even invites me to come up and sit with him in first class. (Just kidding.)

Ray Kroc had a theory – one that has been followed by Fred Turner and now by Mike Quinlan – that if we treat our people fairly and continue to treat them fairly, there is no need for a union. I absolutely agree. People often accuse me of being anti-union on principle. I'm not. I just happen to be of the opinion – of the firm conviction – that a union at McDonald's would answer no need and would only complicate things. It would be a fifth wheel. It would, I believe, clutter what an employee such as Tony Pinto calls the many doors to opportunities that McDonald's endeavours to keep open to its employees. When I talk to crew members about their potential for advancement in the system as it exists, I always point out that Fred Turner started on the grill and Mike Quinlan's first job was in the mailroom. Fred and Mike rose to the very top of the company, and to come up through the ranks at McDonald's is by no means an uncommon story.

In short, I believe that a union is not necessary for our employees. And in an organization such as ours, if something is unnecessary it's not a neutral presence. It's counter-productive.

But when people accuse me of being philosophically opposed to the very existence of unions, I usually tell them of the time I served as chairman of the board of the Ontario Science Centre. At that time, the Centre was facing some really serious labour problems, and so I felt that it would make sense to have an Ontario Public Service Employees Union leader attend and have input at the meetings of the board of directors. This struck many of my fellow directors as unorthodox, but I pushed the idea through. It helped establish some strong and clear lines of communication between management and labour. It helped to avoid a completely disruptive dispute. And, when I left the board, the union presented me with an OPSEU windbreaker and a hat and made me an honorary member of the local. I was touched by this. I'm proud of the jacket and hat. I had them framed. I have them hanging on a wall in my office – a display of solidarity that always surprises my more conservative visitors.

Or, I tell people about my time on the board of directors at the Canada Post Corporation. I served from 1981 to 1984, and if you wanted a real hotbed of labour–management conflict, this was the time and the place to find it. But in 1987, a writer named David Stewart-Patterson published a book called *Post Mortem: Why Canada's Mail Won't Move*. One of the quotes in the book is from Ron Lang, a representative of the Canadian Labour Congress and a fellow Canada Post board member. You'd think that Lang, a committed union man and a rock-solid left-winger, would have nothing good to say about someone who is philosophically opposed to most of his positions. But here's what Lang had to say about me: "You can say what you want about George

Cohon – he wants to operate union-free, but the son of a bitch, when it comes down to a vote, what he thinks is right and what he thinks is wrong, he'll drop down on the right side, the one with a bit of social conscience." Lang went on to say that Derek Oland, the president of Moosehead Breweries Ltd. and a fellow Canada Post board member, and I were "two good, competent, solid people, who said what they thought and many times voted with me against the rest of the board."

Naturally, I like the quotes. But the part that I like best is the bit about Derek and me saying what we think. This returns me to the idea of being direct, of going straight down the middle on things instead of zig-zagging this way and that in order to accommodate the sophisticated strategies of spin doctors and advisors. For instance: recently, in Russia, I noticed that each of the umbrellas – beautiful, bright attention-getters – on the patios outside our restaurants had six panels of white Coca-Cola logos and only two McDonald's. In fact, the Coke logo was entirely dominant, and, as big a fan as I am of Coke, these were *our* restaurants. The umbrellas were the first thing people saw as they approached, and Coca-Cola, not McDonald's, was the brand that jumped out at them.

I didn't like it. I made sure that everyone knew I didn't like it. I spoke directly to the issue. I was told that Coke had covered three-quarters of the cost of the umbrellas. I thought it was too good a deal for them, and not good enough for us. To put it mildly (which I didn't), I was extremely vocal on the subject.

In the same way, I felt an obligation to speak my mind when I was sitting on the public policy committee of the Royal Bank board of directors. When I was giving speeches, people would see my bank directorship and question me about bank profits. In recent years Canadian banks have earned substantial profits.

They've broken the $1 billion mark, and, as a result, they have also earned spectacular headlines.

Historically, banks have always reacted defensively to these kinds of announcements. Consumer groups would be all over them, complaining that the profits were obscene, that interest rates were too high, that the cost of using a Visa card was too great.

So, when people questioned me, I took an active approach. I told them how much the Royal Bank pays in taxes. How many people it employs. How many shareholders it has, and how much they profit when the bank's profits go up. I told them what the Royal Bank does to help small businesses. And I told them about how much the Royal Bank gives to charity.

This information, it seemed to me, reflected well on the bank. Often, people were surprised. They had no idea, for instance, that the Royal Bank gives more than $17 million a year to charity. The Royal is the single largest corporate donor in the country.

I thought the bank should take a more active approach to these kinds of questions. I'd say to my fellow directors, "Look. You're a great success story. You're a great corporate citizen. Tell people directly what you do. Don't be defensive about doing well. Don't wait for your critics to come to you." Fortunately, the top management held the same view, and the Royal Bank now favours a more active approach.

It is possible to teach people how to be direct. As a management "style," the direct approach has obvious strengths. It means that you respond quickly to issues, and in a business as competitive as ours, a quick response has obvious dividends. It means that colleagues and employees trust you; they don't have to work in an environment where things are not out in the open, and where, instead of focusing on policies that are best for the company, they waste time and energy trying to second-guess their bosses and one another. I have found that if a company's executive is secretive and equivocal, a pattern is set that often runs throughout the organization. The reverse is true at McDonald's: People speak their minds because I tend to be forthright. And the entire officer group tends to be *very* forthright – which can sometimes be a little painful, especially when it comes to telling me that I'm wrong.

However – a very big however – being direct has a single, all-important requirement. This is not something, I'm afraid, that can be taught in business schools. If you're going to be direct – with colleagues, with business associates, with employees, or with friends and family – your direction has to come from somewhere.

Earlier in this book, I called this "street smarts" – and, in a business context, that's as accurate a description as any. Throughout the 1970s and 1980s, as we were establishing McDonald's in Canada, it was the most valuable tool I had. There was no standard procedure on how to do what we were doing – no-one knew what the best sites were, who the best suppliers were, what the most popular products would be – and so we had to find our own way. There was little to guide us other than gut reactions, hunches, and intuition. In an even more dramatic way, this was how things were in Russia, of course. But they were also how things were when I was a kid on the South Side of Chicago. I had to learn how to assess a situation quickly – were the two big Irish kids crossing the street toward me friends or enemies, and, with both as distinct possibilities, what options were open to me?

In business I have often had to size situations up in much the same way. I've had to learn who to trust and who not to, using the same intuitive approach. It sounds unsophisticated and not at all the sort of thing that can be taught at business school, but in many instances – with a good deal of money on the line – my analysis of people was really not much more than simply sizing them up. Were they players? Were they honest? Were they dedicated to their job, to their product, to their brand? If we closed a deal on a handshake, would the agreement hold?

In broader terms, "street smarts" could be described as simply knowing yourself. Knowing yourself well enough to have faith in your reactions to situations and to people. It could be called the ability to trust your instincts. Here's an example.

Throughout the latter half of the 1970s, during the period when we were negotiating with the Moscow Olympic Committee, we were using the Paris branch of the Law Offices of Samuel Pisar for our legal advice. We worked with a lawyer named John Huhs, and by the early 1980s, as our negotiations with the Soviets continued, it was pretty clear that we were destined to become one of the Pisar firm's major clients. From our side, it was also pretty clear that our lawyer's role in our discussions with the Soviets and our proposals to various government agencies was absolutely critical. I never doubted that, in the very tricky game we were playing, our lawyer was pivotal. All our moves, in one way or another, keyed off him.

As it happened, Susan and I were in Paris in the early 1980s. McDonald's had, by then, been clients of the Pisar firm for six or seven years – there were times when I was on the phone to John Huhs daily – and so, naturally, I felt our association was a close one.

One evening, during our trip to Paris, Susan and I were invited to the house of the senior partner. Sam Pisar and his wife lived on Avenue Foch in an exclusive part of Paris. I was looking forward to getting to know the head of the firm better, and to solidifying our relationship. I felt we both had a lot invested in one another, and thought that it was a good idea to broaden things from a purely business, to a social basis, and perhaps to friendship.

Trust and understanding are everything in associations as important as the one we had.

But, when Susan and I arrived, we discovered that the Pisars were getting ready for some black-tie society event that evening. We were left on our own; the houseboy brought us drinks. Before they rushed off to their gala, they did manage to spend a little time with us – but we did not feel exactly welcomed. We had, obviously, been squeezed into their social calendar. We were an afterthought. They said goodbye, and hurried off.

When Susan and I got back into our car, I turned to her and said, "Well, you just met our ex-lawyer."

Perhaps I over-reacted. But I don't think so. The Soviet Union was not a sideline for me – I had a lot riding on our negotiations. And my instincts told me that the kind of offhand reception Susan and I were given did not confirm the kind of relationship I felt I needed with so important an associate. So, we changed law firms – almost immediately. A lawyer named Jeffrey Hertzfeld had left Pisar's firm and had become a senior partner in Salans Hertzfeld & Heilbronn in Paris. Jeff had the kind of commitment and energy I was looking for, and he quickly became an irreplaceable member of the Wolf Pack. He played a crucial role in our negotiations throughout the 1980s, in the finalization of our deal with the Moscow City Government, and he continues as a key figure in our ongoing expansion in Russia.

The decision to leave Pisar and go with Jeff was a gut reaction – some people might say an irrational one. In a way it was – it just felt right. But I put a good deal of stock in things feeling right.

When I look back on the all-important years of the 1970s and early 1980s – the years when our sons were growing up, when we were establishing friendships and associations in Toronto and across Canada, when Susan was devoting herself to volunteer work for Mount Sinai Hospital and the Canadian Cancer Society, and when the company was really being firmly established – I'm amazed by how often we did things simply because something – an instinct, a hunch, a faith – told us it was the right thing to do. This was the reason why, in 1975, I became a Canadian citizen: because it felt right to me. At a purely rational level it was a difficult decision. I'd grown up in the States, we had friends and family there. So I had to trust my instincts, and my instincts told me that it was important for me to be an active participant in the life of my adopted country. My instincts were correct: It was difficult for me to renounce my American citizenship, but it was a proud moment for me when I became a Canadian. When I came home that day and met Susan (who had retained her U.S. citizenship), I said, "Now look. If there's one thing we Canadians don't want, it's having you Americans give us any sh— !"

It was just as proud a moment when, in 1987, I was invested as a Member of the Order of Canada. Prouder still when, in 1992, I was elevated to the rank of Officer of the Order of Canada.

Because it felt like the right thing to do. This was the reason Susan and I devoted ourselves so whole-heartedly to raising funds for Israel during the 1973 war. For ten days of fundraising, we opened our house to friends, colleagues, associates. Jews and non-Jews rallied to the cause and invested in Israel by buying Israel Bonds in the country's hour of need. One evening, we met by our pool, and I was going around the table, from person to person, getting their thoughts on what we could do or on what kind of commitment they were willing to make. There was one gentleman there whom I didn't know, and when I came to him, I said, "And, sir?"

In a quiet voice, scarcely above a whisper, he stated a number.

A seven-figure number. That, so he said, was the value of the bonds he would purchase.

I said, "I don't think we've met."

Again, the voice was barely audible. "Albert Reichmann. Olympia and York."

"I'm pleased to meet you."

Susan and I could have given just some money and left it at that. But throwing ourselves into fundraising felt like the right thing to do. And so we did. $22 million was raised, which was wonderful, but it also re-affirmed for us what by then we knew: that in Toronto we had found a warm and generous community. We had found a place that really was our home.

The right thing to do. This was the reason McDonald's got behind Rick Hansen and his 1985–87 Man in Motion tour. Ron Marcoux met Rick in Vancouver, and, although the idea of going around the world in a wheelchair to raise money for people with spinal-cord injuries seemed almost unbelievably ambitious, Ron just felt that Rick was someone special. I remember when he called me, he said, "I don't know, George. I know it sounds crazy, but there's just something about this guy. I think he's going to do it." And when I finally met Rick Hansen in 1987, I knew that Ron's hunch had been right. It was the year of our twentieth anniversary, and to mark the occasion McDonald's raised $1.5 million for the Man in Motion tour. Rick had gone around the world, and when he arrived back in Canada, Susan, Craig, Mark, and I were in Newfoundland to greet him. When he was passing through Ontario, Craig, Mark, and I went up north and bicycled beside him on the Trans-Canada Highway for a day. To me, Rick Hansen is one of our country's true heroes.

Recently, I asked my son Mark about this idea – about trusting your instincts – and he reminded me of what, in our family, we call Roots and Wings. If you have the roots, if you know your basic principles, then you can act on them; you can spread your wings and take flight. We have taught our sons, as our parents taught us, that you can fly as high as you want, but never forget your roots.

Mark has always been passionate in his beliefs and commitments. When he was a student at Northwestern, he led a group of able-bodied students in wheelchairs around the campus to highlight the lack of facilities for students with disabilities. Within a year, enough money was raised to turn one of the university's main lecture halls into a wheelchair-friendly building.

In 1989, when he was in his third year of university, Mark decided that he wanted to lead a Canadian–Soviet Youth expedition to Siberia and the Canadian High Arctic. He was going to raise the funds for the expedition himself, then take on the polar ice cap. And I thought *I* was competitive.

Naturally, the idea made Susan and me nervous. It was a dangerous and demanding undertaking and an unorthodox step for a young man to take after completing college. But, as Mark put it, "Fortunately, I was offered a number of jobs after college – there were consulting firms that wanted me; I could have started off with a job at an ad agency. But spearheading the expedition by raising $500,000 in sponsorships, leading a team of thirty students in a dangerous environment, doing ecological studies, and producing a documentary film taught me more about life than sitting behind a desk working for a Fortune 500 company."

The expedition turned out to be an enormous success, and I'm sure this extraordinary experience was a key factor in getting Mark his current position – he's the youngest managing director of one of the National Basketball Association's international offices. Still, when Mark first raised the idea we – like all anxious parents – initially saw only the risks and the dangers. But the more we discussed his idea with him, the more we became aware of the fact that he was acting on the kind of instinct that Susan and I had always encouraged him to have. We knew he had the roots. Now he wanted to spread his wings. He knew that this was the right thing for him to do. So we gulped. We said a prayer or two. It wasn't easy. And we had a few sleepless nights. But we did what felt right. As Ray Kroc used to say, "Where there is no risk, there is no achievement; and where there is no achievement, there is no real happiness."

We said, "Go for it."

• 9 •

ENCOUNTERS WITH GREATNESS

I have an unusual alarm clock. I bought it in the Frankfurt airport, during a stopover on one of my frequent trips to Russia. It's about the size of an Instamatic camera, and as soon as I saw it I realized that, unlike many of the intriguing, beautifully engineered electronic gadgets that are for sale in German airports, it would be an extremely useful thing for me to have.

I usually come to Russia six or seven times a year, for busy visits of five or six days. The itinerary is always packed – opening new restaurants, visiting possible sites, meeting with government officials, attending civic functions, chatting with customers, seeing old friends, brainstorming with our people at our Moscow office, hosting dinners, making speeches at the centre for Ronald McDonald's Children's Charities in Russia. Days begin early and end late. I seldom stay in one city for two nights in a row. Down time is not built into the schedule. My trips are always blurs of planes and vans and hotels and cell-phone conversations and sheaves of faxes that catch up to me while I have a cheeseburger and a Diet Coke in one of our restaurants or race from arrivals to a waiting car.

As a result of this high-speed pace, I used to find that when my wake-up calls came – always too early – and after I fumbled for the phone in a dark hotel room, I would often lie back in bed and devote myself to two perplexing questions: Where was I, and what was I doing here?

I never liked this early-morning uncertainty. Instead of taking a few seconds to gather my thoughts and prepare myself for the day ahead, I found myself lying in bed in a panic: Was I in Moscow? In Nizhni Novgorod? Was I meeting with a mayor? A governor? An ambassador? Did I have a speech to give? Gifts to present? A problem to solve? A deal to sign? I'm a deep sleeper, and it would sometimes take more than a few seconds to sort this out. It's hardly surprising. One day I'm strolling casually through the crowds, chatting with Elvis Stojko at the Sunshine Games at Variety Village just outside Toronto; the next day, under the watchful gaze of my security guard, I'm having the photograph for the cover of this book taken in Red Square, a stone's throw away from Lenin's Mausoleum. One day, I'm mountain biking through the hills north of Toronto; the next, I'm reading my briefing notes in the back of a speeding car, on my way to a critical meeting with Yuri Luzhkov, the mayor of Moscow. No wonder it takes me a while to figure out where I am. Which is why I was so pleased with my find in the Frankfurt airport.

My new alarm clock allows me to record my own wake-up message – a different one each morning if I want. So, instead of music, or an electronic beeping, or a hotel receptionist's voice waking me, I hear my own voice. I record the message the night before. It fills me in quickly about the day ahead. For example, here's what I awoke to one day on a recent trip to Russia.

"Good morning, George. You're in St. Petersburg. You're going to be opening a new restaurant, attending a tree-planting ceremony, flying to Moscow, meeting with Mikhail Gorbachev, and having dinner with Aleksandr Yakovlev. Go for it."

With wake-up calls like that, who needs a cup of coffee?

We were staying at the Grand Hotel Europe in St. Petersburg. It's a magnificent, pre-Revolutionary building – the kind of hotel that makes you feel as if you've been transported to the time of Anna Karenina (even if you do have to pass through a metal detector before you enter the lobby). The night before, a dinner had been held there in honour of my sixtieth birthday. Let me repeat that (and you'll see why shortly): *my sixtieth!* Anne Collins, the Canadian consul-general in St. Petersburg, had been there – along with Ron Cohen; Ed Garber; Khamzat Khasbulatov, the general director of McDonald's-Moscow; Glen Steeves, the managing director of McDonald's in Russia; Marc Winer, now the chairman of McDonald's in Russia; his wife, Chana; and the entire St. Petersburg management team.

I am always extremely wary of birthdays, especially big ones: forty, fifty, sixty. We have a tradition at McDonald's of pulling outrageous pranks on one another on these momentous occasions – and the stings can be wicked. The worst ever – or the best, depending on how you look at it – was the one we pulled on Ed Garber when he turned sixty-five. Ed has been with McDonald's-Canada from the beginning – I remember him helping me unload the equipment truck at our first restaurant in London, Ontario. He has overseen operations in Canada and has been a major advisor in Germany, France, Italy, and Russia. It would be difficult to find anyone more involved with the company and more knowledgeable than Ed Garber. It would also be difficult to find anyone less interested in the idea of retirement. Which was why, on the very day of his sixty-fifth birthday, we went to unbelievable lengths to convince him that the company was introducing a mandatory retirement age of sixty-five – "immediately and with no exceptions." We had a letter from Mike Quinlan, the worldwide McDonald's chairman and CEO, to this effect. We had a memo from the CEO's office to me that we made sure Ed "just happened" to see; the memo said that, given the unfortunate timing of this unavoidable announcement, someone would have to "look after the Garber situation." We covered every angle absolutely convincingly, and Ed was devastated – so devastated that he almost refused to attend his own surprise birthday party. "That's it," he said. "I'm not going to go in there and pretend to smile. If I'm gone, I'm out of here. Now." But we managed to persuade him to stay, and he sat there glumly. He looked as if he was attending his own funeral. Then we told him we had a special videotaped birthday message from Mike Quinlan. Ed looked up unhappily at the TV screen. Quinlan appeared. And all he said was, "Ed. We got you." The place erupted in laughter, and Ed's jaw dropped to somewhere around his ankles.

Now that was a serious sting.

This was why I'd been looking over my shoulder ever since my arrival in Russia. There had been a very nice dinner in Moscow for me, with many of our McDonald's colleagues and many of my good Russian friends in attendance: Yakovlev and his wife, Nina, were there; Bakatin and his wife, Lyudmila; the deputy mayor of Moscow, Vladimir Malyshkov; the athlete and adventurer Dmitrii Shparo and his wife, Tatyana; and the celebrated children's book writer and the founder of the Soviet Children's Fund, Albert Likhanov. All of our Moscow top management team was there – including Marina Tulupnikova, our first Russian employee, who is now the head of our human resources department and who oversees our 3,700 employees. It was wonderful seeing so many familiar faces in one room. There had been lovely and thoughtful gifts. There had been toasts, and more toasts. There had been speeches – some very amusing, some very touching. But there had been no outrageous prank on this trip to Russia.

At least, not until I was arrested.

The special investigations unit pulled over my car on the way from the St. Petersburg airport to the Grand Hotel Europe. The sunglasses and the machine gun were nice touches. I asked the driver what was going on. He shrugged. "*OMON*. The SWAT team." I rolled down my window, and a heavy-looking character wanted to know if I was George Cohon. I said I was. He glared at me, the way customs officials always used to when I was making my first trips to the Soviet Union. With a jerk of his head, he called over one of his leather-jacketed, two-hundred-pound, brush-cut buddies. He approached the car menacingly, his hands behind his back. Then, with a flourish, he presented me with a bouquet of flowers.

We all had a good laugh, and we continued on our way. Of course, I'd known all along that it was a spoof. Sitting in the front seat of the limo, my security guard had been calm throughout the episode. That was the give-away. Usually, if so much as a stray dog growls near me, he goes on red alert. I could see that he'd been tipped off, and so I'd gone along cheerfully with the roadside interrogation.

I thought, "Well, if that's the best they can do. . . ." I settled back in the car and picked up the copy of *The Moscow Times* that had been left there for me. "Amateurs," I thought smugly. I opened the paper – perhaps the most widely read by Moscow's business community – and there, taking up the entire bottom half of the paper's most widely read page, opposite the editorials, was a monstrous photograph. Monstrous! I couldn't believe my eyes. I blinked. I looked away. I looked back. It was still there.

It was me – or rather, it was my head fixed to the squatting and enormous body of a sumo wrestler. This was a truly appalling vision – all the more appalling because I knew how many influential people in Moscow had opened that paper that day. Who would have seen it? Boris Yeltsin? Yuri Luzhkov? The American Ambassador? The King of Spain was in Moscow that day; I pictured him puzzling over this strange apparition in his morning paper. (The next time I ran into Mark Shaver, the general manager of Coca-Cola, Moscow – at a function at the Ronald McDonald Children's Centre in Moscow – he gave me a curious look and said, "Nice of you to take some time from your sumo wrestling career to come out.")

The photograph was unkind – to say the least. But not half so unkind as the words above the outrageous picture. "Happy 65th George Cohon." *Sixty-fifth!*

Am I a little vain? Am I little anxious about my age? About growing older? Well, if thirty years of spreading my thinning hair over my bald patch is any indication, I'd have to say maybe. Just a little.

There was another birthday dinner for me in St. Petersburg. That evening, at the Grand Hotel Europe, I greeted everyone – Anne Collins, the lively consul-general, Gennady Tkachev, the chairman of the External Affairs Committee – with the same correction. "I'm not sixty-five," I kept saying. "Really, I'm not. I'm only sixty." But by then it had been in the papers. *The St. Petersburg Times*, too, as it turned out. My age was now a matter of public record. It was futile to protest. It was too late for corrections.

They got me.

The morning after my birthday dinner, when my alarm went off in St. Petersburg, I knew as soon as I listened to my message that it was going to be an extraordinary day. I love opening new restaurants; these events, in Russia, are still big deals. There are crowds and marching bands and there is always lots of press.

We had opened two days before in the city of Nizhni Novgorod, with Yurii Lebedev, the acting governor; Ivan Sklyarov, the mayor (now the newly elected governor); Aleksandr Morozov, the head of the district administration; Anne Leahy, the respected and likeable Canadian Ambassador in Russia; and hundreds of local citizens in attendance. Nizhni Novgorod is a lovely old city, at the juncture of the Oka and the Volga rivers. Before the Revolution it was an affluent merchants' town – the gateway to the interior. For many years, after the Revolution, it was a closed city – no Westerner was allowed to visit. It was the city to which Andrei Sakharov had been exiled, and it is the hometown of Yeltsin's first deputy prime minister, Boris Nemtsov. It was also the birthplace of the writer and celebrated communist Maxim Gorky. In fact, the city was called Gorky during the communist era, but now, like St. Petersburg (formerly Leningrad), like Yeltsin's hometown in Siberia, Yekaterinburg (formerly Sverdlovsk), and like almost every street in Moscow, it has returned to its pre-Revolutionary name. But, the city's beautiful central square is still named for Gorky – and the statue of the writer who made famous Stalin's alarming phrase "engineers of the soul" looks a little uncomfortable with the splashy arrival of Western capitalism.

While I was there, I wondered how often the brave, unbending Andrei Sakharov and his wife, Yelena Bonner, had trudged through the grey, sombre square during their long years of exile, and I thought how surprised they would have been to one day find the propaganda posters gone, the red flags removed from the light standards, and the square festooned with golden arches made of bright balloons. Gorky Square had been transformed by balloons and jugglers and a marching band, celebrating the arrival of

McDonald's. Exactly the kind of dramatic contrast between the present and the past that a visitor encounters everywhere in Russia.

These ironic juxtapositions are often astounding. For instance, I learned that Misha Belyanin, who is in charge of our real estate team in St. Petersburg, had served while a student as an engineer in the Soviet Navy. He's a pleasant fellow. One day, I casually asked him what kind of a ship he had served on. He replied, "A submarine."

"A nuclear sub?"

"*Da.*"

"What was your longest time down?"

"Twenty-nine days."

I whistled. "Twenty-nine days. Jeez. Where were you?"

"About a hundred metres off the coast of Alaska."

I guess he could read my expression pretty clearly. He said, "Oh, you shouldn't be so shocked. The Americans were one hundred metres off the coast of Eastern Siberia."

There is still, seven years after we opened our first restaurant in Russia, a buzz about a McDonald's opening, and there are not many events I enjoy more. As is our tradition, we had given our entire opening day sales at Nizhni Novgorod – over 57 million rubles ($10,000 U.S.) – to a local orphanage. As well, our first (non-paying) customers had been children from the orphanage – this, too, is a McDonald's tradition in Russia.

We would be doing the same in St. Petersburg.

We always used to invite President Gorbachev and President Yeltsin to our restaurant openings in Russia, never expecting that they would come. But in June 1993, when we opened our second restaurant in Moscow, we got word that Yeltsin would make an appearance.

His office decided that he would attend, not on our opening day, but on the day after. On opening day, the federal government representative was Viktor Khlystun, the minister of agriculture and food. "We recognize McDonald's activities toward improving the food-service system in Russia," Khlystun said in his speech. "The food-processing plant built by McDonald's is concrete evidence of the company's desire to develop long-term mutually beneficial co-operation with our country. McDonald's method of organization provides a model for other modern enterprises to follow in providing the Russian people with high-quality food products."

Yeltsin would stay for only fifteen minutes, we were told. It would be a quick, short tour. The second Moscow restaurant, one block from Red Square, is the ground floor of a modern, twelve-storey office building that we have constructed. We rent space there to some of the largest multi-national companies in the world. Originally, rent was paid to us in hard currency – one of the solutions we found to the fiscal difficulties raised by our "rubles only" restaurant policy. Now that the ruble is readily convertible, the rent is paid in rubles.

Security was very tight and very obvious the day Yeltsin visited us. This always strikes me as counter-productive because, of course, the first thing that happens when barriers go up and guys in sunglasses appear is that a crowd forms. And, sure enough, a crowd formed. When Yeltsin arrived, the place was bedlam.

He was there with his entourage and his top advisors. I was there with Sasha Tilinin – a fifteen-year-old Russian boy whom I had spotted two years earlier in our Pushkin restaurant wolfing down a Big Mac, a large order of fries, and three apple pies. (Our apple pies are amazingly popular in Russia; in our first three days of operation at Pushkin Square, we sold as many as we sell at an average restaurant in Canada in a year.) I had been extremely

Another milestone: Fred Turner and Ray Kroc help me cut the ribbon and open restaurant number 4,000 in Montreal in 1976. This is the restaurant where the Soviets had their first taste of McDonald's.

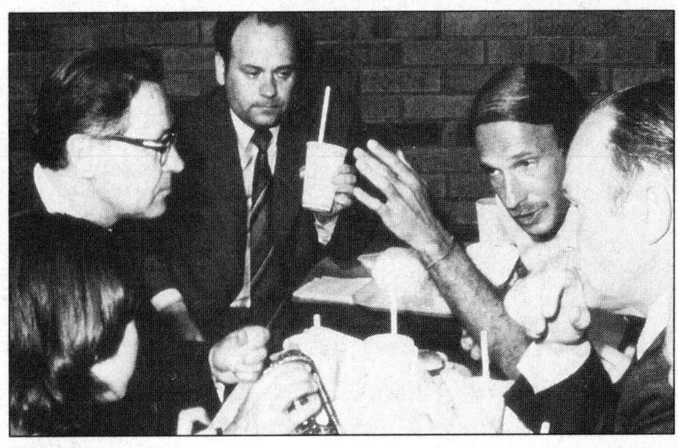

First supper: The 1976 Olympic Russian delegation enjoy their first Big Macs at our restaurant number 4,000, in Montreal.

Finally McDonaldized: During our long negotiations with the Soviets, Sergei Viktorovich Barorakov sat on the other side of the table. He dubbed our team "The Wolf Pack." At last he's come round to our way of thinking.

The Hammer and Sickle and the Maple Leaf: Vladimir Malyshkov and I sign the deal – finally! – while Deputy Mayor Zharov (centre) looks on.

"The ideology will change": Aleksandr Yakovlev has a first-hand look at one of the new ways of life that the reforms he envisioned made possible.

Father figure: I have been the beneficiary of the wisdom, counsel, and friendship of Aleksandr Yakovlev, the architect of perestroika.

Connections: Vladimir Malyshkov, me, and Vsevolod Shimansky. Malyshkov, who became a key player in our deal, first worked under Shimansky, who told him "McDonald's are good people."

News Summary

OFFICE OF THE PRESS SECRETARY

TUESDAY, MAY 3, 1988 -- 6 a.m. EDT EDITION

TODAY'S HEADLINES

INTERNATIONAL NEWS

Plant-Notice Rule Assailed By Reagan -- In a speech before the U.S. Chamber of Commerce today, President Reagan heatedly denounced a provision of the recently passed trade bill that would make companies provide 60 days' notice of plant closings or large layoffs.
(New York Times, Washington Post, Washington Times)

U.S. Drops Plan For Coast Guard Patrol In Gulf -- The Pentagon, facing stiff congressional opposition, Monday dropped its plan to dispatch six Coast Guard cutters to join the Navy fleet patrolling the Persian Gulf.
(Los Angeles Times, Washington Post, AP, Knight-Ridder)

Focus Shifts At Nicaraguan Peace Talks -- Peace talks between the Sandinista government and contra leaders have begun to touch on key military and political questions, and the basic differences between the two sides have become more clearly defined than ever.
(New York Times, Washington Times, AP)

NETWORK NEWS (Monday Evening)

POLAND -- Leading members of Solidarity were rounded up and detained as the strikes spread.

ISRAELI INCURSION -- Israeli forces are conducting a raid inside Lebanon.

GULF -- Secretary Carlucci has decided not to send Coast Guard ships to the Persian Gulf.

BIG MAC TO ATTACK MOSCOW NEXT YEAR

MOSCOW (AP) — Soviets will get a chance to munch "Bolshoi Macs" when the first of about 20 McDonald's restaurants in Moscow opens next year, officials from the city and the hamburger giant announced.... "I think that the McDonald's in Moscow will be the highest volume McDonald's in the world," said George Cohon, president of McDonald's Restaurants of Canada Ltd., a subsidiary of McDonald's Corp. of Oak Brook, Illinois.

This Summary is prepared Monday through Friday by the White House News Summary Staff. For complete stories or information, please call 456-2950.

Headline news! On May 3, 1988, Ronald Reagan looked at the daily news summary prepared by the White House press secretary and learned that strikes were spreading in Poland, the Israelis were raiding Lebanon, things were tense in the Persian Gulf – and McDonald's was coming to Moscow.

"You mean fries don't come that way?" In my famous white boots, on a farm outside Moscow, I make it perfectly clear to everyone present that I have never dug a potato in my life.

Help wanted: A single notice in one Moscow newspaper advertising for crew positions attracted over 27,000 applications.

The young doves of perestroika: A crew rally at a Moscow theatre, the night before opening day at Pushkin Square.

The lines are a'changing: Rumour had it that there were more people waiting to get in to the Pushkin Square McDonald's on opening day than there were in Red Square, waiting to see Lenin's Tomb.

Time flies when you're having fun: On January 31, 1990, fourteen years after I first took the Soviets to McDonald's in Montreal, I cut the ribbon on our first Moscow restaurant.

Build it and they will come: Over 35,000 Big Macs were sold to the crowds on the opening day of the first McDonald's in Russia.

Taste of the West: Soviet citizens in line for their first "Beeg Mek" on opening day at Pushkin Square.

In any language, smiles are free: The Soviet crew on opening day at Pushkin Square.

McDonald's Corporation Chairman Mike Quinlan congratulates me at the Pushkin Square opening while Don Keough, the former chief operating officer of Coca-Cola, looks on.

Moscow Night – and what a night! The evening after we opened our Pushkin Square restaurant, we hosted a glittering VIP reception in the Kremlin's St. George's Hall. Our fundraising efforts raised \$1,100,000 for the Soviet Children's Fund.

Upping the ante: Mike Quinlan of McDonald's and Don Keough of Coca-Cola looked friendly enough during our opening night celebrations. But during our fundraising auction they engaged in a bidding war that knew no bounds.

impressed with young Sasha's appetite. And with his evident enthusiasm. As is my habit, I struck up a conversation with him. He wrote to me after I returned to Toronto. We corresponded. I introduced him to Yeltsin as my top advisor.

When Yeltsin and I met in front of the restaurant, he grabbed me as if we were two long-lost friends. In reality, I'd only shaken his hand in a few receiving lines and chatted for a few brief minutes. But of course, I responded. There is nothing "old-guard" about Yeltsin. He is a politician, and so he worked the crowd for a while outside. Then he said, "Let's go in."

He was fascinated with the operation. He asked about the equipment. He talked to a lot of the young employees. He met the twenty-five-year-old woman manager, Karina, and then he took me aside. He asked, "What does she earn?"

I said, "Let me give you her history."

Yeltsin came within about a foot and a half of my face. He sort of puffed himself up – he's quite an imposing figure – and he said sternly, "I didn't ask you for her history. I asked you how much she earns."

I wanted him to understand that she had earned her position, that she had worked her way through other jobs, and that her advancement and her pay were based on her productivity. So I pretended I didn't understand the translation. I said, "She started by washing floors, washing windows, working on the grill, making hamburgers."

Yeltsin was looking at me pretty severely. Finally, I answered his question. "She earns about one million, two hundred thousand rubles a month." Which, at that point, was about $1,200 U.S.

He was taken aback. "How much?"

"One million, two hundred thousand rubles a month."

He said, "I'm the president of the country. And she earns more than I do."

I looked him right in the eye and said, "She's got a very tough job."

He liked the answer. He broke out laughing, and gave me a huge Russian bear hug.

Then it was time to eat. The president was served a Big Mac. He took the top half of the bun off the sandwich, and ate the hamburger a little cautiously. I waited anxiously. There was so much press present that day, that inside the restaurant we had established a single camera, which would shoot film for all the media. The cameramen asked Yeltsin how he liked his Big Mac.

The following morning, in the United States and Canada, 4,124,100 viewers tuned in to *Good Morning America.* The program opened with the President of Russia looking up from the sandwich in his hand and saying, "*Soli malo.* Not enough salt."

(At our next restaurant opening in Moscow, Yeltsin's wife, Naina, was our honoured guest. We were donating 50 million rubles to a cause that she energetically supports – the Institute of Children's Oncology in Moscow. As it happened, the same cameraman asked her how she was enjoying her Big Mac and told her of her husband's reaction. She said, "It's always the same. No matter what I cook for Boris, there's never enough salt.")

President Yeltsin's visit lasted not the allotted fifteen minutes, but almost two hours. As we were leaving the restaurant, he suddenly asked me if I had ever been to Siberia.

A strange question, I thought, for him to ask of a Western businessman. "No," I said uncertainly.

He went on to say that he was from Yekaterinburg, a town in Siberia, and he wanted to know if I would commit to opening a McDonald's there.

I said, "I can't really respond until I visit the town."

Yeltsin looked very solemn. "I'm the President of Russia. I'm asking you to do this. Will you do it?"

A tricky situation. Yeltsin is not a predictable man. I said, "I'd prefer that our relationship be an honest one. I don't want to tell you that I'll do something, and then not do it. That would be wrong."

This was not the answer he had wanted, but he accepted it – or, at least, he seemed to.

The press was waiting for him. One of the reporters was a woman from CNN, Siobhan Darrow. I'd always liked Siobhan, and so I steered Yeltsin toward her. She asked a few questions. He answered them enthusiastically. Oh yes, he liked McDonald's. Oh yes, it was wonderful for the country. I was beaming – totally unprepared for what was coming.

Yeltsin paused. "I understand now why Mr. Cohon is so successful," he said. "He's a very bright businessman." He pointed at me. "He has agreed to open a McDonald's in my hometown in Siberia."

He gave me a brief, mischievous smile. And then, disappearing into his car, a black ZIL, he was gone.

As I write, there are sixteen McDonald's in Russia – twelve in Moscow, three in St. Petersburg, and one in Nizhni Novgorod. There are still none in Siberia, but no doubt that will change. By the time this book is published, there will be thirty throughout Russia, and by the year 2000, there will be more than a hundred. And I plan to attend as many of the openings as I can.

I love the speeches and the musicians, and the ribbon cutting. I love ushering the children to the counters. I love sitting down and asking customers whether they are enjoying their meal. I love talking with the Russian press. They are so used to politicians – to people who dodge and weave away from their questions – that my directness always startles them. In Russia, the press will usually ask me about the little knot of some half-dozen protesters who often stand off to one side of the huge, jostling crowds at our openings. They're usually old-guard communists or right-wing nationalists.

The protesters hold up signs and chant, and I think the press expects me to be irritated by their presence or to dismiss them as kooks. I think they want me to denounce them. Or – and this would be the kind of official response that the Russian press are accustomed to – they expect me simply to pretend that they aren't there. Instead, I always say, "I'm glad that protesters are present." This usually raises a few eyebrows and starts a few journalistic pens scribbling. I say, "Look. A short while ago there was no such thing as protest in this country. Now people can say what they like in public. They can make their opinions known. This is very important – and if those people want to come out onto the street and voice their opinion about Big Macs and french fries and Coca-Cola, then it's fine by me. That's what freedom's all about."

At openings, I especially love the nervous excitement of the new, young crews. They have worked hard in preparation for the big day. They always look wide-eyed at the gathering crowds and television cameras and photographers. Our Russian crews, contrary to what everyone said to us before we opened for the first time in Moscow, have proven to be enthusiastic and energetic, and, by way of a curious little quirk of history, they have taken on what has become a uniquely Russian characteristic.

One of the training videos we showed our first Moscow crew had been shot at the McDonald's at the Expo 86 site in Vancouver, and that particular crew had developed the custom of waving customers over to the counter when they first stepped into the restaurant. This was a display of esprit that seemed well suited to the celebrations of Expo. Our first Moscow crew picked up on this. When our first customers entered the restaurant on Pushkin Square, they were greeted by crew members waving them over to the counter. "*Podkhodite: svobodnaya kassa!* Here, here. Over here." Since then, every Russian crew has done the same.

What was, originally, a charming idiosyncracy of the Expo 86 crew has been copied at every McDonald's throughout Russia – and I think it says a good deal about the role McDonald's plays in Russia. For someone at a counter to wave and smile and call over a customer is precisely – dramatically – the opposite of the way customers used to be treated in restaurants and stores throughout the Soviet Union. It's a reversal of history no less startling than finding a marching band – with majorettes! – in Gorky Square in Nizhni Novgorod playing "New York, New York." In a way that North Americans and Europeans can't quite appreciate, the enthusiasm of our Russian crews is almost a political statement. It's everything that the former way of life was not. It's as clear a signal as you will ever see that the younger generation – those who have now had a taste of the West – will not allow things to return to the way they were.

Let's keep matters in perspective. It was the efforts of giants such as Mikhail Gorbachev, the ideas of thinkers such as Aleksandr Yakovlev, the struggles of courageous souls such as Andrei Sakharov, and the brave spirit of the Russian people that changed the world. But the achievement of "Burger Diplomacy," I think, is that now that Russia has changed, the country will never be able to go back to what it was. During the coup in August 1991, when Moscow was in a state of upheaval and our crew went out to try to protect our restaurant on the Arbat from the anxious, milling crowds, they quickly realized that our restaurant was under no threat from the Russian people. "McDonald's," people said, "*Makdonalds – u nikh zhe rossiyskaya firma. S nimi vsyo v poryadke.*" "They're a Russian company. They're okay." By then, in Russia, McDonald's had been accepted as a window on a world hidden for a long time, and it continues to play a role in the extraordinary transformation of the country. I remember Aleksandr Yakovlev saying to me that although he expected McDonald's to improve the food industry in his country, he didn't expect us to revolutionize the entire service sector of the Russian economy. But, if you'll pardon the immodesty, it was our people who started exactly that revolution. When people bemoan the so-called commercialization of Moscow, of St. Petersburg, and of cities such as Nizhni Novgorod, I don't ask them to consider the alternative. I ask them to remember it.

An opening – particularly an opening in a city as breathtaking and as steeped in history as St. Petersburg – is more than enough to get me out of bed in a hurry. It was early when the alarm went off. I heard my own voice: "Good morning, George. . . ." Thanks to the wonders of German technology, I knew my itinerary before I opened my eyes.

An opening in Vasilievsky Ostrov, one of St. Petersburg's oldest districts. A tree-planting ceremony at Primorsky Victory Park, with a donation of forty-two Canadian trees to the city of St. Petersburg. Two speeches, a ribbon cutting, a press conference, and visits to our other St. Petersburg restaurants – all before lunch. Not a bad morning. But it was the afternoon – the flight back to Moscow and my visit with Mikhail Gorbachev – that was looming large as I dressed and got ready that morning. All week long, Mikhail Gorbachev had been very much on my mind. I am always fascinated by the reactions I get to the mention of Gorbachev's name in conversations with Russians.

I have an interpreter on whom I rely completely when I am in Russia. Sergei Tsivunin is so quick and smooth, and he knows my conversational habits and my speech patterns so well, that sometimes I feel as if I'm fluent in Russian when he is at my side. This makes it easy for me to strike up a conversation.

It is my habit simply to ask people what they are thinking – to sit down with customers, to chat with people in lines, to stop people in the street and engage them in conversation. To a businessman, this kind of frank encounter is invaluable: a direct line to what the customer is thinking. For a visitor to Russia – a curious visitor – asking questions is always illuminating. At the Nizhni Novgorod opening, for instance, I sat at one of the tables on the outdoor terrace and ended up talking to two policewomen about their meals, about their lives, about their work, and then – I asked the question right out of the blue – about Gorbachev.

Mikhail Sergeyevich? The policewomen began to talk – angrily. Fifteen minutes later, they were still on the subject of Gorbachev.

Even on my way to Russia on a recent trip, changing planes in Amsterdam, I asked several of my fellow passengers what they thought of their former president. I watched in astonishment as comments sparked debates, and debates flared into passionate soliloquies.

There is an old joke about a farmer. One year, his harvest is wiped out by a drought. The next, everything is destroyed by pestilence. The next, there is a catastrophic flood. Finally, in his prayers, he asks, "Why me, Lord?" To which God replies, "I don't know. There's just something about you that pisses me off."

Sometimes, I think that's the way the Russian people feel about Mikhail Gorbachev. There's just something about him – his intellect perhaps, his dignified sense of his own importance, the security of his place in history as compared to the insecurity that many Russians face in their own lives, the temporary hardships that his commitment to the long-term benefits of freedom have brought – that just bugs people. I have heard Russians blame him for everything from the dissolution of the Soviet Union to the break-up of individual families to the rise of the Mafia to the free-fall of the ruble. Communists blame him for being a liberal; liberals blame him for being a communist. Intellectuals see him as the man time left behind – part of the old guard of the Central Committee. There are even those who actually believe the preposterous notion that he is employed by the CIA. And yet, when I ask Russians about his reforms – reforms that required vision and courage and extraordinary political agility – I usually get only grudging acknowledgment that he was in large part responsible for many of the freedoms Russians now enjoy. Religious freedom. Public debate. The right to travel. When I ask if they feel safer now that the Cold War is over, most of them admit that they do.

But. When it comes to Russians' opinion of Mikhail Gorbachev, there is always a but.

I was particularly struck with this in the airport at Amsterdam. I listened to a fellow passenger from Toronto, a pleasant-looking, neatly dressed, older Russian woman, give an anti-Gorbachev tirade at a smoky Aeroflot departure gate. Then I said, "But madam. You wouldn't be here now, in an international airport, with your passport, on your way home to Moscow from a trip to see your children in Toronto, if not for Mikhail Gorbachev."

"*Da*," she said. "That's true. But. . . ." And off she went. Her passion, like the passion of many Russians, was hard for me, a Westerner, to understand. It reminded me of the time I told Gorbachev about Brian Mulroney's efforts to clear his name during the Airbus affair. Gorbachev couldn't quite recall the details of the matter, and he asked me to remind him. I gave him a quick summary of what I'd been reading in the papers of an alleged impropriety and about Mulroney's ferocious and successful defence of his name and reputation. Gorbachev listened. Then he shook his head a little sadly. He said, "And Brian thinks he's got problems."

I first met Mikhail Gorbachev at a government function in Ottawa in 1988, when he was president of the Soviet Union. It was in a reception line, and we were introduced by Prime Minister Mulroney. As is typical at these affairs, we shook hands. Gorbachev said something like, "Ah yes, McDonald's. You are doing wonderful work in our country." The official photographer snapped a shot. Click. Next. I moved on. A few weeks later, the picture arrived with the compliments of the Prime Minister's Office. I sent it out to the framer and when it came back, like all the people the photographer snapped, I hung the picture prominently on my office wall. My encounter with President Gorbachev probably lasted less than five seconds. But from that point on, every visitor to my office was impressed. Here I was with my good friend Mikhail Gorbachev.

I had been pleased to have been introduced to Gorbachev in Ottawa. But I couldn't delude myself into thinking the snapshot reflected any kind of meaningful relationship. And a meaningful relationship was what I wanted. After our first restaurant opened, I became intent on having an actual meeting with him in Moscow. I felt that McDonald's endeavours in Russia and our connections with people such as Aleksandr Yakovlev were putting us at the centre of the reforms unleashed by *perestroika*. I felt that finally, fourteen years after our negotiations had begun, and not long after our first opening, it was time for me to meet the leader of the country, and to discuss frankly our objectives and the challenges we faced doing business in the Soviet Union.

Of course, part of my ambition was to get to know a man who was playing such a significant role in history. But there were also sound business reasons for the meeting. I knew that nothing was ever absolutely secure in the Soviet system – as you may recall, I'd already seen done deals fall through at the last possible second – and I felt that the higher up I went in the Kremlin, the more solid our position would be. I also wanted to make sure that Gorbachev understood the benefits that I believed McDonald's would bring to the USSR. I wanted to impress upon him how ambitious our expansion plans were. Perhaps it was my Fuller Brush background coming through. I was sure that if I could just get my foot in his office door, I would be able to establish a rapport.

Our people approached the Kremlin again and again, and eventually a meeting was set up. I was thrilled at the prospect. Gorbachev's name was in the headlines almost every day. I remember sitting at home in Toronto, watching the news, and thinking, with no small sense of astonishment, "I'll be talking with him in a few weeks."

We asked Gorbachev's people if I should bring my interpreter, Sergei Tsivunin, to the meeting. *Nyet.* They would supply the interpreter. Should I bring any of my McDonald's-Moscow colleagues? *Nyet.*

Just me.

Which is how, in the summer of 1990, I found myself entering the Kremlin through a side doorway that I had never noticed before, on my way to a meeting with President Gorbachev. Alone.

Now, the Kremlin is a little daunting at the best of times. Even if you're a tourist, on your way to the armoury to see the intricately carved ivory throne of Ivan the Terrible, or the fabulous Orlov diamond in the Crown Jewel Room, or the astounding Fabergé egg collection, the Kremlin can be overpowering. So, imagine what it was like to be entering the Kremlin, on my way to meet with Mikhail Gorbachev while he was, absolutely, at the height of his power. This was really the inner sanctum: the guards, the security, the endless corridors, the army of bureaucrats, the assistants and deputies, the vast, hushed reception area. Georgie Cohon, from the South Side of Chicago, was on his way to meet the man who changed the world.

I was very focused. I had been told that I could have fifteen or twenty minutes. I was also very nervous. I consider myself a pretty cool, unflappable character, but this, very clearly, was entry into major-league play.

All I had with me was a single piece of paper on which I'd scribbled the topics I wanted to discuss: a brief history of McDonald's; a summary of our years of negotiations in the USSR; our commitment to our Russian crew, staff, and suppliers; information about our $40 million food-processing plant; our intention to re-invest our profits into further expansion within the Soviet Union; our refusal to use middlemen – the so-called five-percenters – in negotiating our deals.

A single piece of paper. And a camera.

I don't know what possessed me to bring a camera. It was hardly the right prop for the kind of serious discussion I hoped we would have. But for some reason, I dropped it in my pocket, and when I was ushered into the President's reception area, I found myself next to Gorbachev's official photographer. He was standing there, with all kinds of cameras and camera bags slung over his shoulders – a very professional-looking, serious guy. And again, I don't know what possessed me, but I passed him my little idiot-proof, automatic-focus camera.

He looked as if I'd passed him a child's toy. "What do you want me to do with this?"

I replied, "Take some pictures." I decided to kid him a bit. You never know with Russians. They are very proud and stern, but they also have a great sense of humour. If you persist, you can usually make the most stone-faced of them smile. I said, "If the official shots get lost in the mail, I want to be sure I get some."

There was an unnerving, sphinx-like moment of unreadable silence – as there often is in conversation with Russians. Then he laughed.

I gave him one of my Russian Big Mac cards. "Have a Big Mac on me," I said. "Please leave the camera with the receptionist on your way out."

"Okay."

"*Spasibo.*" "Thanks."

So I was ushered into Gorbachev's office. I'm not sure I noticed anything about what the place looked like; I was focused on what was, by then, one of the most famous faces in the world. I was struck by his lively, warm brown eyes. They had a likeable, trusting sparkle. He was friendly and direct, but also quite dignified. We chatted briefly – small talk – and then he said, "Let's have an official picture." We continued chatting while the pictures were being taken, and Gorbachev, who was being very cordial, didn't notice that one of the cameras was distinctly out of place.

After the photographer left the room, Gorbachev continued to ask me questions. I've learned that sometimes big-wigs go through the motions of a meeting – they are often bored or uninformed, and they sometimes think that their presence is all that is required. Gorbachev was different. He sat directly across the table from me and paid close attention to what I said. He was genuinely interested in what McDonald's was doing and extremely inquisitive. Because of his background in agricultural policy and his passionate interest in agricultural reforms, he was particularly eager to know about the network of Russian suppliers we had established. "The farmers," he said. "The producers. This is where you have made an important contribution to our nation." He wanted to know about our meat and our dairy producers. I told him about the seed potatoes we had imported from the Netherlands and of our step-by-step endeavour to establish this variety in Russia. He wanted to know about the vast processing plant we had built in Solntsevo, on the outskirts of Moscow. He wanted to know about our distribution system. He wanted to know about our employees, about our customers. And partway through our conversation I realized that he was using McDonald's to step away from the gloss of economic theory and look at the reality of his reforms in action.

The fifteen minutes I was promised with the president stretched to almost an hour. We got into a very interesting discussion about how to know whom to trust. I realized what he was driving at. I told him that we were interested in a long-term commitment. He referred to the many fast-buck artists who were beginning to arrive in Russia as "pirates and robbers."

At the conclusion of our meeting, Gorbachev rose from his chair. He told me that he would do whatever he could to help McDonald's. He even joked a little; he said his grandchildren would want to go, and so he had to help. He smiled warmly. He said he wanted to help us develop and grow. We shook hands. On a scale of one to ten, the meeting had been an eleven. I left his office so elated, I almost forgot to pick up my camera at the receptionist's desk. Almost.

The world changed once more before I saw Mikhail Gorbachev again. In August 1991, I was travelling the USSR with Susie and Craig, who was, by then, working for Coca-Cola in Moscow. As it happened, we were staying near Yalta, about twenty kilometres from Gorbachev's summer home on the Black Sea. I was exercising on the morning of the 19th, listening to the BBC world news on my small portable radio, when I learned of the coup. A handful of Soviet hard-liners had seized power in what would prove to be a vain attempt to turn back the clock. The day before, at their summer house, Mikhail Gorbachev, president of the USSR and general secretary of the Communist Central Committee, and his wife, Raisa, had been stunned to find their telephone lines cut and their compound surrounded.

As soon as we learned what was going on, we packed up and headed out to the airport, where we had a private jet waiting. At first, the airport officials refused to let us leave. They kept saying, "A state of emergency. A state of emergency." But I happened to know that in Russia even states of emergency can often be overcome with a well-placed gift. I asked the pilot to deliver a package of Big Mac cards, McDonald's watches, and other goodies to the air-traffic controllers. My gift was accepted. Our pilot started the engines.

We flew to Tbilisi, in Georgia, about halfway between the Black Sea and the Caspian Sea, and spent the night there. The next morning, I received word that the acting prime minister of Georgia wanted to see me. I hadn't requested a meeting; I wasn't sure how he knew we were there. And, of course, I was extremely anxious about the political situation. As if in a movie, a big black car pulled up to take me away. I didn't know what to do. But Susie kept things in perspective. She was perfectly calm. She asked, "Is the downtown area open during a coup?" Apparently it was. "Good," she said. "I'll go pick up a souvenir for Mark, since he's missing all the excitement. You and Craig go meet with the acting prime minister."

The meeting was bizarre. Absolutely bizarre. I had no idea what the agenda was going to be, but it became clear soon enough. The acting prime minister was pitching me about opening a McDonald's in Georgia. I tried to duck. I told him that Craig worked for Coca-Cola, and he immediately switched gears. He started pitching for a Coke plant. I said I didn't think this was the most appropriate moment to be discussing opening a restaurant or a Coke plant – after all, the USSR might have been on the brink of civil war. Who knew what the hell was going on in Moscow?

While we were in the acting prime minister's office, a fax came in from Moscow. It was from Boris Yeltsin, the recently elected president of the Russian Federation. It denounced the so-called "State Committee for the State of Emergency" and decreed that "the proclamation of the Committee shall be deemed unconstitutional and the actions of its organizers shall qualify as a coup d'état, which is indeed high treason." Everyone read it, and the gravity of the situation settled in. The subject of opening a McDonald's in Georgia was, for the time being, put to rest.

I had the presence of mind to ask if I could keep the fax. It's one of the strangest souvenirs I own.

Later that day, Craig got word from Coke, ordering him out of the Soviet Union. They felt the political situation was too volatile. So did we. Since the jet we had chartered was not allowed to leave Soviet airspace, we allowed some people who were desperate to return to Moscow to use it. Then we tried to figure out how to get out of the USSR. There was, as it turned out, a flight leaving Tbilisi for Israel, but it was full. Or so we were told until the acting prime minister got on the phone. "If the Cohons are not on that flight, it's not going," he told the Aeroflot official. And so we were whisked to the airport with a police escort and flashing lights, crammed into the three extra crew seats that were available – and sent on our way to Israel.

The coup was the last, desperate gasp of the old guard. It was also the deciding factor in the long and complex power struggle between Yeltsin and Gorbachev. Russian citizens stood firm against the instigators of the coup, who were, obviously, yesterday's men. Moscow streets filled with protesters. Yeltsin made his famous speech from the top of a tank in front of the parliament buildings, and became a hero. He emerged as the courageous man of the people. Less publicly, Gorbachev had steadfastly and bravely refused to negotiate with the plotters. He called them "adventurers and traitors." Incommunicado and under house arrest, he had paced his summer home, worrying about his country and his family. He was completely isolated until, on August 21, with the coup in disarray, my good friend Vadim Bakatin, the former minister of the interior, arrived with a small group of supporters to bring him back to Moscow. (Bakatin's wife, Lyudmila, later told me that when Vadim left for the Crimea, he gave her a list of names of government officials she could trust in case he was killed or captured.)

Gorbachev returned to Moscow, but not, in any real sense, to power. Yeltsin was the victor; Gorbachev was the head of a state and a political institution that were rapidly losing their meaning. As well, Gorbachev had to live with the fact that many of the plotters came from his own inner circle. Both Aleksandr Yakovlev and Eduard Shevardnadze, his two key advisors, had been warning him for weeks about some of the people around him.

The coup increased Yeltsin's stature – and rightly so. He truly rose to the occasion. It also added to the public's perception that Gorbachev's compromises kept him trapped somewhere between Russia's past and its future. They blamed him for the difficulties of both.

The wheels turned. And the next time I met Gorbachev, he was out of power, presiding over a modestly appointed "think tank" at an anonymous-looking academic institution on the outskirts of Moscow.

There are businesspeople who would think there is little point in my continuing to see Gorbachev. It's now a different game. In many ways, Moscow is unrecognizable from the city that I first visited in 1976 – Coca-Cola and Reebok ads have replaced the propaganda posters; kids have skateboards and Chicago Bulls windbreakers; the young women on the streets have a worldly sense of style and flair; and you're more likely to hear U2 or Madonna on the radio than the old communist song, "*Shiroka strana moya rodnaya*." Russia is a different country. The players now are people such as Yuri Luzhkov, the dynamic mayor of Moscow. I have great respect for Luzhkov, and I see him regularly. Or Boris Nemtsov – Yeltsin's first deputy prime minister. I met him when he was governor of Nizhni Novgorod, and, as with Luzhkov, I enjoy a good working relationship with him. I expect that both these men will continue to play prominent roles in Russian political life in the years ahead. By contrast, in the 1996 presidential election, Mikhail Gorbachev, winner of the Nobel Peace Prize, champion of *perestroika* and *glasnost*, and darling of the Western media, received less than 1 per cent of the popular vote. (Prior to the election, when he asked me if I thought he should run, I knew he had no chance. I replied, "You should run for governor of California.") Still, I don't think it's wise to trim relationships to every shift in the political wind. Ray Kroc used to say, "We had principles when we were poor and we have those same principles today." I think the same kind of consistency has to apply to friendships. I admire and respect Gorbachev now that he's out of power just as much as I did when his office was in the Kremlin. He's the same man, after all. I value his advice and his friendship. I try to see him whenever I go to Russia.

The first time I visited him at his new office, I came with a little surprise for him. I'd had one of my photographs of our first meeting at the Kremlin printed on a T-shirt. It was a shot of Gorbachev and me sitting across the table from one another, and I was wearing it under my shirt and tie.

As luck would have it, the same photographer that Gorbachev had had in the Kremlin was there. The photographer and I were ushered into his office. Gorbachev and I exchanged niceties and engaged in some pleasant small talk. It was a friendly encounter, but there was a sad formality to things.

I said, "Mr. President, the last time I saw you was in the Kremlin."

"*Da.*"

"And I want you to know I have kept you close to my heart. That you are no longer in power doesn't matter to me. You were helpful and kind. And I would like to continue our relationship."

Gorbachev seemed touched by this. He is an emotional man, and his feelings are often quite apparent. His eyes widened and he drew a deep breath. "That's very nice," he said. Then he gestured to me to stand beside him. "Here. Let's have my photographer take some pictures."

I said, "Yes. That's a good idea. Let's have *our* photographer take some pictures."

Gorbachev looked surprised. "*Chto Vy imeete v vidu: 'nash fotograf'?*" "What do you mean, '*Our* photographer?' "

So I told him my story about worrying about whether I would ever get the pictures that were taken officially, and of bringing my own camera to the Kremlin.

"And did you ever get the official pictures?" he asked.

"No."

"And did yours turn out?"

"Yes," I said. "Our photographer took an excellent shot."

Gorbachev knew I was leading somewhere. "And where is it?" he asked. "This excellent shot?"

"As I told you, Mr. President. . . ."

Gorbachev looked shocked when I started to unbutton my shirt. He glanced uncertainly at the photographer and at the translator. I could see him thinking, What is this nut up to? I opened my shirt wide, and showed him my T-shirt.

"As I told you, sir. You are close to my heart."

Gorbachev was delighted. I suppose it was an unorthodox thing for me to do, but it had the right effect. The air of sad formality disappeared.

This time, I did receive the photographer's picture – signed by Mikhail Gorbachev. It's the one on the back of this book. Whenever I see it, I always think he looks like a man who hadn't had a good laugh for a long time.

In the car, on the way from the Grand Hotel Europe to the morning opening in St. Petersburg, I took a few minutes to review my notes. There would be speeches at the restaurant – on the front steps in front of the crowd that we knew was already beginning to gather. I was going to speak; so was Anne Collins, the Canadian consul-general. But it was Vladimir Yakovlev, the governor of St. Petersburg and no relation to Aleksandr, who would be the keynote speaker.

The site is a good one, perhaps our best in St. Petersburg – in the centre of Vasilievsky Island, the oldest district of the city and directly across the street from a busy subway station. I would speak as well, and I wanted to make certain that I drew proper attention to the war veterans who would be present at the opening festivities.

It is difficult for a Westerner to fully comprehend the significance of World War II – the Great Patriotic War, as it is called in Russia – in the collective memory of the Russian people. The German invasion, the siege of Leningrad, the battle of Stalingrad, the Soviet Army's 1942 winter counter-offensive – in all anywhere from 26 million to 40 million Soviet citizens and soldiers died in the effort to drive the invaders from the Motherland. The numbers are mind-boggling – the loss of at least the equivalent of the entire current population of Canada – every man, woman, and child.

The tales of courage and sacrifice are truly astounding. Their eventual victory is a source of enormous pride to the Russian people. The Revolution of 1917 has steadily diminished in its historical importance, but remembrance of the suffering and the triumph of the Great Patriotic War remains an unshakeable fundamental of the national identity.

Our openings at Nizhni Novgorod and in St. Petersburg happened to take place in the week leading up to May 9 – Victory Day. As is so often the case in Russia, history seemed very close at hand. All week, I often found myself gazing at the aged faces of Russian veterans, their medals proudly displayed on their chests, and wondering what unimaginable sights they had seen in their youth. A few days before, in Moscow, while addressing some of the hundreds of young children we help at the Ronald McDonald Centre, I drew their attention to the three veterans – two men and a woman – who were seated beside Viktor Korobchenko, one of Moscow's deputy mayors, at the podium. Ronald McDonald Children's Charities (Russia) was founded in 1995, and the centre, which opened in 1996, provides recreation, physical education, and leadership training to Moscow youth with special needs. The kids at the centre, like the kids I meet at Variety Village in Toronto, seem to me heroic in their capacity to focus on their abilities and not their disabilities. I'm always thrilled that McDonald's can help these young people. (As well as operating the centre, McDonald's-Moscow has, over the past five years, raised more than $3 million to help with equipment and medicine for children's hospitals in Moscow, to assist with the special needs of children injured in the Chernobyl nuclear disaster of 1986 and the Armenian earthquake of 1988, to provide wheelchairs for hundreds of Russian children, and as a contribution toward the Moscow Institute for Children's Oncology.)

It is always a humbling experience for me to meet these kids – doubly humbling to be introducing them to "three true heroes." At the Moscow Centre, the three veterans stood up and acknowledged the audience's long and heartfelt applause. Young and old clapped for them. They were presented with large bouquets of spring flowers. I don't think there was a dry eye in the house.

The St. Petersburg opening went well – although the crowd was even larger than we had anticipated, and there had been some pushing and shoving in the square. There were a few teenaged troublemakers, I think – not all of the recent changes in Russia have been improvements. When we opened in Pushkin Square in 1990, the crowd was large but extremely orderly. Everyone waited their turn; indeed, everyone waited patiently for hours in the cold for their turn. For good or bad, that orderliness has begun to disappear in Russian society. Perhaps this marks the end of subservience; perhaps, a shift away from the kind of manners that were once taken for granted – as always, in Russia, it's a two-edged sword.

At St. Petersburg, our people had to stand on the barricades and plead with the jostling crowd in the square to wait more patiently. There was some shouting and some pushing and the odd scuffle, but eventually order was restored.

The speeches were made. Vladimir Yakovlev said, "McDonald's has truly become a significant member of the St. Petersburg community. They are an important part of our local economy and provide hundreds of jobs for city residents." The crowd listened. The ribbon was cut. The band played. The cake was dished out. People filed in for their Big Macs and fries and Cokes. I chatted with Governor Yakovlev's wife; she is the chair of the St. Petersburg Zoo. She was excited about the two experts we were sending out from the Metro Toronto Zoo to help with the city's plans for a major renovation of its facilities. The children we had invited from local schools and orphanages seemed happy. The head of a local orphanage, to which we would donate some 20 million rubles of our opening day sales, grinned at me and raised her milkshake in a salute. I waved back from the table on the upper floor of the crowded three-hundred-seat restaurant, where I was fielding questions from about a dozen journalists. When would the next McDonald's open in St. Petersburg? How many did we intend to build? How much did the new restaurant cost?

We left a full restaurant (always the way I like to leave a restaurant) and headed by car out to Primorsky Victory Park. I had arranged for McDonald's to give forty-two Canadian trees – linden, lilac, maple, and ash – to the park, and before our departure for Moscow there was to be a tree-planting ceremony. My friends in North America are always surprised by how much media attention we get in Russia. The opening of a McDonald's? There are always banks of steno pads, tape recorders, Nikons, and TV cameras. A tree-planting ceremony on a cold grey day in St. Petersburg? Would you believe we had to hire a special bus for the press?

Among the dignitaries present was a veteran – Nikolai Kryukov – a retired colonel of the Soviet Air Force. His medals were emblazoned on his chest. As we were waiting for the press to arrive, we began chatting. I learned that not only had he fought in the Great Patriotic War, but after the war, he had helped establish the park. At first I misunderstood what the translator said. Was he a city planner? A municipal bureaucrat? A landscape architect? He laughed. No, in Russia, in the years after the war, things were not as they are now. Establishing the Primorsky Victory Park meant picking up a shovel and a wheelbarrow and helping to clear the land.

That was all I needed to hear. Russians are very big on pecking orders – the five trees to be officially planted had been lined up in order of rank. The first would be planted by Valerii Malyshev, the vice-governor of St. Petersburg. I would be second. And so on, down to Nikolai Kryukov, the veteran. When, at length, the press arrived, and the ceremony began, I was called upon to speak. I'd been standing there quietly, thinking about my conversation with Kryukov. I'd been looking at his proud blue uniform and his medals, and wondering what it would have been like to have been here fifty-six years before, at the site of one of the war's longest and most terrifying battles.

My prepared speech went out the window. I could think of very little to say. It was a grey, cool day. The leaves had not yet emerged, which gave the park a bare and solemn look. Although the tree-planting was intended to be a happy occasion – McDonald's crew kids, in bright purple windbreakers, had lined the pathway through the park – a sombre mood settled over me. I said a few words, and then simply handed my shovel to Nikolai Kryukov. "You are the one who deserves the position of honour," I said. At first he declined, but I insisted. We traded places. To me, that seemed a much better arrangement. That seemed right.

Then, in the car. Off to the airport. A glimpse, in passing, of the Hermitage. Of Peter the Great's residence. Of the palace where Rasputin died. Of the moored Aurora – the steel battleship that fired the shot that signalled the start of the Revolution in 1917. History on the fly – seen through the windshield of a speeding car.

At one of St. Petersburg's many beautiful bridges, an amazingly surly traffic cop became irritated at our attempt to make a left turn. He was reminiscent of the kind of petty Russian official I often encountered in the old days, at customs in particular. Mean, unreasonable, and menacing in a way that seemed far beyond mere official displeasure at the alleged infraction of some minor law. When faced with this kind of completely irrational power-tripping, I get an inkling – just an inkling, mind you – of how terrifying a police state must be. He waved us over to the side of the road and simply left us sitting there. When we protested, he became even more furious. After five or ten minutes I began to get anxious. After all, I had a plane to catch. I had appointments in Moscow with Mikhail Gorbachev and, later, with Aleksandr Yakovlev. Finally, Natasha Lobanova and Lena Saratova, two McDonald's-Moscow employees, got out of the car and, after chasing the cop around the busy intersection, talked him into letting us go. He accepted one of my cards – a coupon for a Big Mac – and grudgingly waved us on. From St. Petersburg to the airport we argued about what had been the deciding factor in his decision to be so lenient: the presence of two attractive women or the Big Mac? "With certain Russian men," said Lena Saratova, "it is often the combination of women and food that proves effective."

On the plane Ron Cohen, Ed Garber, and I huddled with Khamzat Khasbulatov, Glen Steeves, Konstantin Azhaev, the director of the real estate department, and Marc Winer. During my trips to Russia, it is often on airplanes and in the back seats of cars that I have a chance to catch up with them on the activities and concerns of the Moscow office. We reviewed the opening in Nizhni Novgorod, and went over the first two days' sales figures. We talked about the staff and our management team. Who were the up-and-comers? Who were not doing as well as we had hoped? We discussed what new cities we had our eyes on, and how many more restaurants we could open in our existing markets. We discussed the upcoming Chicken McNugget launch, our new ad agency in Russia, and our marketing plans: TV, print, radio, and billboards. We reviewed our relationships with various city governments – always complex in Russia. Finally, as the jet approached Moscow, we turned to our ongoing discussion of how we could raise more money for Ronald McDonald Children's Charities in Russia. I was pushing the idea of change boxes in our Russian restaurants. The others weren't sure. The question was whether the concept of spare change existed in Russia.

As the plane touched down, I asked Marc Winer for his thoughts on the St. Petersburg opening.

Marc said, "Good. For me the most important thing was that I had a chance to talk with the head of the city region."

I said, "It's important to continue a good working relationship with the city regions. But I liked the festivities today because I had a chance to talk to officials from the city regions where we haven't opened." I smiled. "Yet."

Early the next morning, still feeling the effects of a late-night talk with Aleksandr Yakovlev, I awoke in Room 2264 in the Metropol. My alarm had a simple message. "Good morning, George. You're flying home this afternoon." I climbed out of bed, showered, shaved, got dressed. I looked out my window. I could see that a stage for musicians and dancers had been erected in front of what, only a few years ago, had been the most feared building in the Soviet Union – the forbidding stone headquarters of the KGB. It was May 9. Victory Day.

I had to pack. And I had some calls to make. But on a sudden whim (and playing hooky from my ever-present security guard) I went out onto the street. Moscow had a festive mood to it. It was a beautiful morning – not a cloud in the sky, and I followed the crowds through the cordoned-off streets toward Red Square for the parade.

I stood on the sidewalk in front of the Hotel Rossiya, and watched wave after wave of soldiers come down the ancient cobbled slope between St. Basil's and the red brick wall of the Kremlin. Their boots crunched out the rhythm of their march. Some of the regiments sang, and the deep, booming voices echoed magnificently off the Kremlin walls. The parade was without the display of military hardware that was so commonplace and so threatening during the Cold War years. There were just soldiers marching, lots and lots of soldiers – which was appropriate, I thought. The night before, at dinner at Yakovlev's dacha, I had said, at one point in the evening, "But Aleksandr. Perhaps Stalin was the strong hand that the people needed to stop the Germans." Yakovlev – a veteran himself, and a man who still carries the fragments of bullets in his leg – looked at me sternly. He said, "It wasn't Stalin who stopped the Germans. It was the bodies of thirty million dead Soviets."

An evening with Aleksandr and Nina Yakovlev is always one of the great pleasures of a trip to Russia. I value their friendship and, from the time I first met Aleksandr in 1976, I have paid close attention to his advice. He was the one who assured me – long before an outsider could have seen any such indication – that the ideology of the Soviet Union would someday change. And, as it turned out, he played a prominent role in changing it. This often strikes me as a curious twist of fate, and I was thinking about this as, late in the afternoon of May 8, we drove out from Moscow – past the huge granite-and-glass "monster" dachas of the so-called New Russians – to the Yakovlevs' modest and comfortable country home.

I ended up in Canada – not quite by accident, but almost. But when Aleksandr was posted to Canada it was, as far as Brezhnev and the Politburo were concerned, an exile. In 1972, Yakovlev had published a long article entitled "Against Anti-Historicism" in which, with his customary insistence on honesty, he had cast doubt on one of the Soviet Union's most cherished myths: the harmony of the USSR's many disparate nationalities. Being sent to Ottawa was, from the point of view of the Central Committee, like being sent to Siberia, and so, when I first got to know him, it would have been hard to imagine any Russian political figure more removed from the corridors of Soviet power. Businessmen who devote themselves to clever analyses of who's in and who's out would never have bothered with someone like Yakovlev. He was, in the years I got to know him, without much apparent influence. And yet I liked him. I respected him. I trusted him. As it happened, he was friends with an unknown agricultural economist named Mikhail Gorbachev. Then Brezhnev died. Andropov died. Chernenko died. And when Gorbachev came to power, my friend Aleksandr Yakovlev was recalled to Moscow. Recalled to the very centre of everything.

We talked late into the night at the Yakovlevs' – a conversation that, in a distinctly Russian manner, seemed to touch on everything: from the current political situation in Russia to Pierre Trudeau's love of caviar, from the state of Yeltsin's health to Nina and Aleksandr's friendship with Claire and Farley Mowat, from Aleksandr's memories of the war, to his memories of the unfolding drama of *perestroika*, to his thoughts on the future of his country, to his concerns for his grandchildren, to his current projects.

There was laughter: I kidded him mercilessly about a hopelessly inadequate fence he had built to keep his dog away from three young saplings. "Aleksandr. Your dog can go over the fence, under the fence, and if he wags his tail too hard and hits the fence, it will fall over."

There were moments of great seriousness: Yakovlev described his eight hours in the Kremlin with Gorbachev and Yeltsin, when Gorbachev handed over top secret files to the new president.

And there were moments of insight and wisdom. With Aleksandr, there always are. Earlier in the evening, we had stood on the small veranda off his office. Beside the Yakovlevs' property, a vast, modern dacha is being erected – the country home of a businessman who lives most of the year in South America, and who has made a fortune importing tulips to Russia from the Netherlands. The Russian economy is full of these curiosities: people who find tiny but extremely lucrative gaps to be filled in the nation's new commerce. At dinner I asked Yakovlev what he thought of the phenomenon of the "New Russians" – the BMWs, the limousines, the Armani suits, and the huge, garish houses. He shrugged philosophically. He called them "robber barons" – a term used to describe the legendary figures who established American dynasties such as the Mellons, the Vanderbilts, the Carnegies, and the Morgans – but he used the expression without either condemnation or admiration. I felt as if I was asking him about the weather. He said, "They are just a necessary part of the cycle. This is just an excess we will have to pass beyond. I don't care for it particularly, but it is just part of the process, part of the transformation we are living through."

At age seventy-three, while working on his memoirs and on a book about Buddhism, Yakovlev has also devoted himself to an enormous project – the publication of ten volumes of state documents that he has painstakingly unearthed: secret files – one of which, as he explained at his dinner table, documents the mass execution of 22,000 Polish officers by Soviet troops in 1940.

He has put everything into this project. Late that night, as we were saying goodbye, he said to me, "This is my last big job. I only hope I live long enough to complete it. It is important to have these stories told."

It was long after midnight. The spring nights are chilly in Russia. Nina and Aleksandr had walked me to their gate. I said, "Good night, my friends." We embraced.

The car rattled away, over the country road, through the ghostly forest of birch trees. I turned and watched the two figures fade into the shadows. It had indeed proven to be an extraordinary day. That's the thing about Russia. Most of my days there are.

We had driven out to the Yakovlevs' after the afternoon meeting with Gorbachev. As always, it was slightly surreal to encounter Mikhail Gorbachev in his current surroundings. His office and his "think tank" are, really, the bare minimum that the state could have provided for its distinguished former president: institutional yellow walls, deserted, echoing hallways, fusty brown sofas in the reception area.

He travels a good deal now. He gives speeches. He is busy organizing an international conference on the global economy. Still, I often wonder about how happy he is.

I always try to bring some levity to my meetings with Gorbachev. I think he enjoys my jokes and my irreverent approach to things. But on this occasion, he had a wistful quality that never entirely disappeared. His old friend from his university days, the distinguished Czech politician Zdenek Mlynar, had recently died, and he was obviously saddened by the loss. I asked him about his student days. Did he and Zdenek ever get into trouble together?

"We were serious students."

I showed Gorbachev my ridiculous "sumo" portrait in the Moscow paper. He laughed, but there was a sad undertone to his response. "George," he said. "You should see some of the caricatures they make here of me. Only my sense of humour saves me."

Nervously, I broached the subject I wanted to discuss – the reason I had asked to see him. I asked if he would write the foreword to my book – this book. To my delight, he agreed. And then, because I was in the middle of the process of pulling together the files, and the photographs, and the souvenirs that would help me tell my story – because my office at home was filling up with clippings and videotapes and photo albums – I thought to ask him what he did with all his pictures and diplomas and gifts and awards.

He looked at me. His brown eyes were as full of humour as they were of sadness. It was a distinctly Russian expression; it's often hard to know whether Chekhov's plays are tragedies or comedies, or both. He said, "When I visit the United States, I go to the Carter Library. I go to the Reagan Library. I go to the Bush Library. Here? Here, I keep my mementos in my barn."

"Your barn?"

"*Da.*" He shrugged.

We spoke for almost an hour. He raised the same point that he always raises with me. "In your book, you must talk about the achievements of your Russian suppliers. Of what our farmers do for your operation. That is the important thing."

I listened closely to his advice, but during the interventions of the interpreter, I glanced around the room. His office is by no means cramped, but its modest furnishings and the absence of memorabilia on the walls make it seem strangely ordinary for so extraordinary a man. As I sat there, I couldn't help but think of all the photographs of him that so proudly and prominently grace so many executive offices throughout the world: reception line encounters with greatness. Oh yes, here I am, shaking hands with my old friend, Mikhail Gorbachev. Click. Next. And yet, here, in the office of someone whose handshakes with leaders such as Ronald Reagan, François Mitterrand, Helmut Kohl, and Margaret Thatcher really had meant something – had, in fact, changed the world – there were no souvenirs.

• 10 •

Fathers and Sons

The ghost is on the line. He's in Toronto. I'm in Moscow, in my room at the Hotel Metropol. He's the writer who is helping me with this book, and he tells me he wants to talk to me about the final chapter. I tell him I want to talk to him about the Moshe Dayan story.

"George, we can't get all your stories in. You've got too many. We've got to stop somewhere."

"But we mention it at the beginning, and then we never tell it."

"Well, maybe we should change the beginning."

"But I like it. It's a good story."

"Okay, okay. But you'll have to remind me. You've been telling me so many, I can't remember half of them."

So I tell him – again.

My involvement with the Canadian Council of Christians and Jews, the B'nai Brith Foundation, the Canadian Friends of Haifa University, and the State of Israel Bonds program, especially my term as National Campaign Chairman, has given me a chance to meet a number of Israeli leaders over the years. Golda Meir, Chaim Herzog, Menachem Begin. . . .

"Did I ever tell you about the time Yitzhak Rabin came back to our house after he gave a speech in Toronto, and he and I sat up late into the night talking?"

"George. We can't get them all in."

"All right. But it's a nice story. Just the two of us, sitting by the pool, talking about life, about our families, about Israel, about the Middle East, about everything, until about three in the morning. Absolutely fascinating."

"George."

"Or the one about the time I used a Big Mac card to introduce myself to the captain of the aircraft carrier USS *Independence*, when it was making a call in Acapulco?"

"George."

"I was there with the Canadian officer group, and we really wanted a tour of the ship. Unfortunately, I only had a Russian Big Mac card, and Captain Denny Bird didn't know whether to give us the tour or lock us up as spies."

"George."

"But we got our tour."

"George!"

"All right."

Anyway. One of the ways we raise money for the State of Israel Bonds is by inviting VIPs to town and then getting people out to a big fundraising dinner. When I was National Campaign Chairman in 1974, we invited General Moshe Dayan, the great hero of the Six Day War and the former Israeli defence minister. A truly legendary guy.

Dayan was travelling with his new wife, Rachel Dayan – an extremely sophisticated and elegant woman. They were going to spend a couple of days in Toronto. I greeted them when they

Where supply meets demand: Our Moscow food-processing plant, the only one of its kind in the McDonald's system, ensures that our Russian customers always get what they want.

Quality control: My personal adviser, fifteen-year-old Sasha Tilinin, hard at work.

Mayor Luzhkov and I show off traditional Russian hats. I just bought mine from the Izmayleev open-air market.

Eye to eye with the last head of the KGB: Here I am with my good friend, Vadim Bakatin, the man who dismantled the KGB and whom I almost dismantled on a tennis court.

Inside the Kremlin: This shot of my first official meeting with former Soviet president Mikhail Gorbachev would later end up on a T-shirt – much to Gorbachev's delight.

Ever gracious: When Mikhail Gorbachev expressed an interest in meeting my family and friends, he may not have expected quite so large a gathering. Here, he cordially greets the Cohon contingent, as part of a thirtieth-birthday surprise for Craig.

So this is where the money comes in: Russian President Boris Yeltsin is intrigued by the technology at the Ogareva store.

THE PRESIDENT

OF THE RUSSIAN SOVIET SOCIALIST REPUBLIC

DECREE

In connection with the actions of a group of individuals who have proclaimed themselves the State Committee for the State of Emergency, I HEREBY DECREE:

1. The proclamation of the Committee shall be deemed unconstitutional and the actions of its organisers shall qualify as a coup d'état which is nothing else than a crime against the State.

2. All the decisions made on behalf of the so-called Committee for the State of Emergency shall be regarded as unlawful, null and void on RSFSR territory. Lawfully elected authority in the person of the President, the Supreme Soviet, the Chairman of the Council of Ministers and all the state and local government and administrative authorities shall be in effect on RSFSR territory.

3. Actions of the officials in performance of the decisions of the above Committee shall come within the purview of the RSFSR Criminal Code and shall be legally prosecutable.

THE DECREE herein shall be carried into effect as of the moment of its signature.

[signature]

B. Yeltsin
President of the RSFSR

SENT BY: GEORGIAN MISSION SU ; 19- 8-91 ;

ПРЕЗИДЕНТ

Российской Советской Федеративной Социалистической Республики

УКАЗ

В связи с действиями группы лиц, объявивших себя Государственным комитетом по чрезвычайному положению, постановляю:

1. Считать объявление Комитета антиконституционным и квалифицировать действия его организаторов как государственный переворот, являющийся ничем иным как государственным преступлением.

2. Все решения, принимаемые от имени так называемого комитета по чрезвычайному положению, считать незаконными и не имеющими силы на территории РСФСР. На территории Российской Федерации действует законноизбранная власть в лице Президента, Верховного Совета и Председателя Совета Министров, всех государственных и местных органов власти и управления РСФСР.

3. Действия должностных лиц, исполняющих решения указанного комитета, подпадают под действие Уголовного кодекса РСФСР и подлежат преследованию по закону.

Настоящий Указ вводится в действие с момента его подписания.

Президент РСФСР [signature] Б.Ельцин

Coup d'etat: The official decree from Boris Yeltsin denouncing the *putsch* of 1991. One of my strangest souvenirs.

"I don't want to know her history. I want to know how much she makes!" Russian President Boris Yeltsin and I engage in a little international finger pointing.

Big Mac attack: Russian President Boris Yeltsin bites into his first Big Mac, without the top bun. His only concern? "Not enough salt!"

So why am I laughing?: Yeltsin makes a unilateral announcement to CNN reporter Siobhan Darrow. He tells her that I am going to open a McDonald's in his home town in Siberia.

Mrs. Yeltsin graciously accepts a cheque for fifty million rubles, our Arbat restaurant's opening day receipts, on behalf of the Institute of Children's Oncology to buy urgently needed equipment. When told of her husband's complaint, she said, "No matter what I serve, there's never enough salt."

A new challenge: Boris Yeltsin has played a prominent role in changing the official Russian attitude towards the disabled. McDonald's has supported a variety of programs and tournaments for physically challenged athletes.

Rubles Only: Moscow's dynamic mayor, Yuri Luzhkov, and I put up the brass plaque at the Arbat McDonald's announcing that only rubles would be accepted.

Too Good to Be News: When Boris Nemstov, President Yeltsin's energetic first deputy, joined us at a Ronald McDonald Children's Charity (Russia) golf tournament, which raised $150,000, I had to encourage the western press to cover an upbeat story for a change.

Left: Not a happy camper: My goddaughter, Ksyusha, Vladimir Malyshkov's granddaughter, at her christening. Unlike her godfather, she apparently does not like having her picture taken.

Right: Here I am with Ksyusha, my goddaughter, a few years after her christening. She's a little bigger, and a little happier to see me.

Fathers and sons: Craig and I, Vladimir Malyshkov and his son, Dmitrii, relax after a sauna and a few fierce sets of doubles tennis.

Am I proud of our two sons? Just a little. Here I am putting Craig's professional achievements with Coca-Cola in perspective.

Make time: When I returned to the Ukranian town from which my grandparents and father fled in 1906, I insisted on visiting the one remaining synagogue.

Back to my roots: In Dnipropetrovs'k, the town where my father was born, I was given a warm and cordial welcome. The dapper fellow in the sunglasses is my interpreter, Sergei Tsivunin.

Going strong: Seven years after we opened in Moscow, a McDonald's opening in St. Petersburg still attracts a large and enthusiastic crowd.

Russian veterans of the Great Patriotic War share memories and a lunch at our opening in St. Petersburg.

Changing places: At a tree-planting ceremony at a memorial park in St. Petersburg, I decided that it was the veteran, and not me, who deserved the position of honour.

Forget the CN Tower: When Mikhail Gorbachev visited Toronto, I brought him to Variety Village. I wanted him to see the kind of facility and the sorts of programs McDonald's wanted to help establish in Russia.

Under Lenin's gaze: In this *Life* magazine picture, I'm waiting to deliver a speech to a meeting of the Soviet Children's Fund at the Minsk Praesidium. I was the only North American member of the fund.

Little children should not have to deal with big problems: While the Ronald McDonald Centre in Moscow is not identical to Variety Village in Toronto, the kids who play there overcome the same challenges.

arrived, and Dayan took me aside. He said that his wife would like to do some shopping in Toronto. She had heard about the wonderful stores we have – he mentioned that Mrs. Dayan was particularly interested in Creed's, Holt Renfrew, and David's – and he wondered if Susie would be able to show her around.

Dayan explained to me that for security reasons they didn't travel with credit cards or with cash. He apologized for this imposition. But I told him not to worry. We would look after things, and then straighten it out with him afterward. He expressed his gratitude, and then we got down to talking about the dinner and the activities we had planned for his visit.

When I told Susie, she wasn't exactly thrilled. She was pleased to spend time with Mrs. Dayan. Honoured, in fact. But Susie wasn't much of a shopper. She had our two young boys at home and her volunteer work. Her idea of a good time was not tramping down Bloor Street with an armful of shopping bags. She wasn't all that sure that she would be the best guide to Toronto's stores.

I explained the problem – we would pay for Mrs. Dayan and be reimbursed by the General later. Things would just get too complicated otherwise. I told Susie that I knew she'd rather be doing something else: taking Rachel Dayan to the Art Gallery of Ontario, to the Royal Ontario Museum, to the Ontario Science Centre. But Rachel wanted to go shopping. She was our guest, and I reminded Susie that she was here, at our invitation, for a very good cause. Susie agreed to help.

So Susie went shopping with Rachel Dayan. My instructions to Susie were absolutely clear. I told her not to worry: whatever Mrs. Dayan wanted, buy it. I didn't want her to feel that we were imposing some kind of price limit on her purchases.

Well, in the first store Rachel wanted a couple of pairs of shoes and a purse. Expensive shoes, an expensive purse. Susie got a little alarmed. She got away to a telephone, and called me at work. But I told her not to worry. I told her to enjoy herself. I told her not to worry about the money. I wanted Rachel to have a good time.

At the second shop, Susie called again. She just wasn't accustomed to walking into a store, looking around, and buying. Again, I told her not to worry. It was our job to do anything we could to make Rachel's stay a pleasant one. I really pushed the point. I reminded Susie that it was all for a good cause. I remember exactly what I said to her. I told her to have fun.

So Susie and Rachel carried on, and Susie began to get into the spirit of things. She is an extremely hospitable person, and she didn't feel it was all that gracious to just be there, hovering like a chaperone. She wanted Rachel Dayan to feel comfortable, as if she was just out shopping with a friend. And so, Susie did what I had asked her to do. She followed my instructions. She relaxed. She started to have fun. She joined in.

They cut a pretty impressive swath down Bloor Street and through Yorkville. Our credit card was quite active. . . .

"By the way, did I tell you the one about the time we got a new credit card with the fantastic spending limit?"

"George," says the writer. "We don't have room for any more stories."

"How when I joined the board of directors of the Royal Bank, I got this credit card. The spending limit was something like $10,000. So I called them up, and sort of politely complained. And they agreed to increase it – I mean *really* increase it. The first time I used it was after a two-week holiday at the Four Seasons in Nevis with Craig, Mark, and Susan. I used the card to pay the hotel bill. Then, the next day, when we got back to Toronto, I picked up a new car. And I paid for the car with the credit card. The day after that, Susie pulled into a service station and put twelve dollars' worth of gas in the tank. And they decline the card! It's over the limit, and there she is, stuck. Our third purchase in three days, and we're over the limit!"

"George."

"A cute story, isn't it?"

"Could you stick to Mrs. Dayan, please. We can't keep putting new stories in."

"All right. Where was I?"

"Susie and Mrs. Dayan were burning a hole in your credit card."

They sure were. They were shopping, big time. But I had told Susie not to worry. In fact, I had insisted on it. It was the least we could do to help someone of the stature of Moshe Dayan.

Later, when I asked Susie about her day, she smiled sweetly and said that she hadn't expected to, but that actually, rather to her surprise, she'd had a lot of fun.

The Dayans' visit to Toronto was an enormous success. Dayan gave an excellent speech at the fundraising dinner. As he spoke, I was reminded once again of my reasons for supporting Israel as strongly as I do: because of my heritage, certainly, but also because it is a democracy – the only democracy in the region. During the Yom Kippur War in 1973, when Susie and I opened up our house for fundraising efforts, I made a lot of phone calls. One of them was to Don Fullerton, who at the time was executive vice president of the Canadian Imperial Bank of Commerce. I said, "Don, this is a terrible war, and we need your support. This is not a Jewish issue. It's a question of democracy. Israel is the only democracy in that part of the world."

Fullerton said he'd get back to me – and he did. Right away. "You're right, George," he said when he called. "Absolutely right." The Canadian Imperial Bank of Commerce bought a million dollars' worth of bonds. At the same time other banks were approached, and soon they had also made sizeable purchases. By the end of the year, we had raised $22 million in Toronto – 5 per cent of the entire sum collected in 1973 in Canada and the United States.

The Dayan dinner went extremely well. We raised a good deal of money for the State of Israel Bonds. And when I said goodbye to Moshe Dayan, I felt truly honoured to have met such an impressive figure.

Then, a few weeks later, the bills came in. Mrs. Dayan's were bad enough – but it was Susie's that really took my breath away. It just wasn't like her to go on such a spree. When I asked her about what she had bought, she reminded me of my very explicit instructions. I started to protest, but she told me to relax. She told me not to worry. She told me that I had been absolutely clear. She'd only done what I had asked her to do. We were going to be reimbursed for Mrs. Dayan's bills. As for hers – she smiled. I would just have to pay them – in the name of a very good cause.

"A good story, isn't it?"

The ghost says, "It's a very nice story, George. But where is it going to fit in?"

"You'll find a spot for it."

I always get a sense of real distance when I listen to a long pause during a trans-Atlantic phone conversation. That scratchy buzzing sound makes me picture the cables on the ocean floor, or the satellites in outer space, or whatever. But after about five or ten seconds without a response from the writer, I say, "Hey, here's a thought. Maybe it should go next to the story about the christening of Malyshkov's granddaughter."

"George, we haven't told that story yet."

"That's what I mean. It would be a perfect fit. After the story about Mrs. Dayan you can just slip into the story about the time Vladimir Malyshkov asked me to be godfather to his first grandchild."

"I don't think it's possible."

"Did I tell you the story about how I got the Red Army to dig the trenches for our power lines?"

"Yes."

"Or about how we got the St. George's Ballroom in the Kremlin for our opening party?"

"Yes, George. You did."

"Don't you think it's fantastic what Terry Fox did? Or Rick Hansen? Or how Dmitrii Shparo, after I introduced him to Rick Hansen, became so involved with disabled athletes in Russia – a country where, traditionally, the disabled had been hidden away?"

"Uh-huh."

"And do you think that in 1976 there were very many people who could have guessed that by the year 2000 there would be more than a hundred McDonald's Restaurants in Russia?"

"No. I'm sure there weren't."

"So you see my point?"

"What point?"

"That nothing's impossible. You follow?"

Over the phone, I hear a sigh of resignation. A rustle of pages as he flips open yet another spiral notebook. "Okay," he says.

Then finally he gets the connection between the two stories. "But George, if you're Jewish. . . ."

"Yes."

"Well – are Jews ever godparents?"

"That was the whole problem."

You remember Vladimir Malyshkov. He had been an official in the Russian Federation's Ministry of (Internal) Trade, under Vsevolod Shimansky. But I didn't get to know him until the mid-1980s, when he was with Glavobshchepit, the food service administration of the City of Moscow. Unlike many of the officials with whom we dealt, Malyshkov understood what we were trying to do and could see the benefits of a partnership with us. He was always helpful and encouraging – even when his superiors were not – and finally, in September 1986, it began to look as if his point of view might prevail. Gorbachev announced that as of January 1, 1987, the foreign trade monopoly would be decentralized, allowing domestic companies to enter into foreign trade contracts for the first time. Jeff Hertzfeld, our astute lawyer, wondered whether this might be the light at the end of the tunnel.

It was. On April 28, 1988, we entered into our partnership with the City of Moscow. The official signing ceremony, held at the White Hall of the Moscow City Council, was one of the proudest moments of my life. Vladimir Malyshkov sat with me at the table. He became the first chairman of the board of our joint venture.

We had become good friends. Over the years I had got to know his wife and his children. And when his first grandchild was born – Ksyusha – he asked me if I would be her godfather.

In Russian the word for godfather is *kum*. But in Russian and in English, the concept was unfamiliar to me. I felt uncomfortable. Just a little. I asked about the obligations of being a godfather.

Vladimir told me it was simple: If my goddaughter ever got into trouble, I would be there to help her.

This seemed like a fine idea. It struck me as an excellent tradition. I told Vladimir to tell his wife and their son and daughter-in-law that I would be honoured. Would there be a ceremony?

Indeed there would. A christening. To be held the following week in a town about one hundred kilometres outside of Moscow – which was a problem. This was the late 1980s, and foreigners were not allowed beyond the Ring Road in Moscow without special permission. Vladimir told me not to worry. I was with him. We would be fine.

The town was beautiful. An absolutely gorgeous little spot. We went to a lovely, big old church there. Every pew was full. I was the only foreigner. It was a Russian Orthodox holy day. And as we all started to walk in, Vladimir's wife stopped me. She told me that she had a gift for me, and she produced a little cross on a chain and asked me to put it on.

I gulped. And I thought, oh boy.

If you had twenty rabbis in a room, you would get twenty-five opinions about what I should have done. Some would say definitely not; it is entirely inappropriate for a Jew to wear a cross. Others would argue that it's not any different from a non-Jew wearing a yarmulke at a bar mitzvah; it's something that's done out of respect. I could see both sides of the argument. After all, I'm pretty liberal in my religious beliefs. I thought of all the non-Jews who, out of respect, put on yarmulkes at Holy Blossom Temple in Toronto when they came to our sons' bar mitzvahs.

But I was also carrying some real baggage here. The Kaganovs had been driven out of Yekaterinoslav (now called Dnipropetrovs'k) in the Ukraine at the height of a terrible pogrom eighty-three years before. They had been forced to embrace an uncertain future, to endure all kinds of hardships, and to flee to the United States – because they were Jews.

I often think of my roots and of my grandparents' story when I visit Russia. Once, in 1991, I was in a small office that we had then in the Minsk Hotel in Moscow, when I was told that there were two women from a town in the Ukraine who were waiting to see me. As it turned out, they had been waiting for almost twenty-four hours, but the hotel's staff had not seen fit to alert me.

They were from Dnipropetrovs'k. When I went to the lobby to meet them, they presented me with a magnificent, gold-leaf invitation. On behalf of the mayor, the city council, the local chapter of the Soviet Children's Fund, and various other groups and institutions, they were asking me to return to the city of my family's roots – as an honoured guest.

I took this all in – but then, in true businessman's style, I said I'd have to check my calendar. The two women looked at me with complete astonishment. One of them spoke. She told me that they had never met a Western businessman. They weren't exactly sure how we did things in Canada and in the United States. "But what," she asked, "could there be on your calendar that is more important than an invitation such as this?"

Good question.

I said they could count on me. I'd be there. What did they want me to do?

They explained that they wanted me to open a big children's festival. They wanted me to enter the town's stadium – where thousands of people would be assembled – on a white horse.

I said, "I haven't ridden a horse for a long time."

They said, "Don't worry. We'll sedate the horse."

I told them that we might all be better off if they sedated the rider.

So off I went to Dnipropetrovs'k. I was met by one hundred school children at the airport. I was given bouquets of flowers. I was treated like royalty. At the stadium, I actually managed to stay on the horse while I made my grand entrance in front of thousands of people. I was shown the sights of the town, and during my tour, I asked if there were any synagogues there. I was told that once there had been seventy; now there was one. I asked to see it. I was told there wasn't time.

"We'll make time."

I paid my respects at the synagogue, and later that night, at a dinner in my honour, I thanked the people of Dnipropetrovs'k for their warm welcome. But I added, "It's nice to come back here.

And it's nice that things have changed. But you invited me here because of my roots – and I don't want to ride into town on a white horse and forget those roots. I can't forget the circumstances under which my grandparents and father left this town in 1906."

You could have heard a pin drop.

I'd made my point. I didn't want to belabour it. So, to lighten things up, I told the audience something I had once said to Boris Yeltsin – and that had got a good laugh out of the president. Yekaterinoslav happened also to be the town where Leonid Brezhnev had been born the same year as my dad. "Now," I said. "If my dad had stayed and Brezhnev had left, you wouldn't be in the mess you're in now."

Now, here was the Kaganovs' grandson, eighty-five years after they had fled their homeland, at a beautiful church in a lovely old town outside of Moscow, on a Russian Orthodox holy day, being asked to wear a cross.

We were at the entrance of the church. I had about one second to make up my mind. I looked at Mrs. Malyshkov's friendly, well-meaning face.

I thought, this is heavy stuff.

I put it on. I decided that it was just a sign of the respect I wanted to show to the Malyshkov family and to the gathered congregation. (Were Vladimir, who is now one of the deputies to Moscow mayor Yuri Luzhkov, ever to visit Holy Blossom with Susan and me in Toronto, I'm sure he wouldn't hesitate to put on a yarmulke.) I also wanted to acknowledge my approval of the new freedom of religious expression in Russian life – for this kind of ceremony, like all religious ceremonies, had been officially outlawed only a short time before. Some of the old tensions still exist, of course, but officially, at least, Jews, Christians, Muslims, and Buddhists can now worship openly in Russia. And so in we went – to the dark church, with people chanting, and incense wafting, and mysterious, awesome-looking Russian Orthodox priests in their big robes. It was an overwhelming experience.

There I was – with a cross around my neck and a crying baby in my arms. Now, it's true: I am a co-chair of the Santa Claus Parade, I was voted person of the year by the St. George's Society in 1993 – two institutions that are not exactly hotbeds of Jewish tradition. Still, when I stood at Ksyusha Malyshkov's christening and thought of my own roots, I saw Georgie Cohon, bar-mitzvahed at the South Side Hebrew Congregation on June 17, 1950. I saw George Cohon, member of the congregation at Holy Blossom, a recipient of the 1981 Israeli Prime Minister's Award and an honorary degree from the University of Haifa. I saw George Cohon, trustee of the B'nai Brith Foundation and the National Campaign Chairman for the State of Israel Bonds in Canada. And later, when the Malyshkovs asked me how I had enjoyed the ceremony, I told them, truthfully, that it had been an extraordinary experience. I had found it very moving. I felt honoured to be Ksyusha's godfather and to have been part of such an important service. But I couldn't resist a joke. I told them that it had been amazing. Absolutely amazing. Miraculous, in fact – especially the way the holy water sizzled every time I got near it.

Speaking of miracles. I'm sitting here, in the Metropol, at the end of a phone line that I already take for granted but that I would have practically killed for during my early stays in Room 2264. If I'd had this good a connection calling room service (if there had been room service!) I would have been amazed. I'm looking around at the elegantly appointed suite – the paintings, the bowls of fruit, the vases of flowers, the grand piano, the gleaming woodwork, the fluffy duvet, the comfortable bed, the television tuned to CNN. In the bathroom, there is no shortage of towels or hot water. There's Coke and orange juice and Evian and peanuts in the mini-bar.

And I can't help but think that even here, within the confines of a single hotel room – the room where Dounia the floor-lady once brought me her home-made broth – the changes I have witnessed have been almost miraculous.

"George," says the writer. "Let's talk about the last chapter."

"Okay. But first let me tell you about the time I went out picking potatoes."

There's sort of a moan at the other end of the phone. I take this to be a sign that he is listening.

Because traditional Russian potatoes weren't long enough to be used for our fries, we imported Russet Burbank seed potatoes from the Netherlands. One of our agronomists worked on the collective farms we'd contracted with, overseeing the crop from planting to harvest.

Initially, we had some trouble getting the irrigation that we needed on some of the farms that were supplying us. And then, in one of our early years, we had terrible weather. That fall, things went from bad to worse: rain, rain, and more rain. Then the weather turned cold. It was apparent that we would have to get the potatoes in quickly, or they would spoil.

It was an emergency, and several hundred of our Moscow crew volunteered to go out into the fields and pick potatoes. I was really impressed with their response, and so I decided to go, too. Early one morning, we all clambered into several big, old trucks, and headed out to the farms to pick potatoes.

Now, I had never picked potatoes before. All the way out, bouncing along in the truck, I'd wondered about potatoes, and when we got to the farm, I realized I had to ask. I'm not an absolute expert in potatoes, I guess. It was a fairly embarrassing moment. I literally had to ask someone: Do they grow above the ground or below the ground or what? They might have grown on trees for all I knew.

I got straightened out on the basics of potato growing. And then, everyone wanted to know what I was going to wear on my feet. I was standing in the middle of a group of people, and everyone was looking down at my shoes. I was wearing my loafers. I hadn't thought about wearing anything else – but soon I was told that potato farms are not the best place for Cole-Haan loafers.

Someone went to the farmhouse and found me a pair of boots. Unfortunately, the only kind they could come up with were beautiful, tall, white, winter boots – only slightly more suitable for a muddy potato field than a pair of Cole-Haan loafers. But I put them on, and then trooped into the fields with our Russian crew – terrific kids, all of them, and all of them appropriately dressed in work clothes and dirty workboots. They knew what they were doing – which was more than I did; the first potato I dug up I cut right in half with my spade.

There was a cameraman there from a Moscow television station. And there was a photographer; the picture he took – a shot that ended up in *The New York Times* – was not a picture of our efficient, hard-working crew, but of a ridiculous-looking Western businessman, trying to figure out how to dig potatoes in a pair of clean, white boots.

"Nice story, don't you think?"

"It's good, George."

"And there's more."

A few months later, I was in Moscow trying to find an appropriate site for the Ronald McDonald Children's Centre. I had Toronto's Variety Village in mind as a model for what we wanted to establish in Russia: a complex where kids with special needs could come for sports and fun and for the kind of training and support that they need. And one afternoon, while we were looking, I was touring a sports facility in Moscow. The manager was a very pleasant guy who spent about an hour showing me around. At the end of our tour, as we were saying goodbye, he said, out of the blue, "I assume that you had never picked potatoes before."

I must have looked a little surprised. He said, "I saw you on television, and of course it was quite obvious. No one who knows anything about picking potatoes would ever wear such ridiculous white boots."

This story gets a laugh from the writer. Finally. Grim bunch, these writers.

I say, "And I think I know where we can fit it in."

"Why am I not surprised?"

"I think it can go next to the story about the time in 1973 when Ken McGowen and I got stuck in a broken-down bus in the Sinai Desert with Chaim Topol, who starred as Tevye in *Fiddler on the Roof*, and one of the famous Rothschilds during the Yom Kippur War."

"Another story we haven't told yet."

"I'm sure you'll find a good place for it."

Now, I haven't said very much about Ken McGowen – other than to describe him as my best friend. I suppose that's because when you have a friend as good as Ken, it's hard to put things into words. It's like the problem I have describing my "style." It's so much a part of me, I sometimes have trouble explaining what it is.

You could say we're kindred spirits. Ken is a successful businessman – the founder of Mac's Milk and a director of McDonald's-Canada. But he also has a fun-loving, mischievous, occasionally outrageous side to him, which I enjoy. I remember once going for a walk with Ken in Moscow. He stood on one of those public weigh scales. I guess he wasn't pleased with what the scale was telling him, so he took off his jacket. Then he took off his shoes. Then his sweater. Then his shirt.

By this time a crowd of astonished Russians was beginning to gather.

Ken carried on. Off came his belt. His socks. The crowd, by now, was cheering him on. Off, with considerable fanfare, came his jeans. The crowd went wild. And although Ken threatened to take off his underwear, he stopped just short of complete immodesty – but still managed to get a big round of applause from the crowd.

To this day, Ken claims that he didn't take his pants off; but I remember the event – vividly.

Ken accompanied me on a trip to Israel on a mission for the State of Israel Bonds drive toward the end of the Yom Kippur War. Needless to say, McGowen is not a Jewish name – but that kind of thing is never a big issue with Kenny. He follows his instincts and his heart. When we returned from the trip, I asked other members of the delegation whether they thought we could sell any more Israel Bonds to help with the cause. All of them felt that we had reached our limit. People had already been extremely generous in their support. Ken, the only non-Jew of the delegation, disagreed. I was campaign chairman of the State of Israel Bond drive in Canada, and he advised me to continue our effort. We did – and sold another $7 million worth of bonds.

During the final stages of the war, an international delegation was invited to see, first-hand, what was going on. The Israelis had fought back and had the Egyptian army surrounded at Kilometre 101. We were on a bus with a group of people heading from the Suez back to an Israeli airfield, where we were going to catch a flight to Tel Aviv. Chaim Topol and one of the Rothschilds were in the group. Now, as Jewish experiences go, this was pretty Jewish. Picture it: you're in a bus, in the middle of the Yom Kippur War, in the middle of the Sinai Desert and you've got Tevye from *Fiddler on the Roof* giving directions to your bus driver.

A bus driver who, unfortunately, followed Tevye's directions. We went over a big bump in the dirt road – a bump that turned out to be a big rock. The bus cracked down hard, and oil was going everywhere. We, on the other hand, were going nowhere. I said to Mr. Rothschild, "I'm sure glad I brought my American Express card. I don't like to leave home without it."

With a twinkle in his eye, he said, "American Express? What's that?"

So there we sat, with armies all around us, with helicopters and transports flying over head. Earlier that day, we had stood by the Suez Canal and had looked across its waters toward the smouldering Egyptian tanks that had been abandoned during the battle of China Field – the largest tank battle in the history of warfare. It had been an unforgettable sight.

We had a lot of time to reflect on what we had seen. We were stuck for almost eight hours.

Eventually, we were rescued. Some Israeli soldiers helped us out. We were taken to the airfield, where we were able to get on a military transport plane that would take us to Tel Aviv. And on the plane an extraordinary thing happened.

There were no seats on the plane. It was a big Hercules transport, and the soldiers – about five hundred of them – were crammed in like sardines. Every soldier sat on the floor, with his legs around the man in front of him. They were all tired and dusty and battle-weary. With their gear, there was no room to move. There were, perhaps, about twenty civilians on board, sitting among the soldiers.

The war had been a stunning victory for Israel. Egyptian and Syrian forces had launched a surprise attack on the Jewish holy day of Yom Kippur. But their initial advances had been pushed back. There had been terrible, hard-fought battles, including the battle of China Field. And now, on the Hercules, everyone was talking – about the war, about going home, about friends, and family. But for a second, there was a lull in the hubbub, so that one voice – the voice of one young soldier at the front of the plane – briefly stood out from the rest. Then there was a shout from the rear – a shout that just went straight to everyone's heart. An older man, a soldier, shouted out "Josie!"

They were father and son – neither had known that the other was on the plane. In fact, they hadn't known whether the other was even alive until that moment. But there was no way they could move; there just wasn't an inch of space. So the soldiers at the back hoisted the father over their shoulders, and the soldiers at the front did the same with the son. They were both passed along, by their comrades, overhead, toward the centre of the plane. They met there, and they stood and embraced, right in front of Ken and me.

"It was a magical moment."

"It must have been."

"So that story has to go in. And, in fact, something else quite magical happened to me on that trip."

"Yes?"

On the same plane I met a young soldier – an American. He was from Florida, and he had come to Israel to make *aliyah* – the Hebrew term for returning to Israel. He'd been in several heavy battles in the war, and he was going directly to another army encampment when we landed; he wouldn't have a chance to call his family. So he asked me if I would call for him when I got to Tel Aviv. He gave me the number in Florida. And so, of course, it was the first thing I did when I got to my hotel room. It was the middle of the night in the States, and I woke his parents up. They must have been terrified when they heard the phone ring at that hour. The father picked up the receiver, and I said, "I just saw your son. He asked me to call and tell you that he is fine.

"The best phone call I ever made."

"I guess."

"So those stories have to go in. Absolutely have to. I still get choked up when I tell them."

"Okay," says the ghost. "I agree. They're lovely stories. We'll put them in. But, George. Please. Can we focus on the final chapter?"

So, we do.

He thinks that the last chapter should be "reflective." He wants me to take a little time to sit, if I have a few minutes while I'm here in Moscow, look back over what we've written, and jot down some notes: my thoughts on the stories we've told, the events we've described, the life I've lived. He's on the phone from his office in Toronto, and he's going on about the "mood" and the "tone" that he thinks the last chapter should have.

But that's not what's on my mind. I've got questions about the book's title, about the book launch, about the jacket. Are the mock-ups of the cover ready yet? Have the invitations gone out for the launch? All my royalties from the book are going to go to Ronald McDonald Children's Charities. McDonald's covers RMCC's administrative costs, so every penny I earn from my book sales goes directly to kids. I'm excited by this, and I think readers will be excited to know that they've helped out with such a good cause. But I want to supplement my royalties, and my dream is to raise $1 million for RMCC at the book launch by selling one thousand special editions of the book for $1 thousand each – all proceeds to RMCC. I happened to mention this idea one day to Joan Kroc, Ray's widow, and she said, "George, if you raise $1 million for children at your book launch, I'll match it with another million." Once, thirty years before, Ray Kroc had offered me $1 million – to buy back the McDonald's licence for most of Eastern Canada – and I turned him down. Now Joan was making me an offer I couldn't refuse: the $2 million we raise at the book launch will be the seed money for an RMCC endowment fund. I was overwhelmed by Joan's generosity, but didn't quite have the nerve to ask, "Is that $1 million Canadian or U.S.?"

So I wanted to know. Have we started on the press kit? Have we set up the interviews, the signings, the book tour? I can't help myself. I'm a salesman. A front counter kind of guy. Both my sons are embarked on successful careers, and both have the same strong sense of marketing – Craig with Coca-Cola; Mark with the NBA. Craig's wife, Jeanette, works in international marketing for CNN. All three of them use an expression that I like. They talk about the point where the rubber meets the road – and that's the place where I function best: at the counter, at the cash register, at the spot where the product passes to the customer.

I'm told that many authors stay away from the selling side of things. They feel that's not their department. Certainly, they'd never dream of talking about it as openly as this in their books. When, on the telephone, I raise the idea with the writer, he sounds a little horrified at the prospect.

"You want me to write about what?"

"About the book. That's what I'm thinking about all the time. That's what I'm working on. That's what my energy is going into."

"Well, George. I don't know. It's not a very orthodox approach."

But I'm not very orthodox. I never have been. Writers might be reluctant to get involved in cover design and book launches and marketing schemes. But I'm not a writer. If I were, I wouldn't have someone at the end of a telephone line who keeps saying, "George. Will you please focus on the last chapter?" I may be a bit of a butterfly, but I'm a salesman. A pretty good one, actually. I may not know how to dig a potato, but I know how to sell good fries.

Marketing is my area of expertise, and so I'm driving everyone a little crazy with my ideas and suggestions about this book: What's the hardcover pricing strategy? Which is the best cover shot? The most catchy cut-line? What about a promotional video?

How do we best target our advertising? My publisher probably wishes I'd get off his turf. But I throw my marketing ideas at him the way I throw my stories at the writer.

I'm not the most relaxing person to be around, I know. Just ask Nancy, my executive assistant, when I call in from the car and ask her to track down some historical information on the Hotel Metropol, set up a meeting with Vickers & Benson, pull my correspondence with Yitzhak Rabin from the files to send to the writer, set up an appointment with Rick Hansen for when I'm in Vancouver, and patch me through to Khamzat Khasbulatov in Moscow. Just ask Peter Beresford about the time when he kept coming back to me with some new, completely unprecedented concession from the Kremlin regarding our opening night party, and I kept saying, "That's not bad. But I think we can still do better." That's just the way I do things – when it comes to books, or openings, or hamburgers. I'm not modest in my aspirations. Am I competitive? Well, unless you've never played tennis with me, or you skipped a few pages in the middle of the book, you know the answer to that. Do I have an ego? Well, I'm on page 327, and I'm still talking about myself – so the answer to that seems clear enough. But, apart from these, there is another reason that I'm so enthusiastic about this book – a reason that is very important to me. Just yesterday, while visiting the Ronald McDonald Children's Centre in Moscow, I was reminded of why I want to make sure the book does as well as it can.

I had gone out to the centre to meet some of the kids and to have a tour of the facilities. The centre is in Krylatskoe, near the rowing lake in Moscow, at the site of the 1980 Olympics – a fact that, when I think of the bus at the Olympics in Montreal in 1976, always makes me feel that things have come full circle for me in Moscow.

As always, visiting the centre was a moving experience. The kids are terrific, as is the staff. But as I was leaving, just outside the gym doors, I ran into a father and his little son. We started talking. The father was a professional musician – an intense young man who had recently returned from tours to the United States and Europe. He was obviously devoted to his art. And to his son. The boy, who was about five or six years old, was seriously disabled – he suffered from hydrocephalus, what we used to call water on the brain. He was in a wheelchair. His speech was difficult to understand. His movements were awkward and constrained. He appeared to be mentally handicapped, as well.

Now, I may have had children on my mind. I often think how lucky Susan and I have been to have had two healthy kids, both of whom have grown into such accomplished young men. Perhaps I was thinking about the father and son I saw embrace in the aisle of a military transport plane somewhere over the Israeli desert. Or perhaps I was thinking of the pride and love I felt and that I saw in Susie's face on the day our son, Craig, married Jeanette.

I may have been thinking about a young boy named Sasha Tilinin whom I met one day in the Pushkin restaurant in 1991; we started chatting, Sasha and I. He was thirteen then, and, after I returned to Canada, we started corresponding: "How do you do Mr. George. I am Sasha. You got acquainted with me in Moscow McDonald. . . . I live in Kaliningrad, Moscow region. If possible, ring me please when you visit Moscow." Now Sasha is nineteen and works part time for McDonald's as a crew trainer while he continues his education. He's a bright, likeable, outspoken kid; when he was only fifteen, I introduced him to President Yeltsin as my special advisor. Now when I visit Russia, it's always a pleasure to see how much he is maturing and learning.

Perhaps my thoughts of Sasha had led me back farther.

Perhaps I was thinking about being a kid myself, in South Side Chicago – of riding my bike out to the beach, or going to the movies with my sister. Maybe I was thinking of my love for my mother and father, and the admiration I always felt for my grandparents, for the courage they showed in leaving the fears of the old world for the hope of the new.

There is something about that bond between parent and child that affects me strongly. And standing outside the gym door at the Ronald McDonald Children's Centre, I felt a wave of sympathy for this brave young man and his son that completely overwhelmed me. Fate had given each of them a very, very difficult path to follow – and yet the love between them was strong and obvious. The father told me how much the centre meant to his son – how often they came, and what a great addition it was to their lives. Places like the centre did not exist in Russia before; kids such as the little boy whose hand I was holding used to be hidden away.

He told me about his son's operations and about the difficulties and worries they faced. But there was no self-pity in his voice; he was proud of how well his boy was doing. His voice was full of affection and there was something quite matter-of-fact about his manner. I might almost have been standing beside a little-league field, talking to a dad about the problems his son was having hitting curve balls.

We spoke for about ten minutes. Then I shook the father's hand and wished him well. He said thank you to me. And I said, "No. Thank *you.*" As I headed toward the car, I thought: Well, there's the reason. That's it. It doesn't ever get any clearer than that. That's why it's important to try to help.

"So," I say to the writer, "it might be good to talk about the main reason I wanted to do this book in the first place. I think people might be interested."

"Okay. But the book will do a lot better if it has a last chapter."

"All right," I say.

The writer tells me his idea. He says that in the last chapter I should be reflective. He thinks I should look back, sum up, come full circle. Tie things together. He tells me I should sit down at the writing desk in my room and conjure up recollections of the past: my grandparents' long journey to the United States, and my long journey back. And so, after we talk about this for a while, after we finish our long-distance conversation, and I hang up, I sit in Room 2264 and try to reflect.

I have a Hotel Metropol scratch pad in front of me. It says, "A Member of Inter-Continental Hotels and Resorts, 1-4 Teatralny Proezd, Moscow 103012, Russia." And, after about two minutes of my fiddling with the pen, that's still all it says.

I hate sitting still. I get up and walk to the window. I sidle around the potted fern, pull open the sheers, and look up the street toward Lubyanka Square and the former KGB building. The sidewalks are busy. It's a beautiful day. And so, of course, I do exactly the opposite of what I've been asked to do. I don't sit down and reflect. I take off my suit and tie. I pull on my jeans and a T-shirt. I tiptoe down the hall, because I don't want my security guy to know I'm going out. I don't want a bodyguard tagging along. I just want to go for a walk. By myself. I just want to look at Moscow.

I go through the lobby, where, as usual, there are vast floral displays, and bustling, attentive bell-hops, and waiting drivers, and well-dressed businesspeople on cell phones. The Metropol has a buzz to it these days – the kind of electricity that you might feel in the lobby of a good hotel in New York, or London, or Tokyo. I stroll around the side of the hotel, to Teatral'naya Square, past the façade of the Bolshoi. The famous theatre is currently under restoration and, like so many institutions in Russia, it is going through a difficult period of adjustment to the new realities.

I walk along Okhotnyi Ryad to Manezhnaya Square and then toward Red Square. Red Square, where on one memorable day in 1989 Susan and I were ushered by the gravely solemn, almost zombie-like guards into Lenin's Mausoleum for a private viewing – just Susan, Vladimir Ilyich Lenin, and me, there in the darkened chamber. Red Square, where, now, the spirited and sophisticated young women swinging by in their leather mini-skirts would turn heads on the Champs Elysées or Fifth Avenue. Red Square, where lovers now walk arm in arm and stop to embrace outside the Kremlin walls and where, not long ago, Anton Lange, the photographer who took my picture in front of St. Basil's for the cover of this book, did fashion shoots for *Vogue, Elle*, and *Cosmopolitan*. Where, if you wanted, you could wear a button or a T-shirt that says "Stalin was a monster" or "Sakharov was a hero" and not get thrown in jail for your beliefs.

I pass the monolithic GUM department store – where, on my earliest trips to Russia, a grim-looking salesclerk measured my waist with a length of string when I bought a pair of jeans. And where, now, people actually smile. Where Russians and foreigners alike can purchase Benetton clothes and Diesel jeans.

It has been more than two decades since my first trip to Russia. Now, as I walk toward the Moskvoretsky Bolshoi Bridge over the Moscow River, thinking about all that has happened since the first time I stood, awestruck, in Red Square, it seems as if a great deal of time has passed. On the other hand, as I look upstream in the direction of Christ the Saviour Cathedral, it seems a short time for a city, for a country – and, as a matter of fact, for the world – to have been transformed.

Not long ago, we had to beg Soviet officials to meet with our McDonald's team; now, Russia is a different place. On a recent Saturday morning, Yuri Luzhkov, Moscow's mayor, invited me out to see the retractable roof that is being constructed at the 110,000-seat Luzhniki stadium. I have an excellent working relationship with Mayor Luzhkov. We have agreed to expand our operations well beyond the twenty restaurants we originally envisioned. Changes in the Russian laws allow us now to control 80 per cent of McDonald's-Moscow, and the City of Moscow 20 per cent. The mayor, who dislikes sitting still almost as much as I do, plays soccer with some friends there once a week, and he wanted to talk to me about putting a McDonald's in the stadium. While we were discussing his plans, I noticed that the Israeli soccer team was waiting to come onto the field for a practice – they were on tour in Russia. I stood there, and I could only shake my head in astonishment at how much had so suddenly been transformed.

I have seen astonishing changes – political, economic, and social. And I have been fortunate enough in my visits to this extraordinary, haunting, and beautiful country to get to know a few of those brave people who made these changes possible.

But let's be clear – I tell myself as I turn back from the river and head up the grey, curving streets, back toward the Metropol – all is not well, and it would be a terrible mistake to leave the impression that it is. There is environmental degradation, and there is economic confusion. The proposal to ban "non-traditional" religions – religions that are neither Russian Orthodox, Jewish, Islamic, nor Buddhist – seems to me a backward step. There is dislocation and there is poverty: I only have to look down the block to see beggars on the corner, a drunk asleep at the entrance to a park, a cluster of homeless gypsies on a slope of grass, and, across the street, a sad, bewildered-looking man – perhaps an out-of-work academic or a laid-off clerk – standing with something in his hands. I look more closely; it is a toaster. He is selling an old toaster because, presumably, he is hungry, or his family is hungry, and he has nothing else to sell.

Juxtaposed to this are the BMWs and the Mercedes rushing by. The jewellery stores and the Armani suits. The caviar, the champagne, the five-hundred-dollar-a-night hotel rooms, the tell-tale bulges in the jackets worn by bodyguards, and the glass-and-granite monster dachas that the "New Russians" are building outside the city.

This is Moscow today. This is Russia – the good and the bad side by side. The city, and the country, have never failed to intrigue me – within the space of a few blocks I can go from something close to exhilaration to something very much like despair. For a Canadian, this is a particularly extreme range of emotions to experience. This year, the UN Human Development Report recognized Canada as the best place in the world to live, and whenever I visit Russia, whenever I walk through the streets of Moscow, I am reminded of how lucky we Canadians are. We enjoy a standard of living, a cultural life, a cherished environment, and a political and economic stability that are the envy of the world. We have problems, of course, serious ones. Jobs – particularly jobs for our young people – are perhaps the most serious issue that we face. But it only takes a trip to Russia to put Canadian problems into perspective. No one can talk glibly about breaking up a country such as Canada after seeing what political and economic uncertainty really looks like.

Whenever I return to Canada or to the United States, I am often frustrated by the questions I am asked about Russia. I am always asked by somebody or other about crime. About bodyguards, and graft, and ostentatious displays of wealth. In part, this is a result of the Western media's focus. Inevitably, the Russian stories covered by the international press are stories of desperation, and crime, and unrest. The triumphs of small businesses – especially apparent under Yuri Luzhkov's administration in Moscow – are not considered news. Not far from Red Square, a vast underground shopping mall is under construction; it will be three storeys deep and as big as Toronto's Eaton Centre. But the people I speak to in Canada and in the United States don't hear much about this; they hear about the Mafia. They don't read about a Ronald McDonald Children's Charities (Russia) golf tournament that raised 877 million rubles ($150,000) for local children's charities; they read about the extortion of a much smaller sum.

I try to get across to these people how much I love Russia, and how exciting it is. I try to tell them how much I enjoy the Russian people, and how much I admire their strength and their determination and their courage. I try to describe their enormous love of life and their passion for their country. Somehow I laugh harder when I am in Russia – sharing jokes with good friends such as Vadim Bakatin or Aleksandr Yakovlev. Just as – when I see an old war veteran standing proudly at attention in a wind-blown park in St. Petersburg or when I meet a father and son at the RMCC in Moscow – I am more frequently moved to tears. I try to explain to Canadians and to Americans what Aleksandr Yakovlev once explained to me: that for all of the confusion and hardship, and for all of the shocking contrasts of poverty and wealth, this is a period of transition in Russia. It is necessary, a stage to go through. It is a time of enormous, almost unimaginable change – change that inevitably brings difficulties and injustices. But a period that – most importantly – brings something that was not here, on the streets of Moscow, in much abundance before. Something that, as I head back toward the hotel, I decide can be best described as hope. Hope – to be cherished and nurtured and protected by the older generations who fought so hard to win it back and who must pass it on to the younger: to people such as Mikhail Gorbachev's granddaughters, Kseniya and Anastasiya, and Boris Yeltsin's grandsons, Boris and Gleb, and Aleksandr Yakovlev's six grandchildren, and Boris Nemtsov's daughter, Zhanna, and Yuri Luzhkov's two youngest children, Alyona and Olga. And to the young son of the musician, and to Sasha Tilinin. Hope is something we always owe to our children. My grandparents gave it to my parents and my parents gave it to me. And our children's generation will only pay us back when they, in their turn, pass it on.

Renée Glenn Eph Walter Jerry Marcia Judy Dima Avie Nelly Charlie Lynn Luc Elizabeth Michael Lou Ghislain Stuart Nastya Gordon Misha Carrie Mark Geof Harrison Courtney Dorothy Sankaran Aleksandr Wally Carlo Reg Shane Marvin Victor Phoenix Will John Marsha Dan Ira Byron George Larisa Todd Lola Herman Darrell Arleen Donna Tundra

ACKNOWLEDGEMENTS

"None of us is as good as all of us." – Ray Kroc

I have always thought of Ray's philosophy as one of life's great solutions. Better than anyone, Ray understood that the day-to-day working relationships between staff and crew members, the communication and support between managers, owner-operators, suppliers, and the company itself, the shared goals and camaraderie of our workers, our management teams, and our executive is the glue that holds McDonald's together.

But Ray's belief in McFamily and the company's ongoing emphasis on teamwork raises a problem for me now. The value we place on the energy and talents of *all* our personnel, *all* our suppliers, and *all* our associates is our greatest strength. Which means I don't want to omit anyone in expressing my thanks.

When it comes to family, the list is easy enough: Susan, Craig and Jeanette, and Mark; my sister, Sandy, and my brother-in-law, Maury. My aunts and uncles, cousins, nieces, and nephews.

Clarke Ming Tom Laura Julia Laurier Russ Devy Oksana Josie Nina Manon Bruce Sergei Maria Angela Garth Sharon Vladimir Domenic Jean Michel Slava Louie Richard Cathy Dianna Volker James Evgeni Jeanette Sam Harvey Rachel

Linda Wallace Mel Karey Sarah Cynthia Darryl May Riva Elvio Darlene Jane Bev Mike Kathleen Harriette Rita Leigh Rodger Tanya Norma Lyn Dorri Dmitrii Adam Marcel Shelly Rich Donald Den Victorya Amanda Rem Heather Steve Thomas Philippe Juhani Rosa Shannon Tony Deborah Andrey Nicki Carolyn

Henry Irv Ralph Gwen Sherry Robert Claude Pilar Ramzan Lorri Jim Yves Carl Annette Nadyaze Clinton Julietta Suchilla Dennis Daryl Gary Malcolm Gunther Lyne Colin Doug Gord Pauli Mary Anne Juliette Christopher Greg Charles Stephane Peggy Natalie Darcie Vivien Hal Michelle Elena Josette Jayne Les Marty Elie Wayne

Ed Erica Julie Ben Ferne David Karin Randy Leslie Helen Irene Anatoliy Sylvie Bery Dinah Rod Joan Yana Ottavio Bud Dee Natali Ross Audrey Olia Dounia Margann Yuri Cliff Beth Jackie Alexander Eric Rick Stephen Barb Ian Drew Louis Dave Peter Raymond Logan Gail Konstantin Aly Dmitry Mary-Mae Steven Serge Cindy Jas Elaine

And, of course, my parents and Susan's parents – who I only wish were here to read this book (and point out its errors). To my family, as always, I owe more than I can say.

Not many men have been as fortunate as I in the counsellors they have been given. In the writing of this book, and in many of the events this book describes, I relied on Mikhail Gorbachev, Aleksandr Yakovlev, and Fred Turner for their guidance and advice. I am grateful for their encouragement, humbled by their contributions, and honoured by their friendship.

I owe a great debt to Ray Kroc – mentor and friend. I am also indebted to Mike Quinlan for his friendship and his inspiration in my professional life, and for his encouragement in the writing of this book.

I continue to be lucky with my friends, both inside and outside the McFamily. I'm not sure what I find more valuable – the good counsel they give me or the good times we share. All of them deserve to be gratefully acknowledged here.

I would be remiss if I didn't thank all of the officers and top management of McDonald's in Canada and in Russia. The companies rest on their shoulders.

Fred Karen Muhammad Chris Jordon Pavel Honey Jessica Sheilagh Glen Howard Pierre-Andre Sasha Alexandr Igor Diana Wendy Bob Galina Anton Marie Lena Felicia Holly Andrew Melody Rosie Gloria Catherine Jean-Marie Shirley Yetta Roberto Roger Sonia Alla Ginny Geoff Simone Craig

Carole Jon Gerry Harry Nicole Joy Elliot Cynthya June Nick Cam Jasper Ron Patrick Ulia Debbie André Gilles Karina Judi Max Bonnie Jeff Joe Gale Nathalie Hazel Alexey Pearl Buddy Alex Albert Lee Perry Vaychesval Tina Cinzia Inna Daniel Mary Oleg

Normand William Kim Jack Krys Dean Trudy Rudy Valery Andrei Frank Jacques Keith Shazeeda Herb Trevor Ken Cheryl Joseph Dow Nan-b Oxana Mac Sui-lun Joann Marc Kathryn Pierre Anita Kathy Scott Jimmy Jean-Marc Irina Rocco Stig Terry Nadine Armand Gregory Jeffrey Roy

Ash Adrienne Aida Pam Mary Ann Grant Howie Gerard Natasha Glenna Maureen Rory Maribelle Deane Anne Norman Cutelin Amy Marcy Kseniya Dale Rhoda Benjamin Sergey Lionel Ted Carol Kostya Marina Nikolay Janel Anna Norm Denis Phil Sylvain Rona Marie-Josee Guylaine Graham Chuck Carol-Ann Morena Dick Larry Paul Elly Alain

Francois Sandy Lawry Tradd Kyle Janet Sylvia Barry Rodney Oswald Olaf Sveta Richmond Nancy Marilyn Isabelle Mona Brad Mats Leonard Sydney Kong Ursula Khamzat Marlene Vadim Loondeo Mila Gerald Debby Philip Susan Teresa

But this is where things start to get difficult. Through all of these friends, I have made others, and through these, others still. The list goes on.

And so, I have decided that the best I can do here is to acknowledge my failure to thank everyone who deserves to be thanked. There are hundreds, perhaps thousands of people who, in a wide variety of capacities, have played an important and valued role in my life. They do not, in these pages, get the credit they deserve. I apologize for this. But the reason is simple: there are just too many of you.

Having too many people to thank is a problem when it comes to publishing a book. However, when it comes to living a life, it is not a problem at all. It is my greatest blessing – one for which I will always be grateful.

– George

P.S. To David, the very accomplished and talented writer, from George, the author and storyteller: Thanks for putting my thoughts into words. Remember the deal we made at the start of this book: If it does well, I'll take the credit. If it falls short of our expectations, you take the blame.

Dani Mikhail Terri Helmut Ann Myrna Erinn Patty Olga Stan Jean-Paul Allan Leonor Sherri Chana Janis Hany Diane Pattie Lyle Rebecca Janine Badur Pasha Zinaida Vera Svetlana Bill Nikki Kevin Kristine Tatyana Melissa Eugeny Mario Guy Arlene Tim Belinda Don Edward Rob René

Joanne Neil Brian Alan Lou Anne Jo-Anne Jill Jenny Prle Shaleha Banff Jean-Louis Marg Josée Ray Ludmila Becky Jean-Yves Louise Margarita Gaston Shari Lev Bernie Jacquelyn Vlad Martin Adrian Sandra Tatiana Laurent Rosemary Mohamed Alexandra Ferdinand Maury Barbara Zina Al Jacqui Andy Boris